Glam Italia!
101 Fabulous Things to Do in Venice

Insider Secrets to the Renaissance City

ISBN: (paperback) 978-1-7323799-7-8
ISBN: (eBook) 978-1-7323799-8-5

DISCLAIMER
The author is not a travel agent. All opinion and views expressed are those of the author based on personal travel experiences. Business and websites recommended by this author may change ownership, rebrand, or close through no fault of the author. The author has not received any compensation or sponsorship from any recommended business.

Cover art and all images by Marta Halama © Corinna Cooke
www.MartaHalama.com
Photography by Tracy Battaglia, Fully Alive Photography
Photography Karianne Munstedt
Formatting: Polgarus Studio
Cover Design: eBook Launch

Contents

No one forgets the first glimpse of Venice.
Whether arriving by plane, boat, train, or car, there is that startling moment when one looks across the waves and finds what should not be there – stone towers, rich churches, and packed buildings rising out of the sea.

The extraordinary beauty of Venice only adds to its improbability.
How does such a city exist?

– Thomas F. Madden

1.
Introduction

Venice, its temples and palaces did seem like fabrics of enchantment piled to heaven.

–Percy Bysshe Shelley

I love Venice. Venice is a sensory explosion. Even after coming here for decades, stepping out of the train station into the magnificence of this city still takes my breath away. Every. Single. Time.

Venice doesn't gradually warm you up to her beauty. You don't pass through the ugly outskirts of town enroute to the pretty part. There's an immediacy to arriving here. You leave the old world, cross the causeway, and it hits you right between the eyes and right through the heart. You've stepped into a dreamlike world that cannot possibly be real. Except it is.

Maria di Blasi says of Venice, "Your eyes don't know where to land." I think of this all day long. Venice is a visual banquet. You'll never forget gliding along the canal between rows of palazzi lined up like gorgeous old kings and queens with jewels sparkling at their throats, or seeing the moonlight dancing along the waterways, bathing the most beautiful piazza in the world in a dreamy blue light.

Venice is a city full of stories and secrets. Mercurial and never static, her moods and rhythms ebb and flow with the tides. She is a mystery wrapped in an enigma. Her very existence is impossible. At moments she's decadent, occasionally she's ghostly. She is always maddeningly beautiful.

You learn the sounds of Venice. Once you've quieted the riot in your mind, listen for the almost imperceptible swish of gondolas gliding by, like secrets in the night. By day you learn the calls of gondoliers approaching blind corners, and the chugging sounds of early morning barges and delivery boats; the rolling click-clack and running steps of delivery men racing down narrow walkways, carrying goods to local stores. Venice is a symphony of sounds –just not the ones we're used to. Here, there are no car engines revving, no motorcycles or scooters, no clip-clop of horses.

I'm sometimes asked, "Yes, but does Venice smell?" It does –of fresh roasted coffee at Torrefazione, of flower stalls and vegetable stands scattered across the city, of fresh fish caught that morning and displayed at the Rialto Market, of wood shavings at the *remeri* where they handcraft oars for the gondoliers, of the briny waves lapping against the *fondamente.* As you walk past Venetian restaurants, the fragrance of seafood risotto and pasta floats through the air, reminding you it's food time again, even though it feels as though you just ate. You know what it doesn't smell of? Pollution. The smells we associate with big busy cities –car exhaust, smoke from fires –none of that is here.

Venice is a tactile experience. Not just visually textured, you'll feel her textures under your fingers and under your feet. You walk everywhere in Venice, over bridges and along *calli* (Venetian streets) which are whispering stories collected from 1000 years of footsteps. Almost nothing here is entirely flat. Beneath your shoes the streets weave, bend, and roll. Running your fingers across carvings on a well in Cannaregio, a column outside the Doge's Palace or a church exterior dotted with talisman *paterae*

(circular bas relief decorations), you'll wonder how many others in the last thousand years have done the same? How many souls left traces of their energy in these stones? Are the porous surfaces absorbing your life force too and keeping a tiny piece of you here? Venice will imprint a piece of herself on your soul. She's like a lover who never truly lets you go.

Here, you will encounter the tastes of Venice –and, Good Lord, you *need* to eat your way across the *sestieri* (neighborhoods). Venetian cuisine is light and fresh and bursting with flavor. But rest assured, friend, you can eat your own weight in Venetian food every single day and not gain an ounce, partly because calories don't count in Italy (my theory) and partly because you'll be walking *everywhere*. You'll eat a seafood risotto for lunch, stop for late afternoon cicchetti, find yourself twirling pasta later that evening, and *still* wake up with a flat belly the next morning! This is lucky, because mornings in Venice start with coffee and a pastry. My Venetian mornings start at Rosa Salva with the perfect Italian pastry, cappuccino, and a view to die for. And I frequently repeat the process a couple of hours later across town at Caffe del Doge, because *why not?*

In a lifetime of travel, I've learned that mass tourist crowds don't ever really see a city. They visit the same handful of sites that someone (heaven only knows who) once deemed "the most interesting", and they miss everything else. But Venice is full of fascinating things, and once someone points out these details and places, you can't *un*-see them. They become part of your own secret Venice story. In this book, I'll acknowledge the most famous sites, and then I'll direct you to cool details near them. Stick with me and you'll see details and places you'd otherwise walk right past without even knowing.

Before we go any further, in case you don't already know me from my other books in the *Glam Italia!* Series, allow me to introduce myself. My name is Corinna. I'm not a historian or an art historian –I'm a makeup artist. I'm a storyteller with a passport full of stamps, who has spent her life traveling the world and painting faces. Along the way, I fell in love with Italy.

Many years ago, a woman told me she desperately wanted to visit Italy, but not on a cruise or a bus tour. She dreamed of doing the things she'd seen in my social media photos. She too wanted to sit in beautiful piazzas drinking coffee or wine, she wanted to meander through little neighborhoods, and eat spaghetti at a sidewalk table on a quiet, tree-lined street. Her dream was experiencing Italy "off the beaten path", even in the most well-traveled Italian cities. However, her husband had zero interest in traveling. His (absolutely genius) solution was for me accompany her to Italy instead. And just like that, my little travel business was born. It turns out the world is full of women dreaming of exactly the same thing, so for nearly a decade I've spent my summers taking small groups of women on private tours of Italy.

Along the way, I learned that most people have the same set of concerns, stresses, and worries when planning their trip to Italy. It is these worries preventing them from travelling independently and forcing them onto bus tours and cruises instead, meaning they missed out on the greatest experiences these destinations had to offer. I realized I knew the answers to their questions and their concerns, so I wrote my first book to address them. In no time, *Glam Italia! How to Travel Italy: Secrets to Glamorous Travel (On a Not-So-Glamorous Budget)* was topping charts around the world.

Millions of people travel to Rome every year, but I knew the majority only saw the most overcrowded tourist sites and didn't get to really *experience* that magnificent city. So I wrote *Glam Italia! 101 Fabulous Things to Do in Rome* to guide them away from the crowds towards the even more sensational lesser-visited sights –the secret spots where you find the very best of Rome. It's impossible to see this side of Rome and not fall head over heels in love with her.

When that book also shot straight to the top of the charts, I followed up with a third book, *Glam Italia! 101 Fabulous Things to Do in Florence*, which tackles the same issues when visiting Florence and guides you through a unique set of experiences in the Renaissance city.

And now I get to share the magic of Venice with you!

As you look back on your time in Venice, you won't only remember what your experiences looked like, you'll remember *how they made you feel*. And that's what love is really, isn't it? Love is not how something looks but is an intensity that you feel to your very core. The things we love, we treasure and take care of, and on this journey together I know that you will fall in love with Venice, treasure her and want to take care of her.

When traveling somewhere new, the key things I want to know are – where to stay, which neighborhoods are good and which to avoid, which of the big touristy things are not to be missed, and where are the special places only a local would show me? I want to know where to get a killer cup of coffee. Where are the coolest shops? What local foods must I try? How should I get around? Furthermore, I find that if I understand the history and *why* everything is the way it is, I get a better sense of a place. And I am going to share all of this with you in Venice.

As an aside, I love reading books set in the cities I travel to. I think it's fun to turn a corner and see the breakfast spot where the *Commissario* takes his morning coffee, or the palace where a wacky historical figure held her wild parties, or the neighborhood a travel writer lived in during a sabbatical in the city. With this in mind as we explore Venice, I will recommend books I have loved which are set here. Who knows? You might love them too. I hope they might add another layer of magic to your Venice experience, as they did for me.

I don't like it when guidebooks talk *at* me –I want them to talk *to* me. So in this book, I'm going to talk to you the way I talk to my friends when we wander around Venice. You'll see lots of words *italicized* –this is the way I speak, and if were we walking Venice together, it's how I would tell you these stories.

So, who is this book for? If you want more than the regular guidebooks provide, if you are interested in random, quirky things to look for, if you enjoy intriguing stories both ancient and recent, if you want to feel you've really connected with a place, and you want to have the trip of a lifetime, then I wrote this book specifically for you!

So, let's explore Venice together.

Andiamo!

2.
Map of Venice

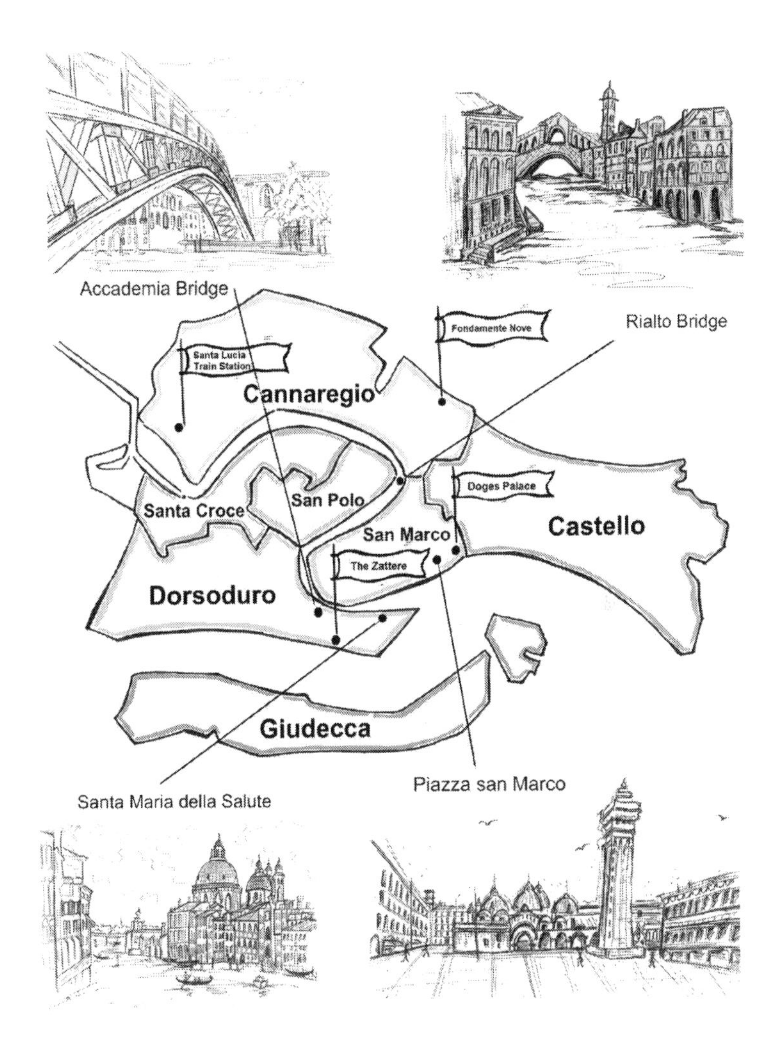

3.
How To Use This Book

His clothing marked him as Italian. The cadence of his speech announced that he was Venetian.

–Donna Leon

With so much to look at in Venice, it's easy to miss little intriguing details. So, because I know it's easy to be overwhelmed by all that's in front of you, I'm going to point out a handful of interesting features to look for wherever we go, and whenever possible, I'll tell you an anecdote about them.

First let me say (and I'll say it again), Venice is *small.* You can walk everywhere –and I realize that when you're planning your trip, being told this doesn't help! Any town you've not been to before will seem huge (even if it's tiny) and looking at a map, trying to gauge the distance from one neighborhood to the next, is tricky. Arriving in a new city for the first time, it's always hard to judge the time needed to go from point A to point B, so everywhere we go in Venice, **I'll include the nearest vaporetto stop and what's nearby**. This doesn't mean you need to go there by vaporetto (I recommend walking), but it'll give you a reference point. If you get yourself turned around (and you probably will more than once), you'll be able to find your way back to the closest vaporetto stop or landmark. It should also make it easier to group things together. I'll use the same landmarks over and over, to help you get familiar with the city and to form an idea of how close everything is. Remember –the more efficiently you manage your sightseeing time, the more time you can spend sitting in a gorgeous *campo* with a cappuccino or a spritz, soaking up the life around you.

I recommend you also read the chapters of this book that you don't think will interest you, because there is likely to be a story in there that will enrich your experience of Venice. For example, Ca' Dario in the **Ghosts** chapter and the Palazzo Venier dei Leoni in the **Peggy Guggenheim** chapter both have fascinating stories, and even in a city bursting at the seams with intriguing tales, these stories will make that stretch of the Grand Canal even more thrilling. You might not be planning to visit any museums, but after reading the **Museum** chapter you might decide you must visit Ca' d'Oro, or that you can't miss Ca' Rezzonico. Whatever interests you in Venice's past, there is a museum for it. Many museums have only a few visitors, even when Venice is exploding with tourists, so you'll enjoy most of them unfettered. This book is packed full of information, and I think you'll be surprised by how many quirky, fascinating places you'll definitely want to see. On your way from one attraction to the next, you might recognize a cicchetti bar, artisan workshop or church from this book, and decide to drop in for a quick visit. Often these unplanned visits will become your favorite experiences. Plenty of them require only a few minutes.

Once, a local guide passionately talked about an artist he considers the greatest painter in the world. With hand gestures emphasizing his point and the breeze making his hair fly, he mentioned a church I hadn't heard of and had no intention of visiting. The church is considered a museum of this artist's work. A couple of days later, while lost, I walked past it. I recognized the name from his story and dropped in to see what the drama was about. It was *phenomenal*! San Sebastian became one of my most beloved churches in Venice, and Veronese became one of my favorite Venetian painters. When I left the church that day, I texted my guide friend the name of the church, and he sent back: *Told you so!*

I've thought about this experience often while writing this book. In some ways, I think that is the essence of great travel, where someone tells you a story about a random place, and although you're not really interested, you pop in anyway, and *BOOM* you have an experience that turns your trip on its ear.

So read it all, let it swirl around in your brain. Some things will make it onto your must-see list, others will fall into an 'If I'm nearby' category, and others will just be a point of recognition (then you'll walk inside and it will rock your world). I suggest choosing an item from each chapter to experience –a cicchetti bar, a coffee shop, a museum or church, a place to sip an aperitivo. You may not get to them all, but it will help you to refine what goes on your list in a city with endless things to see and do.

I'm not going to provide any recommended daily itineraries –that would align too closely to the mass tourism model. Instead, my advice is to bookend each of your days in Venice with a killer coffee somewhere wonderful in the morning, and an aperitivo with a view in the late afternoon. In the middle, I suggest you wander, eat, slow down and enjoy.

Venice is a banquet meant to be savored. Love it, respect it, and soak up every glorious minute of your time here.

4.
An Exceedingly Brief History of Venice

Italy will never be a normal country because Italy is Italy. If we were a normal country, we wouldn't have Rome. We wouldn't have Florence. We wouldn't have the marvel that is Venice.

–Matteo Renzi

Venice officially began at the stroke of noon on Friday 25 March, 421AD. That was the moment they dedicated the first church of Venice, the church of San Giacomo, on the little islet of Rialto. To this day, they celebrate 25 March as the birthday of Venice.

The last Doge abdicated on 12 May 1797, and for roughly 1400 years between, the city grew, adorned herself with maddening opulence, and became the center of the trade world. When the merchant trade spread elsewhere and the riches waned, Venice became the party capital of Europe. Fourteen centuries later, she is one of the most visited cities in the world.

The early Venetians were refugees, fleeing from the barbarians, Huns and Visigoths invading from the north. They created sanctuaries on the marshy outcrops and islands of the lagoon, protected from attack by the waters surrounding them. They stabilized and built up the existing land to build their empire, while respecting and maintaining the delicate balance of the lagoon. From mudflats and salt marshes, these wily characters built a series of islands into their own wonderland. (See more on *how* they did this in the next chapter.) Meanwhile the rest of Europe entered the bleakest time in history – the Dark Ages.

In 697, the 12 founding families elected their first duke (*doge*) Paolo Lucio Anafesto and started a republic that would survive for 1000 years. Initially the seat of the doge was on the island of Malamocco, but in the early 800s, the doge moved to the more geographically protected area of Rialto. There they built the first ducal palace and the first Basilica San Marco.

Venetians became master ship builders. The combination of their ship building prowess and their location between the east and the west made them a mercantile superpower. Venice was the access point for goods coming from the East, Asia, the Middle East, and North Africa into the rest of Europe and Britain. This trade brought extraordinary wealth. Before long, Venice became a banking and money-lending superpower. The merchant trade riches and mercantile pragmatism influenced local politics and strategic thinking. All colors, creeds and races mingled here.

The republic got involved with the lucrative crusades (which ultimately were barbaric looting and pillaging in the name of Jesus). The worst of the crusades was the horrific sack of Constantinople in 1204. This gave Venice an unbelievable booty haul but marked the beginning of the end of Christianity in the East.

Venice helped itself to the islands and ports essential to controlling the trade routes from Venice to the Black Sea, also securing the overland routes to China and Russia, meaning Venetian ships could sail safely all the way from the lagoon to Byzantium. The cash flowed and the era of *La Serenissima* (the Most Serene Republic of Venice) had arrived. (Of course, I'm leaving out a lot of the story, but by the late 13th century Venice was the wealthiest city in all of Europe.)

Venice had become one of the largest cities in Europe. Politically stable (for 1000 years), the economy flourished, and the citizens enjoyed a standard of living not seen anywhere else. Opulent, exquisite palazzi, churches and government buildings popped up everywhere, and Venetians became renowned for their lavish dress and jewels, perfumes and cosmetics.

Although brutal, the political machine was also brilliant. Their system guaranteed that no single person ever held absolute power, while regulating itself with a series of checks and balances. No single family ever dominated Venice –the city didn't have its own version of the Medici. Every branch of the Venetian government watched over the others and held everyone accountable. The *Libr0 d'Oro* (Golden Book) was a list of the nobles of Venice. Members of the noble class held every position of power, including the doge. The book produced the Great council and the Minor council, even the terrifying Council of 10. Magistrates, heads of supreme courts, clerks, committees and a host of seditionist seeking spies, all came from the book. This clever system kept the republic running for a thousand years.

Everything was going swimmingly until Venice made a fatal mistake. After the sack of Constantinople, they didn't monitor the growing power of the Ottoman Turks. In 1453, Sultan Mehmet the Conqueror conquered Constantinople and blocked the sea trade routes. Then, in 1497, Vasco da Gama rounded the Cape of Good

Hope, opening new sea routes to the East, marking the beginning of the end for Venice. Throughout the 16th and 17th centuries, Turkish power in the area surged and Venetian merchant trade dwindled. Venice became a party city. Its power diminished and in 1797, the last doge abdicated. They voted the Republic out of existence and the diminutive Francophile Napoleon swooped on in.

After French rule, Venice became the property of Austria until 1866 when they handed it over to the brand spanking newly united Italy.

5.
How Venice was Built

Venice is a city built on water. It is preposterous. If you couldn't see it with your own eyes and touch it with your fingers, you would think it was some poetic fancy. It really shouldn't be there at all. But it is. And it is beautiful beyond words.

–Russell Norman

Venice is an engineering marvel and a tribute to the absolute genius of human beings. Everything here is manmade. Buildings float on the water like a glorious facade, as if by magic.

Her story starts at the beginning of the 5th century. The Roman Empire had collapsed, and Barbarians from northern Europe were looting and pillaging their way across Italy. With nowhere else to go, the Veneti (the people of the Veneto) escaped into the lagoon. This marshy wasteland comprising tiny, muddy islets gave them no solid land to build upon, so they had to get really, *really* creative. To make them buildable, they had to strengthen the islands, drain them, enlarge them, all while maintaining the fragile lagoon ecosystem. You have to wonder who thought the whole thing up and how they figured out such a complex solution. But figure it out they did.

They dug hundreds of canals into the marshy sludge, shoring them up with wooden pilings. Next, they pounded wooden poles up to nine meters tall, down through the sludge and silt, until they hit hard clay, strong enough to hold the weight of the buildings that would eventually be on top. How did they know (or guess) they'd hit solid ground at 10 meters? Imagine if they'd given up at five?

The pilings were placed as closely together as possible, then stones and rocks were wedged into the gaps to stop the silt from rising between them. Wood rots in water (even the water-resistant oak and larch they used), but for wood to rot, it needs both water and air. Once the pilings were below the waterline, there was no oxygen, so the wood was protected. The lagoon water was full of silt and dirt, creating a specific type of sediment which was absorbed by the wood, which was then petrified, essentially turning it into stone. Some of the remaining pilings are 1000 years old. (The original buildings from the 5th century are long gone, but buildings from 1000AD are still here.)

With the wooden pilings secured and their tops leveled off, they added two layers of wood to build the beginnings of a foundation. A double layer of bricks or masonry went on top of this foundation. The weight of the buildings pushed down on the dirt and mud, squeezing out the water and compacting the soil.

As you wander around Venice, it's wild to think there are millions of tree trunks below you acting as pilings, and that some have embedded there for over 1000 years.

Random Facts

- Venice has no forests, so the logs used for pilings came from Croatia, Slovenia and Montenegro.
- These huge logs arrived by water, rowed across the Adriatic Sea.
- Over 10 million oak poles were used for the pilings below Venice.
- The Rialto Bridge was built on around 30,000 pilings.
- The church of Santa Maria della Salute stands on over 1,000,000 pilings, which took more than two years to embed.

How it Works

As I've explained, wooden pilings were driven into the clay, the wood became petrified and stone-like, and a platform was placed on top to act as a foundation –but *why* does it work? Venice is constantly moving, so why don't the houses and palaces fall down? How have the front walls of the palaces not sheared off into the water?

In 2010, I stumbled upon a British TV show with an architect who travels through Italy, explaining how the architecture works. In the first episode of *Kevin McCloud's Grand Tour*, after a romp through France and Northern Italy, he arrives in Venice. Look it up on Vimeo –the show completely changes the way you view palaces along the Grand Canal.

Here is how he explains it: Normal houses, like your own, have four external walls connected to each other, which support the roof. If there's any big movement, the house falls down. Clearly, that wouldn't work in a floating city. Venice is in movement all the time and the front facade of a palace or house, being the closest to the water, is the most susceptible to the rise and fall of the tides and the overall movement. Looking at the palaces along the Grand Canal, you'll notice that none of the facades go straight up and down –they all lean. They do this because Venetian houses are divided into three sections –the two internal walls (the ones from the middle section) take all the weight of the floor above. The *internal* walls support the ceiling and the roof above. The *external* walls do nothing except look pretty. In fact, they lean slightly backwards toward the internal walls, relieving the stress and stopping them from shearing off and dropping into the water. (McCloud goes inside a convent under renovation and shows you exactly how it works. It's fascinating!)

Much of the architecture we see today in Venice is from the 14—15th centuries, in a style known as Venetian Gothic. These buildings, like the beautiful Ca' d'Oro, have a light style that lifts your eye upwards with spires and arched windows.

Other Architectural Nuances to Look For

At first, Venetian architecture can seem overwhelming –there is so much happening, it's ridiculously beautiful and dramatic, and your eye doesn't really know where to focus. One way to approach it is to look for clues in the architectural styles. For centuries Venice was the center of the trade routes between Western Europe and the Middle and Far East and was home to merchants and traders from all over. It was a cultural and architectural melting pot, and you can still see the foreign influences in the architecture.

- **Byzantine Influence**. From roughly 900 to 1300AD, there was a Byzantine influence to Venetian architecture (think Constantinople). The best example of this is Basilica San

Marco with its spires and rounded domes on top, golden mosaics inside and shimmery textures on the exterior.

- **Islamic Influence**. This happened from 1300 to 1500. Perfect examples of the Islamic Gothic architecture are the Doge's Palace and Ca' d'Oro. Look for loggias with closely spaced columns, lacey stonework, pointed arched windows and pretty quatrefoils. Rooflines with vertical decoration, and exterior walls with colored patterns (like the pink and white of the Doge's Palace).

- **Venetian Renaissance.** This started a little later than the Renaissance in Florence and was used by mostly non-Venetian architects. If you've read *Glam Italia! 101 Fabulous Things to Do in Florence*, you'll know Brunelleschi pioneered a style of architecture based on balance, symmetry, and harmony. A perfect example of the Venetian interpretation of this is the church of Santa Maria in Miracoli. When you visit, feel how your mind is calmed by the harmony of the marble exterior.

- **Venetian Baroque**. You also see the curly, swirly baroque influence in some Venetian architecture. The best example of this 17th century architectural style is the big white church of Santa Maria della Salute.

- **Ecclesiastical Gothic.** Another style of Gothic architecture to look for in Venice is Ecclesiastical or Religious Gothic. You'll notice this because it looks familiar, yet also out of place. Brought over from the mainland by Franciscan monks, the first example of this style was the church of Santa Maria Gloriosa dei Frari. The Gothic churches built all over

Europe in the 13th century were huge and heavy, with towering, vaulted structures and weight-bearing stone (which would have collapsed if built on Venice's marshy and unstable bog). Building materials in Venice had to be light, and flexible enough to work with some shifting and sagging below deck. This required some extra ingenuity for the gothic style. The Frari church has high brick walls and a vaulted structure, but a brace runs through to keep it stable. Venetian Ecclesiastical Gothic churches don't have the lacy, skeletal windows associated with other Gothic churches of that era. Two other beautiful churches built in this style are SS Giovanni e Paolo in Castello and Madonna dell'Orto in Santa Croce.

Is Venice Sinking?

Technically, Venice has been sinking since the beginning, but over the past 100 years the city has sunk nine inches. Experts worry that global warming will cause sea levels to rise so high that Venice will eventually be submerged.

One of the most pressing issues facing Venice right now is the impact of visiting cruise ships. Even though tugboats tow them in and out of the lagoon, these gargantuan floating Vegas's cause enough vibration to rattle windows and make palazzo walls shake. (Read more about this in the **Sustainability** chapter.)

6.
Arriving, Departing, and Getting Around Venice

There is something so different in Venice from any other place in the world, that you leave at once all accustomed habits and everyday sights, to enter an enchanted garden.

–Mary Shelley

Even when you *know* there are no cars in Venice, the lack of wheeled vehicles can still be startling. I can't tell you how many times I've arrived with a Glam Italia group of travelers, and had at least one person flip out when they realize they can't get anywhere by car! No Ubers, no four-wheeled taxis, no land-bound airport shuttles, rain or shine.

So how do you get around in Venice? Mostly on foot. Be prepared to walk and walk and walk.

My first major piece of advice to you is to throw fashion to the wind and invest in good walking shoes and/or sandals. Italy is about walking everywhere, and good shoes are the cornerstone of a glorious trip. You don't have to get ugly shoes, just make sure they're broken in, comfortable, and support your lower back. If you're wearing covered shoes or sneakers, add extra insoles with a nice squishy cushion in the heel.

Venice is a series of tiny islands connected by endless little bridges. You will walk up and down the stairs of these bridges all day long. Most are only a few steps up and a few steps down, but it all adds up. Be warned –when it rains in Venice the bridges get slippery. I had one traveler several years ago insist on wearing expensive designer flip-flop sandals –even though I begged her not to. When a rain shower passed through Venice, the bridges got slippery and BOOM over she went. Her pricey slides slid right out from under her. She went airborne and landed with a resounding thwack on her bottom and lower back. We'd shopped at the Prada a few days prior, and this was her first day toting her gorgeous new Saffiano leather shoulder bag, which flew up in the air as if in slow motion. Somehow, I caught it just as it hit the wet ground, *before* it slid over the edge into the canal. Her pride was hurt more than her bottom, but she limped for a few days and had a God-awful bruise for several days more. The Prada bag, however, sustained minimal damage!

Arriving in Venice

The most common ways to arrive in Venice are by airplane or by train. (I sincerely hope you don't come here or leave here by cruise, but if you do, the cruise line will cart you back and forth, so you won't need to find your own way around.)

Venice Marco Polo Airport (VCE) is on the mainland, approximately 13km away from Venice. The airport is small, modern and easy to navigate, and there are several ways to get from the airport into Venice.

From the Airport to Venice by ...

Bus

The least expensive and quickest option is to take the ATVO coach to Piazzale Roma (next to the train station) or the #5 ACTV bus from the airport to Piazzale Roma via Mestre. Both cost €8 one-way.

You can purchase tickets for the ATVO at four locations: the ATVO ticket counter at baggage claim, the airport arrivals exit, online from the ATVO app or the website, and from the attendant at the bus stop. The attendant can help you with timetables and schedules too.

- **ATVO coach.** Exiting the arrivals area at door D, go to the #2 bus stop. There are signs for buses/coaches to Venezia Piazzale Roma and Venezia Express. **You must validate your ticket in the machine at the bus stop before boarding the bus**. The coach takes 20 minutes, departing regularly from 5.20am—12.20am.

- **ACTV #5 bus.** The ACTV #5 bus is a regular public transport bus to Piazzale Roma, making several stops along the way. It also takes 20 minutes and operates from 4am—1am. You can buy an Aerobus + Nave ticket that lets you hop on the vaporetto at Piazzale Roma without having to buy a separate vaporetto ticket. **Validate the ticket when you board the bus**.

If you have luggage, the ATVO is the better option as the regular bus doesn't have a luggage hold underneath. If traveling with only carry on and a personal bag, either option works.

Once you get to Piazzale Roma, you need to get a vaporetto (water bus) or a water taxi to your destination.

Car Service or Land Taxi

You can book a regular taxi or car service from the airport to Piazzale Roma. (This is also how you get to the cruise terminal.) The ride takes 30 minutes and costs €60 for up to four people with one piece of luggage each. There is an extra fee per additional suitcase. You'll find official taxis along the sidewalk when you exit the arrivals terminal.

The Alilaguna Waterbus

This is the public service waterbus from the airport into Venice. This waterbus is much smaller than the regular vaporetto and fills up quickly. This is the slowest route into Venice's city center. From the airport to San Marco takes a little over an hour. The cruise terminal takes around an hour and 45 minutes. Boats arrive every 30 minutes and fill up quickly, so have a backup plan during the high season.

The Alilaguna has three routes:

- **Line Blu** loops around Murano, back along Cannaregio and Castello past Fondamenta Nove, across to Lido, back to San Marco, then around Giudecca ending up at the train station at the bottom of Cannaregio.

- **Line Arancia** goes to Fondamenta Nove then loops in the opposite direction up the Grand Canal. It stops at Guglie, S. Stae, Rialto, S. Angelo, Ca' Rezzonico, Giglio and San Marco before heading back through the Giudecca Canal to the train station. Chances are you'll be needing the orange/arancia line.

- **Line Red** only operates April through September. This one loops around Murano and Lido, cuts back to San Marco and then takes the Giudecca canal to the cruise terminal.

Alilaguna tickets cost €15 and pay for one suitcase and one personal bag. Additional luggage costs €3 per piece. You can purchase your ticket at the public transportation desk in the arrivals area at the airport, from the ticket booth at the dock, or from the ticket machine. **Validate your ticket *before* boarding.**

From the arrivals area of the airport follow the signs for boats and water taxis. The walk takes 10 minutes.

If arriving with the Alilaguna you probably will need to take a vaporetto from the stop to wherever you are staying. Check the Alilaguna website to see which line is best for you. Go over the options with your hotel or vacation rental ahead of time to make sure you get the correct line, have purchased the correct tickets, and know where to disembark and make any necessary connections to get to your final destination.

Private Water Taxi

This is the most expensive and (providing it's not raining and the water isn't rough) also the most glamorous way to arrive at the city center. For around €120, the water taxi carries up to four people, with €10 more for each additional person. This is the best way to get the most staggering views when arriving into the city, and the taxi will take you as close as possible to your canal-side accommodation.

The disadvantage of this method of transport is that it's tricky to disembark. Depending on the tides, the ground you step onto can be slippery, and then factor in dealing with your luggage. There can be a gap between the water taxi and *terra firma*, and the taxi driver can't anchor to help you out of the boat. You may still have a significant walk to your accommodation too.

A few years ago one of my Glam Italia travelers had to get an impossibly early train to Milan to catch her flight home. There were no vaporetti that early, so she had to take a water taxi. I swear it was like watching a Fellini movie –the sun was rising over the lagoon and had turned the world an intense shade of rose gold, mixed with the remaining shadows of the night. Water taxis are gorgeous polished wooden boats, and the taxi driver was movie star handsome. It had us both in fits of giggles. He pulled the boat out into this impossibly beautiful light and then took off, with Erin's long blonde hair blowing out behind her. It looked like a Vogue magazine shoot or a beautiful piece of cinema. I kept thinking I too must make an exit like that before I die. Except instead of wearing travel pants and sneakers, I want to be wearing a long dress. (Also, it is probably only glamorous if someone is there to catch it on film, but whatever.)

The ride takes 30 minutes. You can purchase tickets online in advance from Conzorzio Motoscafi or buy a voucher at the water taxi ticket desk after exiting baggage claim. From the arrivals area, follow the signs to the boat piers and taxi dock, and present your voucher to the attendant at the taxi dock.

Arriving by Car and Parking at Piazzale Roma

If arriving by car, you will park at Piazzale Roma, then either walk over the Calatrava Bridge (if you don't have luggage) or take a vaporetto. Depending on where you are going, you may need to take one vaporetto to the train station (Ferrovia) and then a second to your destination. It's all quite easy though.

Arriving by Train

I normally arrive by train. There are two train stations: Venezia Mestre is on the mainland and is not the station you want (unless you're staying in Mestre) and **Venezia Santa Lucia**, which *is* the station you want.

Unless you're staying immediately next to the train station, you'll take a water taxi or a vaporetto to your destination. (Be sure to ask your hotel/vacation rental which vaporetto stop you need and get really specific directions from the vaporetto stop to the hotel/apartment.)

Rather than dragging your suitcase around trying to figure out which yellow and white platform is the ticket booth and which is the one for your waterbus, I propose a solution. As you exit your train platform onto the main concourse, with the trains behind you, *veer left*. Before you get to the end, you'll see a small public transport ticket office. The crowds walk right past it and out into the mayhem, trying to find where to go next. But you, my friend, can slip in here and buy your vaporetto ticket calmly and without the crowds. The people working here will tell you which platform you need (lettered A, B, C, etc), which vaporetto you need (the #1, #2, #5.1, etc) and which direction you want the vaporetto going –the one heading to your left or the one going right. They make it so easy and you don't have to worry about pickpockets while you're figuring out how to use the ticket machine outside.

This also means when you exit the train station, you can relax and enjoy the view rather than trying to figure out where to go.

Insider Tip: When exiting the train station, rather than banging your luggage down the stairs, veer to your right. A smooth ramp lets you glide your suitcase down to the fondamenta, protecting your back and your sanity.

When you're exiting the train station with suitcases, expect to be bombarded by porters offering to take your luggage to the vaporetto. Politely but firmly, tell them no and keep walking. Expect at least three or four of them to bug you between the exit and getting to your vaporetto stop.

How to Use the Vaporetto

The vaporetto (waterbus) is the primary public transport in Venice. This is how you travel around the city and the lagoon islands.

Compared to other European cities, public transport in Venice is really expensive. Purchase a day pass if you plan to be moving around all day. If you are only doing one or two trips, it's better to buy individual tickets. Remember, Venice is tiny and you can walk everywhere. I only use day passes when I'm going to the islands, heading to Lido to go to the beach, or bouncing around lots of places in one day. Otherwise, I walk everywhere.

PRICE

A single vaporetto ticket costs €7,50 and is good for 75 minutes.

A vaporetto day pass costs €20.

A two-day pass costs €30.

A three-day pass costs €40.

A seven-day pass costs €60.

In comparison, a ferry ticket for crossing the lagoon or a canal is €5. (For example, from Zattere to Giudecca is €5 on a ferry, € 7,50 on the vaporetto. From San Marco or San Zaccaria to San Giorgio, €5. Lido to S. Elena or Giardini, €5. Don't worry –I'll tell you all about these places as we move through the book.)

Visitors aged 6 to 29 years old can buy a **Rolling Card**. It costs €22 for three days. The card itself costs €6 but it can also get you discounts at museums and can be pre-loaded with extra tickets and passes.

A **Venezia Unica Pass** is great if you'll be in town for a while. You load your vaporetto pass onto it but also entrance to museums, wifi access etc. The pass is valid for two years.

The **Venezia Unica Carta Venezia** costs €100 and is valid for 5 years. You sign up for it at the Venezia Unica office with your passport. Once you have the card, you can load it with 10 single vaporetto tickets for €14, or a monthly pass for €37 (valid for a calendar month, starting on the 1st of the month). It also gets you discounts on the Alilaguna and the airport buses.

Where to Buy a Vaporetto Ticket

As counterintuitive as it may seem, you can't always buy a ticket at the vaporetto stop. Some stops have ticket machines, others don't. There are ticket points scattered around town, Tabbachi shops sell them (look for the sign with the big T outside) and apparently some supermarkets do too. You can also go to a ticket booth with a human in it and ask them. The big stations like Fondamente Nove and San Zaccaria have ticket booths operated by people, as well as ticket machines.

The use of your ticket starts when you validate it. *Every* vaporetto stop has a validation machine. Most have gates that won't let you through unless the machine beeps your validation. (Tap your ticket against the machine and you'll hear the beep.)

***Every time* you board a vaporetto, you must validate your ticket,** even if you have a multi-day pass. If you don't validate your ticket and the guard checks it, you will get a big fine. The same rule applies to public transport all over Italy. A ticket is open until validated, so theoretically you could buy one €7,50 ticket and use it over and over, which is why validation is required. There are no exceptions and they won't accept, "but I'm a tourist, I didn't know". It's not worth it – validate your tickets. Italy used to have a lot of trouble with tourists breaking the rules, so in 2018 they started levying fines left and right. Some busy vaporetto stops now have a uniformed armed guard. (This is also to keep the passenger volume in check and to make sure they follow mask mandates.)

The vaporetto routes are color coded like a subway map. You can google where you're going to find the nearest vaporetto stop or use the ACTV website. Most of the big tourist sites and museums have vaporetto stops named for them, like *Rialto Market, Rialto, Ca' Rezzonico, Ca' d'Oro, Accademia, San Marco*. This takes out much of the guesswork. (Throughout this book, I'll list the vaporetto stops nearest to everywhere we explore.)

The ACTV vaporetto stops are clearly marked on most Venice maps, and the yellow and white floating platforms are easy to spot. Large stops such as San Marco/San Zaccaria and Fondamenta Nove are hubs for multiple routes and have multiple platforms. The direction of the boat is shown on a sign. For example, it might say #1 towards San Marco, or #1 towards Piazzale Roma.

Make sure you are getting on the correct vaporetto. A sign on the side of the vaporetto has the color-coded number of that line, and the stops it's going to. Inside the waiting area, you will also see the same sign with a *You Are Here* indicator highlighting the upcoming stops.

Smaller stops will have boats going in each direction. When the vaporetto pulls in, the sailor opens the gate, lets the disembarking passengers off, then allows the new passengers to board. He normally calls out the direction the boat is going. If you're not sure, ask him. He's busy, so rather than trying to get chatty, just ask him your stop. "Ferrovia?" (Or wherever you're going, in a friendly voice.) He will shake his head and say "No", or say "Si". Simple. You can also ask locals who are waiting for the vaporetto to arrive.

Along with color coding, each vaporetto line is numbered. The #1 goes up and down the Grand Canal. It makes 21 stops, zigzagging back and forth across the canal, and takes about 58 minutes total.

The #2 has two very different routes, one through the Grand Canal, the other through Giudecca, both ending up at Piazzale Roma.

The #1 and #2 are larger boats and are called *vaporetti* (or one *vaporetto*). The smaller #4.1, #4.2, #5.1 and #5.2 are technically *motoscafi*, although I think most people just call them all vaporetti.

Insider Tip: During the tourist season (April to October) the #1 gets packed. As in *crazy* packed, making it perfect for pickpockets. Avoid using the #1 during busy times unless you have to.

Also remember this isn't Disneyland –real people live here, real people who have to get to and from work and the dentist's office and the doctor and everywhere else that you and I go by car/bus/subway. It becomes impossible to go about their day when the vaporetto is full of tourists overloading the space with their suitcases and travel paraphernalia, and who won't get out of the way.

Avoid the #1 during rush hour and when it's full of tourists. You will literally find yourself pressed up against someone's underarm or otherwise too close to their BO. (Not kidding.) I do however recommend taking a run up and down the Grand Canal on the #1 early in the morning, later in the afternoon, or any time it's *not* packed. I honestly think riding the Grand Canal is one of the great joys if you can score an outdoor seat up front. (Another option is to ride along the Grand Canal in a private boat. It costs around €120 for an hour, but is worth it, if it fits your budget.) The view is stunningly beautiful and I never, ever get tired of it.

A few years ago, I sat next to a very nice elderly Venetian gentleman on the #1. I asked him a couple of questions and we ended up chatting for ages (as in, three trips up and down the Grand Canal!). I had time and am fascinated by everything, so he told me amazing local stories as we rode along. He told me stories about the palazzi, and the people who lived in them, which ones were haunted –all kinds of amazing details. On the way back up the canal he pointed out where he met his now-deceased wife, where they went dancing, where they got married, important places in the story of their life together. On our third pass he talked about growing up in Venice and what it was like to live there. It was one of the best afternoons ever. I spent three hours on the #1 and learned more that afternoon than I had in years. And he seemed incredibly happy to have someone to tell his stories to.

Walking in Venice

Venice is a fantastic walking city. It used to be much trickier in terms of perpetually getting lost, but now with the GPS on your phone, you can walk anywhere easily and relatively quickly. Sometimes the

GPS gets confused inside the narrow alleyways, but just step into an open space or campo, and your phone will find the satellite, regroup and off you go.

From the water, you'll see the beautiful palazzi. On foot, exploring the sestieri, you can spot endless tiny details you'd otherwise miss. You'll stumble upon gorgeous little local eateries, bars to stop at for *un caffe* or a spritz and to admire the staggering views. The best things I have discovered in Venice have been while wandering aimlessly, turning corners just because they're there, and walking through doorways just because they're open.

Venice gets crushed by mass tourism (which I'll mention again and again in this book). The cruise ship tourists and other mass tourism folks tend to stick to the same handful of places, from the Rialto Bridge to the Bridge of Sighs. This means that even on the busiest days the rest of the city is wide open for travelers like you and me to wander and explore. And there's no bad part of town. You can't accidentally wander into a street full of gangsters or criminals. There is negligible crime in Venice. It is a *very* safe city, with one of the lowest crime rates in Europe. Venice is incredibly safe to walk around at night. Your biggest worry at night will be getting lost in the mist, but your GPS will guide you home. (I don't think I've ever seen it misty or foggy at night when I've been there during the spring and summer.)

One winter when I stayed near Campo Santo Stefano, a dense fog rolled in late at night, making the beautiful well in the campo suddenly seem quite menacing. I know the area well and was staying only a couple of blocks away down a straight calle (if you saw how close it was on a map you would die laughing). I turned to head home, which basically meant walking to the end of the campo, turning left, following the calle to the end and to the palazzo, something I could do blindfolded. Except in the midwinter fog, which was so dense I could barely see in front of myself. Somehow I managed to get myself turned around. I walked for 30 minutes instead of five and wound up back at the well in the campo, right where I had started! To this day I have no idea how I managed it. Venice is full of ghost stories with similar endings, so at least it's not just me.

Another of my fantastic nighttime escapades happened several years ago when I was staying in Castello, on the edge of the lagoon. My friend and I had been across the Grand Canal at bar Foscarini in Dorsoduro. It wasn't foggy, but night was falling, so I asked the bartender Paolo how to get back to the apartment. He told me to walk through Piazza San Marco, go between the lions and I would find my way back. We said goodbye and headed off, only to arrive back at the bar 40 minutes later! Somehow we had *crossed back over* the Grand Canal, something I can't see how you can possibly do accidentally. We were crying laughing at the stupidity of it and at the same time incredulous that we had pulled off something that crazy. Paolo didn't skip a beat, still polishing glasses behind the bar, and merely said, "I told you, Corinna –walk between the lions!" To this day, every time I walk home through the piazza, I hear Paolo telling me to walk between the lions. And now I always do.

I love to walk Venice in the wee hours. Whether you stay up extra late or get up extra early, make the effort at least once to walk through Venice before sunrise. The city belongs to you and the ghosts, and it is *beautiful*. Especially if there's a little mist floating around. There is something ethereal about catching Venice in the space between the dead of night and the sun creeping up toward the horizon. As you enter the morning blue hour, you'll see photographers emerging to capture the magic. Get to the Riva degli Schiavoni or opposite at the Punta della Dogana as the sun crosses the horizon, bathing you and all of Venice in the morning golden hour. I watch it rise over the lagoon, then turn and watch it light up the palazzi along the Grand Canal. It's a sight you will never, ever forget!

My one caution about nighttime walking in Venice is to take extra care when it's foggy out. In the blink of an eye, a mildly foggy night can turn thicker than pea soup, leaving you unable to see your hand stretched out in front of you –or a canal or waterway you could fall into. I don't actually know anyone who has fallen in, but theoretically, it could happen. (No doubt I will be the idiot it happens to.) Ask the front staff at your hotel if it's a safe night to go walking. I've not encountered fog that thick during the April through October season, but that might just be luck.

Getting Lost in Venice

Chances are you will get lost in Venice –it's part of the magic of this mercurial city on the water. Getting lost is a glorious way of discovering new and wonderful things, so let's unpack this a little.

The Grand Canal cuts Venice in half, so you don't have far to go before you'll find an easily identifiable landmark. There are signs everywhere pointing you to the major landmarks. You will see signs saying *per San Marco* (to San Marco) or *per Rialto*, etc, so identify a couple of landmarks on either side of the Grand Canal. Maybe Piazza San Marco and Ca' d'Oro on one side and Santa Maria della Salute and the Rialto Bridge on the other. Then if you get lost, ask anyone to point you in either direction and you'll find your way again.

Insider Tip: Keep your phone charged (and pack a small external phone battery) so you can always fall back on your phone's GPS.

Crossing the Grand Canal

Only four bridges cross the Grand Canal. The #1 vaporetto zigzags back and forth from one side to the other, but what do locals do when they can't wait for the waterbus? There is quite a distance between the Accademia Bridge and the centuries-old Rialto Bridge, so a series of gondola-style boats cross at strategic points along the canal. These are the *traghetti* (one *traghetto*).

Also known as a *gondola parada,* traghetti are unadorned, with no luxury trimmings or brocaded cushions. They're manned by two oarsmen instead of just one and carry up to 10 people.

In the 1950s there were 30 traghetto routes. Now there are seven, with only two of those in constant use. The two most reliable operate between the Rialto fish market and Santa Sofia (by Ca' d'Oro), and between San Toma' and Sant'Angelo.

The other five traghetti run between the following:

- Fondamenta S. Lucia (train station) –Fondamenta San Simeon Piccolo
- San Marcuola –Fondaco dei Turchi
- Riva del Carbon –Fondamente del Vin
- San Samuele –Ca' Rezzonico
- Campo del Traghetto –Calle Lanz (by the Salute church).

On street maps of Venice, a straight black line cutting across the Grand Canal marks traghetto routes. The stop is a small wooden pier and you'll see the traghetto shuttling back and forth. It won't wait for long.

There are two prices –€2 for a tourist and €0,70 for residents and Venezia Unica pass holders. You pay the oarsman as you board or disembark. Be sure to have coins. Don't give him large bank notes.

A great way to differentiate between the locals and tourists is to watch them board a traghetto. Most Venetians stand stoically, even in rough weather. I, on the other hand, would fall over the edge if I tried standing, even if it was glassy smooth, so like most non-residents, I sit. Try to face backwards –once it pulls out from the dock, the traghetto will turn.

This is not a means of cross canal transport for anyone with luggage, a wheelchair, or a stroller. If you fall into any of these categories, just grab the #1 vaporetto, which has a flat deck for you to balance on with ease.

7.
Figuring Out Venice

To build a city where it is impossible to build a city is madness in itself, but to build there one of the most elegant and grandest of cities is the madness of genius.

–Alexander Herzen

No doubt you've heard about getting lost in Venice. But Venice is tiny and if you keep going, you'll either run into a building or the sea, so you can't get catastrophically lost. And you can't wander into a dangerous neighborhood, because there aren't any. This is a city like no other. It's not designed like anywhere you've been before, and for many of us, it makes no sense at all –which is part of why I love it so much! In this chapter, I'll explain how the city functions, what everything means, and how this unique place works.

Venice by the Numbers

Venice is a series of 118 little islands separated by canals and *rios* and connected by 435 bridges. These islands live in a shallow lagoon in an enclosed bay between the Brenta and Sile rivers and the Adriatic Sea. The city looks like a fish. The Grand Canal runs through the middle with three neighborhoods (*sestieri*) on either side (one *sestiere*, two *sestieri*).

On one side:

- **Cannaregio**, the most populated
- **San Marco**, the most famous
- **Castello**, the largest.

On the other side:

- **Dorsoduro**, the "hard back" of Venice
- **San Polo**, the littlest sestiere
- **Santa Croce** at the base.

Three islands next to Venice each belong to a different sestiere. The cemetery island of San Michele is part of Cannaregio. San Giorgio Maggiore is part of San Marco, and the Giudecca is part of Dorsoduro.

Canals and Rii

Over 150 waterways run through Venice, crossed by its 435 bridges, and these are called *rii* (the plural of *rio*).

There are also three canals in Venice:

- The most famous is the **Grand Canal**, running through the middle of the city.
- Until 1861, when the railway connecting Venice to Mestre opened, the **Cannaregio Canal** was the principal thoroughfare into the city from the mainland. *Cannaregio* comes from *Canal Regio* or Royal *Canal.*

- The third canal is the **Giudecca Canal**, flowing between Dorsoduro and the Giudecca. Cruise ships use the Giudecca Canal.

Venetian Addresses

Street addresses in Venice are super confusing. They're like a secret code known only to psychics and mailmen. Buildings opposite one another can have street numbers differing by hundreds. A narrow alleyway throws off the sequence of numbers. But that's Venice for you –she's all smoke and mirrors, wisps of thoughts swirling in the fog. Nothing is as it seems, yet it somehow is.

Addresses seem inconsistent. In some, you'll see the street name, the sestiere and the street number. But not always. As a non-Venetian, don't expect it to make sense. For example, the *osteria* opposite an apartment I once rented –*Osteria Al Bacareto* is on the corner of Ramo de la Piscina and Calle Crosera (Calle Crosera has a shoe etched into the wall as it was once a cobbler's street), but its address is Campo San Samuele 3447.

An address might just be the name of the sestiere, followed by the street number. An address might read: Santa Croce 1327. This means it is in the sestiere of Santa Croce and it is door number 1327. Or you may see a street name in there too, such as Santa Croce, Ramo Orsetti 1425.

The key is that the buildings in each sestiere are numbered according to walls rather than streets (*calle/calli*). From the start of the *calle*, numbers follow in sequence along your side. At an alleyway or side street the numbers will turn the corner, go to the end, and swoop back. Within each sestiere, it can feel as though blocks of house numbers are random, so don't expect to use them to find your way.

Here's my advice for navigating in Venice –when you're trying to find a landmark (or shop or hotel or museum or church) in Venice, just type the name into your GPS. It's *much* less confusing than trying to find it using the street numbers. When trying to find a private home or rental apartment, ask for the closest landmark. From there, GPS the street address. This actually works out well for me. I'm terrible at street names –I can name the streets I drive in and out on in my Phoenix neighborhood, but despite living here for years I couldn't tell you the name of a street two blocks from my house. I remember the names of the streets I use the most and pretty much none of the others. Venice is a labyrinth. Most locals couldn't tell you all the street names, anyway.

It makes it confusing to use physical street maps, but with the GPS on your phone telling you to turn left in 20 feet then cross the next bridge, it's relatively easy to make your way across town to the most random location.

The History Behind the Address System

During the Venetian Republic, there was no street numbering and streets had no official names. Addresses used the parish name plus another identifier, "the street with the meat shop" or "along from the church". The system worked for 1000 years.

When Austria occupied Venice, their administrators wanted street names, so they asked what the street was known for, then labeled it, like Shoemakers' Street, Fishermen's Street, Hatmakers' Street, and the street name was painted on the wall at the street corner. These same street signs (*nizioleti*) are still there to be seen today. (The nizioleti are in Venetian dialect, not Italian.) A few years later, they passed a law to number the buildings. Each building needed its number stenciled in black on a white background. The numbers later changed to red, but you can still see this system today.

In each sestiere, they chose a starting point for the numbers. In San Marco, the starting point was the Doge's Palace, which has the official address of San Marco 1. Cannaregio started at the church of Santa Lucia (though the church was later demolished to make way for the train station). Castello starts at the Basilica of San Pietro. In Dorsoduro it's Santa Maria della Salute, Santa Croce's is the Ponte San Pantalon and San Polo starts with the Palazzo dei Camerlenghi by the Rialto Bridge. The total number of houses in each sestiere is written on another nizioleto. San Marco's is near the Fontego dei Tadeschi, telling us the last building in the sestiere is number 5562.

Throughout this book, I'll provide street addresses, but essentially I'm just being polite, because trying to get anywhere via a street address will only confuse you. First, look for the sestiere (Cannaregio, San Marco, Castello, Dorsoduro, Santa Croce or San Polo) to know which side of the Grand Canal you're on, then group several things together. I'll also include the vaporetto stop for each listing, which I find is the most helpful direction when trying to find my way somewhere.

Street Names

Everything in Venice is different, which adds to the magic. There are no roads, no cars and trucks, not even the ubiquitous Italian vespa. So it stands to reason they have different names for the various thoroughfares. Here is a breakdown:

Strada: There is only one *strada* in Venice, the Strada Nova in Cannaregio. Built in the 19th century, this is a long, wide, winding street full of shops.

Calli/Calle: Venetian streets are called *calli* (one *calle* two *calli*). Venice has 3000 calli. A calle can be anywhere from just under 60cm wide to 6 meters wide. For reference, the average American male shoulder width is 41.1cm. The narrowest calle in Venice, measuring only 53cm wide, is Calle Varisco in Cannaregio, near Fondamente Nove. (Look for the Doric column at the entrance.) The second narrowest calle is in Castello, a short walk from Calle Varisco. Calesela dell' Ochio Grosso (the narrow street of the big eye) measures 58cm across.

Ramo/Rami: Calli leading to a dead end or to a campo can be called *rami* which means "branches". They can also be smaller streets connecting to bigger streets. There are 367 rami in Venice.

Salizada/Salizade: These are calli that were once important, like embassy streets. *Salizade* were the first paved streets in Venice. Sometimes you still see them paved with terracotta bricks in a herringbone pattern, such as outside of Madonna dell'Orto. There are 42 salizade.

Ruga/Rughe: This is a type of street that was used for commercial business. The name comes from the French '*rue*'. There are 10 *rughe* in Venice.

Rio Terà: Sometimes a *rio* had to be paved over. These became known as *Rio Tera'*, roughly translated to "buried rio". Most rio tera' still have water flowing beneath them. Venice has 53 rio tera'.

Sotoportaghi/Sotoportego: These are underpasses or short walkways with buildings above them, technically a street-level passageway running below part of a house. Look up as you walk through and you'll see the classic wooden beam ceiling as is in every Venetian house.

Fondamente/Fondamenta: A *fondamenta* (foundation) is a walking bank that faces the water. It has places to load and unload boats. Some have docks for the vaporetto. They can be small and private or big and bustling like Fondamente Nove, which is a hub for multiple vaporetto lines. Some fondamente are very long. The Fondamenta delle Zattere stretches most of the length of the Giudecca canal, lined with bars and restaurants. (Unless cruise ships are passing, the Zattere is a gorgeous place to enjoy an aperitivo with a view of Giudecca island.)

Campo, Campiello, Corto

In Italy, the town or village square is called a *piazza*. In Venice, there is only one *piazza*, the Piazza San Marco/St Mark's Square. Here, the other town squares are called *campi* (one is a *campo*), which means "fields". In the beginning, these actually *were* fields. Covered in grass, some were orchards or gardens, others had sheep and horses grazing on them. Campo di San Pietro di Castello with its grass and trees gives you an idea of how they must have once looked.

The campo was the social center of the community. Each of the 118 little islands was a separate community with its own campo. This was a meeting place for the residents, surrounded by houses. In the morning, the local market would be in the campo. It was also where children played. Away from the tourist crush, you'll still see children kicking soccer balls in the campo, playing games of chase, especially in the afternoons and long summer evenings.

Every campo has a well. This was the only water source for the community before the construction of the aqueduct, bringing water from the mainland. The campo wells are fascinating during the day, but I find them deliciously eerie on foggy nights.

Traditionally, the campo would have had a church with an adjacent cemetery, but Napoleon banned burials in the campi and moved Venice's cemetery to the island of San Michele. Most campi take the name of their church. Some were named for the important family living there, others for the merchant trades carried out in that space.

Smaller campi are called *campielli* (one *campiello*). A campiello can be a section of a calle, or just a smaller town square, part of a micro-community. They can be a central communal space for a group of houses and doesn't normally have its own well. A campiello is small, intimate and almost an extension of the homes surrounding it, like a big courtyard. However, a *corte* (courtyard) normally has only one entrance, through a gate or a *portico*.

The Bridges of Venice

The 118 islands of Venice are connected by approximately 435 bridges. Only four bridges cross the Grand Canal: The Constitution/Calatrava, the Scalzi, the Rialto and the Accademia.

Famous Bridges

Ponte delle Tette (Bridge of the Boobs)

During the Republic, around 10,000 sex workers plied their trade in Venice. In 1412 they were restricted to the Carampane di Rialto neighborhood, turning it into the city's Red-Light District. In 1514, the profession even had taxes levied on it. Sex workers had curfews, couldn't work on holy days, could only leave the neighborhood on Saturdays, and had to wear yellow scarves to identify themselves when they left. This bridge got its name because prostitutes were permitted to show their boobs from windows in the buildings surrounding the bridge, and to stand topless on the bridge holding lanterns at night. (I'll tell more of this story in the **Venetian Masks** chapter.)

When you cross the bridge, look for a big white *nizioleto* or street sign that says: Sestiere S. Polo, Ponte de le Tette.

Address: 1951 Calle Agnello
What's Nearby: The bridge is midway between Campo San Polo and Campo San Cassiano, near the Rialto Market.

Ponte dei Pugni (Bridge of Fists/Punches)

This bridge is where they once held fist fights. Although it now has railings, the idea was to punch your opponent until he fell into the cold, sewage filled canal. These fist fights were a popular spectator sport in Venice dating back to the early 1600s. Such fights took place on several bridges around Venice, but the most famous fighting bridge was the Ponte dei Pugni, near Campo San Barnaba in Dorsoduro. Four white marble footprints mark the starting point for the fighters. They restored these in 2005, so be sure to look for them when making your way across!

Address: Campo San Barnaba 30123, Dorsoduro
What's Nearby: This is a quick walk from Ca' Rezzonico. La Barca S. Barnaba (the floating market) is beside the bridge.

Ponte del Chiodo

This is the last remaining bridge in Venice without railings or parapets. (There's another on the island of Torcello, known as the Devil's Bridge.) The Chiodo Bridge dead-ends at the front door of a house. Look a little closer and you'll see that the steps are both wider and shallower than regular steps, making the bridge extra interesting visually. Chiodo means "nail" and was the surname of the family who owned both the bridge and the home. The home is now a B&B.

Address: Cannaregio 3749
What's Nearby: The Church of the Misericordia, Vino Vero and the Jewish Ghetto.

Ponte Dei Tre Archi (Bridge of Three Arches)

Dating back to 1681, the bridge is in Cannaregio and is the only one left in Venice with three arches. Two bridges cross the Cannaregio Canal, this one and the Ponte delle Guglie. Along with the four bridges that cross the Grand Canal, these are the six main bridges of Venice.

Address: Cannaregio
What's Nearby: The Jewish Ghetto.

Ponte dei Sospiri (Bridge of Sighs)

This bridge connects the Doge's Palace with the prison next door. Contrary to popular myth, the sighs weren't the romantic kind. They were the sighs of the convicted, getting their last look at Venice before descending into the dungeons below.

Address: Rio del Palazzo
What's Nearby: Doge's Palace, Piazza San Marco.

The Wells of Venice

As you explore the *campi* and *corte*, keep an eye out for the wells of Venice. They can seem spooky at night, especially when the fog rolls in, but during the day they are quite marvelous. Some have intricate stonework, and all are fascinating.

There was always plenty of fresh air and fresh fish to survive on in Venice, but in the beginning there was one crucial thing missing –fresh, drinkable water. Venice was built on swampland in a salty lagoon, with no underground water supply. The *Veneti* needed a solution, and quickly. The answer was to filter rainwater. Wide spaces were needed around each well, making the campo the perfect location.

The engineering of these wells is absolutely brilliant. No campo is flat, the pavement slopes down towards the well, guiding rainwater into the guttering. The water is then filtered and cleaned through layers of clay and sand below. (I'm leaving out several steps here, but it ultimately filters through the *canna de pozzo*.) The *canna* (a tall tunnel made of *pozzoli* bricks) was as deep as the tank and the bricks allowed water to penetrate and pass through, cleaning it one last time.

The wells were so important, the Grand Council ordered more to be built. In 1322 (50 more wells) in 1424 (30 wells) and in 1768 (55 wells). Supervision of water access was very strict. Local priests and block leaders were the only people with keys to their assigned wells and would unlock them twice daily for the residents to collect their water ration. The ringing of the "wells bells" notified citizens of the unlocking of the wells every morning and evening.

Along with being an absolute necessity, building wells was very expensive. Rich Venetians flaunted their wealth by "gifting" wells to the city. The Republic rewarded them with an inscription or bas relief on the *vere da pozzo* (the visible or decorative part of the well). Look at the decoration of the wells to see if you can spot which family donated them.

Another indirect donor of wells was the Vatican. Venice welcomed hundreds of churches and cloisters, most of which required private wells. In a clever move, Venetian law made it mandatory for the church to give free access to its wells to the citizens of Venice, twice each day.

In 1858, a census counted 180 public wells and 6000 private ones, along with 556, which were closed or removed. (The most famous removed well was the one in Piazza San Marco, which kept getting contaminated, making the water smelly and undrinkable.)

Not just anyone could create a well. It was an amazing feat of engineering, it was expensive, and it required specialized workers. Venice created a guild called the *Confraternita dei Pozzieri*. The confraternity were the only people allowed to build wells. Membership was prestigious, and the knowledge and expertise passed from father to son. However, their membership came with a caveat –they could only build wells for the Republic of Venice.

Venice has three signed wells. Bartolomeo Bon signed the Pozzo at Ca' d'Oro in 1427. Creators Nicolo' Conti and Alfonso Albergetti signed the two bronze wells in the Doge's Palace Court in 1556 and 1559.

The growing population needed more water, so in 1386, they created the *Corporazione degli Acquaroli*. This corporation filled the wells with water from the Brenta River, ensuring enough water to last all year. They stored the water in closed bowls to ensure its purity. In 1609, the peak of Venetian population, the *acquaroli* dug an artificial channel to speed up bringing the fresh water to Venice. The canal was 1 meter wide and 13.5km long, starting at the Brenta River and ending at Moranzani on the mainland. The acquaroli would fill their boats, row to Venice, then use wooden pipes to fill the wells from their boats. They also sold water to citizens for immediate consumption, like street vendors.

The Venetian water system relied on careful maintenance and rigorous control of access. This entire enterprise was wildly successful for centuries, until the fall of the Republic, and the subsequent decline of city administration. Without experts to maintain the delicate balance of the water filtration and the functionality of the wells, quality diminished. The only answer was to modernize the water system by creating an aqueduct. Work began in 1881 with construction of a cast-iron pipe beneath the lagoon, connected to the water supply in Moranzani. The project was completed in 1884 and celebrated with a fountain in the middle of Piazza San Marco.

Today there are still around 600 wells in Venice and about 142 fountains. Make sure you check them out in every campo and corte you visit.

The Bricole

In the canals and the lagoon, you'll see wooden pilings strapped together, leaning into each other. These are *bricole (bree-COH-leh)*, the guardians of the lagoon, keeping boats safe for 1000 years. They act like street signs in the water, telling the boatmen where the channel is too shallow, stopping them from running ashore. They tell the boatmen where they can safely traverse, even in very low tides.

INTERESTING FACTS ABOUT BRICOLE

- *Bricola* means dolphin. When you see them, think of dolphins arching out of the water, guiding ships and boats to safety.
- They make bricole from oak, but not just any old oak. The lagoon has a very fragile ecosystem, so introducing the wrong wood, or wood containing bugs/parasites/viruses, could be disastrous. This oak comes from European forests, mostly from Germany, France and the Balkans, and is certified by the Forest Stewardship Council (FSC) and the PEFC (Program for the Endorsement of Forest Certification).
- Unlike the pilings below the houses of Venice, bricole only last between 5 and 10 years. Their longevity depends on where they are in the lagoon, how strong the waves around them are, and which microorganisms are present in their specific stretch of the lagoon. Where they are in relation to the cruise ships plays into it as well, with the toxic pollutants from the ships and the catastrophic undertow that pulls on all of Venice's pilings taking a toll.
- Although embedded in the bottom of the lagoon (unlike the pilings underneath Venice), a section of a bricola is in moving water so has both water and oxygen present and, unlike the building pilings, is not impervious to rot. Keep an eye out and you will spot signs of rotting at the waterline.
- The bricole are monitored and hopefully get replaced before they break off and float into the path of approaching boats.

- A bricola's life isn't over when it leaves the lagoon. Companies refurbish and treat the wood, making it into flooring, furniture and decorative pieces. You can even purchase souvenirs made from re-purposed bricole.
- In 1789, a study counted 8000 bricole. Today over 20,000 bricole guard the Venice lagoon.
- On 8 December 1439, the Venetian Senate enacted the first laws concerning bricole. Most of these laws are still in effect. All new channels in the lagoon must be marked with these wooden posts and the posts checked annually. The major difference now is the addition of reflectors and lights to some.
- The *Dame (dah-meh)* are a group of five posts bound together. One is taller than the others, and usually has a light attached to it. The Dame mark the beginning of a canal.
- Before you can pilot a boat in Venice, it is mandatory to learn the laws and rules of the lagoon, and the rules of the bricole. You can't just rent a boat and go for a joyride.

The Pali da Casada

Look for colorful striped poles in the water in front of houses and palaces in Venice. These are the *pali da casada,* ("the poles of the house"). For centuries, they helped guests ensure they'd arrived at the correct palace at night. An oil lamp would sit on top of the *palo*, shining a light on its colors. Now you will see a *cappellozzo* symbolizing the lamp. Look closer and you'll notice different designs of *cappellozzi*, as chosen by the family.

The pali are always painted in the family colors. Until 1562, they also painted gondolas in the family colors. (After 1562, all gondolas were painted black.) Now that people living in the palazzi no longer own private gondolas, the pali poles are purely ornamental. You're not supposed to moor a gondola or a boat to them.

Not all pali are painted in stripes. Some, like those outside of the Palazzo Contarini Fasan in San Marco, are a single color –in this case bright blue covered in gold. The neighbor's pali da casada are gold and blue stripes. You can see both across the Grand Canal from the church of Santa Maria della Salute.

The Foscari family colors were white and red with a white top. Look for them outside of Ca' Foscari (the university) on the Grand Canal, then spot those specific pali da casada all over Venice outside of various properties owned by the Foscari. Once you train your eye to look for them, it's fun to look for the different pali da casada as you stroll Venice.

Operating a City on the Water

Every aspect of Venetian life happens on the water. I love to be on the Grand Canal in the morning watching barges and delivery boats delivering supplies to the city. Everything that gets delivered by cars, vans, and trucks at home, arrives by barge or boat in Venice. You'll see UPS boats and Amazon Prime boats, police boats, construction boats, ambulances and fire engine boats.

The trash collectors are my favorite. The *spazzini* (sanitation workers) wheel their specialized hand carts up and down over bridges, collecting trash bags and bringing it back to the green and white trash barges waiting at the mouths of the larger waterways. These larger trash barges have crane arms to pick up the carts and dump trash into the appropriate tanks. Trash collection has always been tricky in this city of narrow alleys and waterways. Add 25 million tourists per year, seagulls ripping open trash bags and scattering refuse, and a proliferation of rats, and it becomes even more difficult. Rather than leaving trash bags outside waiting for collection, in 2016 the local trash company put a new system in place. Trash collectors now go door to door from 8.30am until noon, filling their carts. (If you're not home you can take your rubbish to a trash barge.) Trash boats are fitted with special compactors that make recycling super-efficient. Paper products are collected on Mondays, Wednesdays and Fridays. Glass, plastic, and cans on Tuesdays, Thursdays and Saturdays. They collect general waste every day. There are also eight collection bins around the city for used oil.

Road Repairs

In a city where nothing is easy, I find the process for road repairs interesting. When streets need repairing, you can't just tear up pavement, fix what's broken and lay down new asphalt here. Streets in Venice are either waterways, or covered waterways (*rio tera*), so repairs are incredibly intricate and difficult because before anything can be done, someone must remove the water.

To do this, they erect *cofferdams* on either end of the afflicted *rio*, sealing it from the neighboring waterway. Then the crew drain it and remove the gray, smelly sludge and silt accumulated over who even knows how many decades. A crane scoops out the sludge, dumps into a vehicle that then transfers it to a collection barge. This part of the job takes several smelly days to complete and has multiple complicating factors:

1. The ancient pilings below Venice. The moment the pilings make contact with the air, they begin to rot, so they have to be protected during the canal cleaning. Pilings exposed to air

have to be replaced. They still use the same type of wood they've used for centuries.

2. The issue of public utilities. Water mains, electric power lines, fiber optic cable, and all the stuff used to run any city, are submerged below the canals and waterways. They must be secured and protected while the cleaning is happening.

The Emergency Room

The *ospedale* (hospital) is *fascinating*. Visitors and workers don't emerge from a parking lot, they exit a vaporetto or walk in from Campo SS Giovanni e Paolo. The main hospital entrance is a must-visit. It's the prettiest hospital in the world.

The *pronto soccorso* (emergency room) entrance is on the lagoon. From Fondamente Nove you can watch ambulances racing in and out. It's intriguing to think Venetian paramedics perform emergency medicine on fast boats in rough water –the same life-saving acts our paramedics perform on land, in a steady ambulance on a flat road. Can you imagine inserting a needle into someone's arm on a rocking, bouncing boat? How on earth do they move a wounded patient from a bobbing boat onto *terra firma*? It's so interesting!

Along the side of the hospital, you'll see ambulances parked diagonally along the Fondamenta Mendicanti. Imagine ambulance crews running along here in the pouring rain or thick fog, tearing off into the night. It also gives you some insight into how much more complicated life can be for Venetians.

Daily Life

Life in the most unique city on earth, comes with a price. Even without millions of tourists jamming the central city during the travel season, life in Venice has complications. Consider everything you do in life that involves a car, or land transport, and then remove the car. That includes getting your kids to school in a rainstorm, grocery shopping, and going to the doctor. Imagine having a knee injury or a broken leg, and having to cross 20 bridges to get to the doctor's office or hospital. For the elderly, simple things like going to a dentist appointment involve multiple sets of stairs up and down bridges. It's tricky in the sunshine, and treacherous in the rain.

An unwritten rule when visiting Venice is *stay out of the locals' way.* Please don't walk side by side through a narrow calli. Keep to the right. Let locals pass. Don't block the bridges either. Remember, this is how residents go about their day. Be cognizant of the elderly, give them room to get through, and it doesn't hurt to offer to help carry their wheelie shopping bag/cart over the bridge for them.

8.
Where to Stay in Venice

When I went to Venice, I discovered that my dream had become – incredibly, but quite simply –my address.

–Marcel Proust

How to you decide where to stay in a city you've never visited before? Nobody wants to book a hotel in a bad part of town or find themselves too far from the action. So, let's look at how to choose where to stay in Venice.

Venice is one of the safest cities in Europe –violent crime, race and gender related crime, any kind of physical attack are all uncommon here. You are extremely safe walking around at night –you are more likely to fall in a canal than get mugged! Any major tourist city in Europe has pickpockets and some measure of property theft, but in Venice, they rate even these crimes low to moderate.

Usually when you're travelling, the areas around train stations are frequently troublesome, but in Venice, the Santa Lucia area is lovely. (It's not my first choice to stay in purely because there are other neighborhoods I love more and stay in regularly.)

There is no bad part of Venice. However, I do have several criteria for when I'm looking for accommodation here.

Stay *in* Venice

Some people recommend saving money by staying in Mestre and commuting daily into Venice by train. *I emphatically disagree.* You came to experience Venice –so why stay on the mainland? Venice has great accommodation at all price points, so I don't see the financial benefit of staying in Mestre. In addition, day trippers are the single most economically damaging aspect of tourism to Venice.

I used to make this mistake myself, thinking my tour groups were better spending a day in Venice than missing out altogether. I didn't know how damaging this was to the local economy. (Later on, I'll give you the statistics, but they are quite staggering.) Our spend would include a local guide, meals, tickets to the Doge's Palace or Ca' Rezzonico, gondola rides, and vaporetto rides. Then we would have apertivo hour, do some souvenir shopping, and buy food to eat on the train home. I never spent less than €100 per person, normally closer to €150—175, so I thought I was doing the right thing by investing in Venice's local economy. I wasn't. We spent much more than the average day tripper, yet we were part of the problem. We weren't investing in the city's infrastructure.

Venice doesn't need more day trippers, it needs more overnight stays. In Italy, you pay a nightly tourist tax to the city you stay in. In Venice, this covers the cost of collecting your trash, using the toilets (that sewage has to go somewhere, and it's not free) and maintenance of the calli and bridges. It also contributes to emergency services and the cost of running the city. Your morning coffee, evening aperitivo and every random little expense you don't even think about, all contribute to the local economy of wherever you're staying. It doesn't seem like much, but the little things add up. They impact the economy and the livelihood of local Venetians. Once I understood this impact, I changed my tours so that now we spend a minimum of three nights in Venice.

So, let's all stay in Venice.

A Room with a View

In a city as beautiful as Venice, try to get yourself a room with a view, preferably of a canal or rio. One of the great advantages of staying on the Grand Canal or Cannaregio Canal is observing Venetian life from your window. In the early mornings you'll see the barges and delivery boats delivering groceries to the supermarkets, goods to the shops, and moving things from point A to point B. Everything that happens by delivery van or truck at home happens via boat and barge here, and it's cool to watch.

Evenings spent on your balcony watching nightlife are glorious. A few years ago we stayed in a gorgeous palazzo next to the Sant' Angelo vaporetto stop. One evening a palazzo across the canal hosted a ridiculously glamorous party. From our window seats, with icy cold glasses of Friulane, we saw guests arriving in their gleaming water taxis. Tuxedo-wearing greeters helped ladies in gowns and gents in tuxes alight from the boats and guided them inside. It was like watching a movie! Enormous chandeliers sparkled inside the palazzo as we watched the event through its massive windows. Later, we returned home from dinner in time to see them dancing, and then finally their boats pulling up to escort them home. It was gorgeous!

Another benefit of staying on the major waterways is seeing the sunrise, sunset, golden hour and blue hour from your window, with the light playing over the palaces lining the canals. It really is incredible. This, however, is prime real estate and is probably your most expensive accommodation option.

There are plenty of minor waterways with fabulous Venetian views, that really aren't expensive. You can watch the boats and hear the water slapping the walls below from just about anywhere, without breaking the budget. And you'll never forget that magical sound.

Go High

Don't book a ground-floor apartment in Venice. At the best of times, Venice is humid and ground floor apartments get the worst of that humidity. In *The Venice Experiment*, author Barry Frangipani talks about constantly wiping down the walls of his family's ground floor apartment with a bleach solution to stay ahead of the mold. During the year they lived in Venice, despite their valiant efforts, the mold ruined their shoes and many belongings. They are Floridians, yet they still found it overwhelming.

The ground floor can also be noisy, especially on busy waterways with workers making their early morning commute. Ground floor apartments frequently get flooded during *acqua alta* high tides.

Humid, watery places get lots of mosquitos. Although science might not support this, I'm convinced more mosquitos hang out down low than up high. I get eaten alive in Venice if I'm not covered in DEET. I probably glow in the dark from it by now. When I am down low, if there is a single patch of skin I've missed, an entire squadron of mosquitos will find it.

However, my major freak out about ground floor accommodation in Venice is rats. The city on the water always has to contend with rats and you see rat traps everywhere. (I am rodent-phobic and can spot a rat trap at a thousand paces.) You often see what looks like chicken wire over ground-floor windows. This is there to stop rats getting inside (which frankly gives me the heebie-jeebies).

Interestingly, when Italy first opened after Covid and the tourists were all gone, the rats were too. The lack of tourists dropping trash meant the rats were on sabbatical. For centuries, stray cats kept the rat situation under control, which worked swimmingly until two things happened –a British do-gooder spayed and neutered the feline rat patrol, drastically diminishing their ranks, then mass tourism left the felines with nowhere peaceful to hang out and sun themselves. So, like many of the locals, they left.

No Elevators

Don't expect elevators in most buildings in Venice. Hotels have them and some apartment buildings do too, but that doesn't mean they'll be working. (This applies all across Italy, not just Venice, and is reason enough to travel light. It only takes one trip to the 4th floor with no elevator to cure people of traveling with a heavy suitcase.)

If climbing stairs is a problem for you, I suggest either a ground-floor apartment that doesn't back onto water or staying on the first floor. Otherwise find a hotel where there's a greater certainty the elevators will be working.

Map Your Route

This is super important. Map. Your. Route.

Until you've seen this city, it's hard to comprehend the difficulties of getting around Venice with luggage. There are no door-to-door taxis here. Unless you're staying at one of the big hotels, you and your suitcase will have to get from point A to point B on foot, come rain or shine. This means dragging your bags across uneven cobblestones, up and down the steps of bridges. It's actually against the law to bang your bags up and down steps. Your apartment or hotel may *seem* close to the vaporetto stop, but nothing is a straight (or easy) line here. There may be a considerable walk, navigating multiple little bridges.

A private taxi in Venice won't actually deliver you door to door either. It will deliver you *to the closest point where he can unload you.* The driver will try to help you and your suitcases. But the boat might not line up perfectly against the edge of the walkway, and the water may be rough. You and your luggage may have to "mind the gap" and disembark onto wet pavement from a boat that's rocking.

I always look for accommodation close to a vaporetto stop, but also with few/no bridges in between the stop and the accommodation. Arriving by taxi is cool, but the vaporetto is easier when you're wrangling luggage. Trust me, try it once in the pouring rain with rough water and you'll see there is method to my madness! (When it rains in Venice, it *rains.*)

I've given up staying at plenty of spectacular apartments with my tour groups because the drama of getting them to and from with their luggage is just not worth the stress.

Avoid Crowds

I like to stay in neighborhoods far from the tourist crowds. Until you've seen it yourself, you can't imagine what the streets of Venice look like when multiple cruise ships are visiting. Five ships in port means around 20,000 extra visitors to the city, and they're all squashed into an area about a mile long. Cruise passengers mostly hangout between the Rialto Bridge and Piazza San Marco, but it isn't like rush hour in Manhattan. These groups look overwhelmed and move *really slowly*. They absorb all the space and won't let you cut through the group, panicked by the possibility of losing sight of their umbrella waving cruise guide.

Moving through these crowds is a nuisance, and with luggage it is a nightmare. It ruins something as simple as wandering down the street for coffee, and it is not the Venetian experience you've been dreaming of. I'm guessing your dream involved beautiful scenery, all the intricacies of this gorgeous city, lovely places to sit with a morning coffee or an early evening spritz. I'm pretty sure you didn't want to be surrounded by sweaty, fanny-packed tourists blocking the view.

The good news is that most of Venice is far from the crowds. Once you get about 5 minutes' walk from San Zaccaria/San Marco (where you still find some tourist-overflow), I love the Castello neighborhood. I've stayed here for so long it feels like my Venetian home.

Cannaregio has some tremendous areas. The younger party crowd loves the Fondamenta dei Ormesini, which is bopping until all hours of the night. If you want something a little less noisy, Cannaregio also has plenty of wonderful, quiet neighborhoods too.

Away from the major tourist spots, San Marco is gorgeous. I recently had a group staying near the Campo Santo Stefano and it was like living in a dream. I love that their impression and memory of Venice is of that place, those streets, the coffee shop on the corner –it captured the sheer magic of Venice.

Dorsoduro is lovely. The masses don't seem to congregate there, so you can enjoy a more peaceful version of Venice. Also, there are tons of great places to eat and drink.

The Zattere side of San Polo is nowhere near as crowded as the Rialto side, and blends into Dorsoduro's loveliness.

In Santa Croce, one of my friends stayed in an unbelievable apartment in San Giacomo dell' Orio. They watched the Tuesday night tango just down the street and discovered endless eateries and coffee bars all around them. Surrounded by Venetians, not tourists, they enjoyed authentic food at non-tourist prices.

Which brings me to another good reason to avoid the mass tourism areas –tourist pricing.

I like to meander over to my local coffee joint, rather than hustle through crowded streets. Once there, in calm surroundings, I sip my breakfast cappuccino or caffe macchiato at local prices (around €1,20). I also like to drop in on a local bacaro for an apertivo in the early evening, at non-tourist prices. People sometimes say Venice is an expensive place to eat and drink. I say, "Only where the tourists go."

Some of my friends stay on Lido, and love the resort feel of the island. Just know it looks nothing like the Venice across the water. The lagoon islands are pretty, but they require a substantial commute to see anything else. I recommend staying in Venice on your first trip, then maybe try staying on one of them on a subsequent visit. If you experience Venice the real way, you'll always want to come back.

Hotels

Some of the most beautiful hotels in the world are found in Venice. If you are going 5-star you can't beat the Aman, the Danieli and the Cipriani (on Giudecca). There are loads of amazing luxe hotels in Venice.

When choosing your hotel, look at how close it is to the vaporetto stop. Ask the hotel how close a taxi can bring you. Does the hotel have a transfer service from the station or airport? (Most don't.) Find out how crowded the area is. For 5-star travelers, this may not matter to you. Or you may prefer a location where you can stroll to reasonably priced meals and experience the city without drowning in tourists.

Before you book a hotel or apartment, read reviews and look for common threads:

- What is the neighborhood like? (Loud? Smelly? Overpriced? Over-touristed?)
- Are the beds comfortable?
- How is the bathroom?
- Are the towels soft?
- Are the reviews recent?

If there are no recent reviews, ask yourself why.

9.
What to Eat in Venice

If I were not King of France, I would choose to be a citizen of Venice.

–Henry III

In *Glam Italia! How To Travel Italy: Secrets to Glamorous Travel (On a Not-So-Glamorous Budget)* I explain that Italian cuisine is entirely regional. As you move across the country, food changes, ingredients are different. The shapes, textures and types of pasta and the sauces that go with them are different. Even the bread changes.

You also find differences *within* each region. Italian cooking uses seasonal, locally sourced ingredients. Although a dish may be specific to a particular region, it may not be on that day's menu if the core ingredient is not in season. This is especially true in cities, towns and villages not pillaged by mass tourism. (Some busier, more touristed places keep popular dishes on the menu year-round, to keep the visiting clientele happy.)

The Veneto region of Italy (of which Venice is the capital) reaches from the mountains on the Austrian border, sweeps down through the lowlands, and ends with a dramatic flourish in the Venetian lagoon. The region is separated into seven provinces, each with its own distinct cuisine –Germanic up north, and oceanic when it reaches the lagoon.

For several centuries, Venice was the center of trade and the most international European city. Citizens from everywhere rubbed shoulders in the calli, influencing commerce, architecture, religion and, yes, food. This influence is still felt (and tasted) today. Exotic herbs and spices made their way to Venice and into the local cuisine.

Pepper, ginger, saffron, cinnamon, cloves, nutmeg, and others appeared in everything from risottos to cakes, cookies, and pastries. The first defining characteristic of regional cuisine in Italy is the form of carbohydrates. In Venice, pasta is not the main carbohydrate – instead you'll find *polenta* and *risi* (rice). Pasta is on every menu, but it's not the star of the show here the way it is elsewhere.

Polenta

Polenta comes in several forms. Originally made from multiple ground meals mixed into a type of porridge, now it's mostly made from cornmeal. You'll see it whipped into a mashed potato-like consistency or in bread-like form, sliced and sometimes toasted. It may be white, made from *biancoperla* maize or it may be yellow. They often serve a mushy form of polenta with meat, game, and piquant dishes. One of my favorite Venetian appetizers is *Sarde in Saor*, a pickled sweet and sour sardine, sometimes served on a slice of polenta and drizzled with a balsamic reduction.

Risi

Rice is big here, especially in endless fabulous risottos –often seafood risottos, but you also see plenty of vegetable versions. *Risi e bisi* is a rice dish made with pancetta and peas, traditionally served to the Doge on the Feast of Saint Mark (25 April). You must try risotto at least once while you're in Venice (or 10 times), even if you're not a fan of the dish at home.

Bigoli

Bigoli is a thick Venetian spaghetti made with buckwheat (or whole wheat) flour and eggs. One of Venice's oldest and most famous recipes is *Bigoli in Salsa*, made with a sardine (or anchovy) and onion sauce.

SEAFOOD

Seafood is king in Venice. Expect to find it on every menu, everywhere. For 1600 years the people of Venice have been fed and nourished by the lagoon. If you're lucky enough to be there in the right season, *moeche* will be on the menu. Everywhere. It is a lightly fried soft-shell crab from the lagoon. It is sensational and is a must-try food.

Sarde in saor, the sweet and sour sardines I talked about with polenta above, is served multiple ways. This dish isn't for everyone, but those who love it, *love* it, and it is one of my favorites.

Venetians have the most incredible way of frying things. It is always light and crispy and doesn't weigh you down or fill you up with fat. I particularly love the mixed seafood dish, *fritto misto,* fried in a light crispy coating. It's whatever came in fresh that day, but expect some combo of shrimp/prawns, scallops, sardines and calamari. Make sure you try it.

Even though they're surrounded by water and have access to all the fresh fish you can imagine, a dried cod dish from Norway (*baccala'*) has been part of the local cuisine since the 1400s. And it is fabulous. You'll see it prepared in different ways, from the incredible *baccala' mantecato* (cooked and whipped into a mousse, served on crostini) to fried (divine). You may see *baccala' alla vicentina*, a tomato-free baked dish from nearby Vicenza, or *baccala' in umido*, a dish made with tomatoes, onions, olive oil and white wine. It is always delicious.

You may see local delicacy *nero di sepia* or *seppia nero* made as a risotto, pasta dish or served with polenta. It's black cuttlefish ink, sometimes referred to as squid ink (cuttlefish and squid are in the same family). You also find cuttlefish dishes that aren't black. The black ink dishes taste great but color your teeth and lips black while you're eating them.

Venice is a fish lover's paradise, where you'll find sea bass, bream, sole and many more. A stroll through the daily Rialto fish market shows you the extraordinary variety of seafood that local restaurants can choose from.

FRUIT & VEGETABLES

The main vegetable market is just beyond the fish market. Most of Venice's fruit and vegetables grow on Sant' Erasmo, the largest island in the lagoon. You'll also find fruit and vegetable stands scattered around the city every morning. Most of them pack up and leave by the early afternoon.

MEAT

I don't eat red meat, so can't give any personal recommendations, but there is plenty of red meat in Venice and my Glam Italia travelers rave about it.

Carpaccio is thinly sliced raw red meat or fish. You'll see it on lots of daily specials. In 1950, Countess Amalia Nani Mocenigo's doctor told her to stop eating cooked meat. Giuseppe Cipriani of Harry's Bar decided raw meat was too bland, so he invented a sauce for her, made with mayo, mustard, tomato and cream. He named the dish "carpaccio" after the Venetian painter Vittore Carpaccio, who had an exhibition in Venice at the time. (Cipriani also named his most famous cocktail for another Venetian artist, Bellini.)

Another meat dish you may see is *brasato all Amarone*, which is beef braised and cooked in Amarone wine.

Polpetta

You see these everywhere –deep fried meatballs, specific to Venice. Ground meat is mixed with herbs and bread, rolled into balls, then rolled in polenta and deep fried. You can also find amazing fish versions and even vegetarian ones. The recipe was conceived out of necessity. It stretched the supplies of meats and put leftovers to good use. *Polpette* are in pretty much every cicchetti bar in the city. Put them on your must-try list.

Tramezzini

You see *tramezzini* (one is a *tramezzino*) all over Italy. Normally I'm not a fan, but the Venetian ones are next-level fantastic. Tramezzini are triangular sandwiches made on white bread with the crusts cut off. The first ingredient apparently is usually mayonnaise, but from there things get interesting. In Venice they use delicious combinations of fillings, packed to near overflowing. Expect to find *porchetta* and *raddichio*, asparagus and egg (it doesn't sound exciting but just wait until you take that first bite), shrimp and some kind of delicious pink sauce, crab, salmon with fine slices of gherkin, even tuna and olives. There is magic in the tramezzini in Venice. The flavor profiles work better here. This silly simple little sandwich takes on gastronomic importance, and you'll want them all the time. They are a perfect snack, ideal for a quick lunch, and I often have them for breakfast at Rosa Salva. They are addictive, and at only €1,50 are affordable on any budget.

I'm sure the reason this ostensibly British food became so successful in Venice is the climate. Maybe the dampness and humidity of the lagoon stops the bread from drying out and curling up. At any time of the day, each bite is soft and tender, and the local venetian ingredients make the flavors explode in your mouth.

Try at least one while you're here in Venice. (But maybe skip them elsewhere.)

Cheeses of the Veneto

The Veneto region has many local cheeses. Here are some of my personal favorites. There are, of course, plenty more totally fantastic cheeses from the region.

Asiago

Asiago is a semi-firm/hard cheese and comes in fresh (*Asiago Pressato*) and aged (*Asiago d'Allevo*) varieties. The aged type has further sub-categories –*Mezzano* (aged 4—6 months), *Vecchio* (aged 10 months or more) and *Stravecchio* (aged 15 months or more). Asiago has a rich, piquant taste. The older Stravecchio is wonderful in risottos and pasta dishes, while the Mezzano is tremendous on a cheese board served with fig or pear jam.

Ubriaco

Have you been to Treviso? It's a gorgeous, artsy little city only 30 minutes from Venice by train and is well worth a visit. Among other things, Treviso makes amazing cheeses, and one of my favorites is the drunk *Ubriaco* cheese. It is an aged, cow's milk cheese, and during the last few months of the aging process the cheese is soaked in dry, sparkling Prosecco along with skin and seeds from the wine-making process. If you think it sounds fabulous, try eating it –it's wonderful! this cheese was created during WWI when farmers hid their cheese from soldiers, in wine barrels. It has a soft texture that gets crumblier as it ages and has a rich and fruity flavor profile.

Casatella Trevignana

This cheese was traditionally homemade on pretty much every farm near Treviso, hence the "casa" part of its name. A soft cheese that pairs beautifully with the crisp white wines from the region, *Casatella Trevignana* is creamy and a little sweet. You'll find it often served on grilled polenta, on crostini, or on a cheeseboard.

Montasio

Another cheese from Treviso, *Montasio* is named for a plateau in the mountains of Friuli Venezia Giulia, but it is produced throughout Treviso and as far as Padova. This is a naturally lactose-free cheese (added bacteria eliminate lactose) so is extra good for anyone with lactose intolerance. It also contains tryptophan and a level of calcium known to be a stress buster, which might be God's way of telling you to eat some before bed. This is another really delicious cheese.

Acidino

This goat's milk cheese acidifies naturally. Once drained and molded, you'll find anything from salt to chives, watercress, thyme or even cumin added. *Acidino* is mild, has a little zing to it.

Basajo

The only blue cheese on this list, *Basajo* is a creamy, semi-soft sheep's milk cheese. It matures for 5—6 months, gets covered in raisins, and then soaks for three delirious drunken weeks in a sweet wine called *passito*. The wine soaks into the cheese, making it crumbly. It has notes of wild honey offsetting its naturally peppery, tangy sharpness. Basajo melts in your mouth. In September, try basajo with ripe figs and a glass of passito. You might pass out from its gloriousness.

Bastardo Del Grappa

How could I not include a cheese called *bastardo*? This is a smooth, creamy, fabulous cheese comes from the area of the Veneto called Monte Grappa. It is made from cow's milk from two separate milkings (one in the evening and the next the following morning) and in the old days, they made it from mixed milk, hence the "bastardo" moniker. It is aged for 120—180 days, is pale yellow with a rough rind and scattered little holes throughout the body. The flavor is intensely beautiful and pairs nicely with the local white wines.

Morlacco

Also from Monte Grappa, this is another wonderful cow's milk cheese. Unlike the intensity of bastardo, *morlacco* is delicate and creamy, with a milky, buttery taste and just a hint of grassy, lemony notes. It ages 20 days but can be allowed to mature up to three months. You'll find it often served with berries and jams and medium to full bodied white wines.

Pizza

Pizza is a food from Naples, which is now served everywhere. In Italy, pizza is made by a *pizzaiolo*, not a generic cook. It is made to order (never cooked from frozen) and is baked in a domed, wood-burning oven for 60—90 seconds, and then eaten immediately. Wood-burning ovens take all day to reach 800+ degrees Fahrenheit, so it is a nighttime food. No one has pizza ovens in their homes, so it's also a social food, eaten in a pizzeria, surrounded by other hungry Italians, where it is served whole, not sliced, and eaten with a knife and fork.

As every Italian will tell you –never, ever, under any circumstances, put pineapple on a pizza. Not ever.

Variations of pizza across Italy all follow these core rules, which brings me to my next point –wood-burning ovens are NOT allowed in Venice because having an open fire is considered too dangerous for the city. The ban includes pizza ovens (and is why glass blowing is restricted to the island of Murano). Therefore, in Venice all pizza is cooked in an electric oven and, unless you actually watch the *pizzaiolo* making your pizza, it has probably been frozen. (With all the amazing food available in Venice, why would you choose a frozen pizza?)

There is, however, one exceptional exception …

Birraria La Corte

If you want fantastic pizza in Venice, this is where to go. Birraria La Corte in Campo San Polo is owned by the Zambon family. They only use quality Italian ingredients, there's no frozen food, no MSG, no preservatives. Their pizzas are exclusively made with San Marzano tomatoes and *Mozzerella Fior di latte d'Agerola* (from Naples). All their vegetables come from Sant' Erasmo island, except for the red onions which are sourced from Tropea. The *nduja* (Calabrian spicy pork sausage) is actually from Calabria. Their oven is top-of-the-line new technology. It is the closest thing you can get to a wood-burning oven in Venice. Their topping combinations are chic and unusual and their pizza is phenomenal.

Address: Campo San Polo 2168.

On the Sweet Side –*Dolce*

Venetians love pastries and sweets, as evidenced by the multitude of *Pasticceria* (pastry shops) all over town. They excel at the craft too. The windows of the Pasticceria are always full of artistically created delectable bites for those with a sweet tooth.

In the **Coffee** chapter of this book, I'll tell you about my two favorite pastry shops, Tonnolo and Rosa Salva. Both should be on your must-see list for an awesome cup of coffee and an authentic sugar hit.

There are far too many varieties of cookies and pastries to list, but I will tell you about just a few.

Buranelli cookies come from Burano and are sold everywhere. They come in two distinct shapes –a *bussola'* which is round with a hole (*buso*) in the middle, and an *essi*, which is an S shape. They are perfect with coffee or with a dessert wine after dinner (like eating *cantuccini* with *vin santo* in Tuscany). You find buranelli in every pasticceria and they frequently bring a couple with your coffee at the end of a meal.

Sfogliatine come from Treviso. They are crunchy cookies made from layers of thin puff pastry and cream. They crumble everywhere when you take a bite, but they are so light and lovely you won't care.

Pinza Vineta is a cake from the Veneto which traditionally was prepared for the Epiphany (6 January). A batter of polenta flour, plain flour, raisins, figs, apples, orange zest, fennel seeds, butter, sugar, yeast and grappa is placed on a baking tray and baked until golden brown. It is often served with a glass of dessert wine or grappa.

Frittelle are an almost donut-like fried dough, but a thousand times better, and they show up around *carnevale* time. Frittelle are available plain or with a variety of fillings, from pastry creams to pine nuts and raisins. They are fried, then rolled in fine sugar. If frittelle are available when you're in Venice, you must get some from Tonnolo, the best pastry shop in town.

Zaeti/Zaleti are cornmeal cookies, which can be small or up to scone-sized, depending on where you find them. Their name comes from the word *zalo'*, which is Venetian for yellow. Flavored with lemon zest and rum-soaked raisins, they're traditionally made without sugar. Often grappa is splashed into the dough. They are great for dipping into coffee, and are a popular breakfast choice in Venice, although they are also a good snack or can even be served with dessert wine or grappa at the end of a meal.

Eating Out in Venice

Here is my most important piece of advice –**avoid tourist restaurants**! One of the huge downsides of mass tourism is the homogenization of local cuisine. Restaurants in any city burdened with mass tourism have to offer what the tourists want unless there is enough local clientele to keep them afloat.

Mass tourism forces the migration of a thousand Venetians to the mainland each year. Without their business, local eateries are forced to cater to the cruise ship clientele in order to stay afloat, and non-regional items start slipping into menus. Stalwart local restaurants, unable to make the newly inflated rents, have had to sell out to foreign money (in the case of Venice, an enormous amount of Chinese money).

Every year I come back to Venice and find that yet another restaurant/bar/shop is no longer Venetian-owned or run. Now more than ever, it is crucially important that discerning travelers like you and me are hyperaware of this, support Venetian businesses, eat at Venetian restaurants, and leave the tourist joints to the mass tourism folks.

Before we go any further, I want to clarify that I am not vilifying people from other countries. If I'm going to a Chinese restaurant, I don't want to find Italian chefs and waiters. If I am going to Vietnamese restaurant, I won't knowingly go to an Indian-owned establishment, nor would I go to an Indian restaurant owned and run by Mexicans. As a rule, I find that the people of each country and culture best understand the nuances of their own cuisine, and the magic of their food is all about those nuances. Without that, it's all just McDonald's.

Yes, there are always exceptions, especially at the fine dining level or specialty foods, but that's not what I am talking about here. I am talking about having some guidelines that you and I can use when walking down a random calle or fondamenta in Venice, looking for a nice place to eat.

While writing this, I flew to Venice with a friend to "walk the book", as I do when writing all of my *Glam Italia!* books. I wanted to look for new things and ensure the businesses I intended to tell you about here were still open in the post-pandemic world. On this visit I also took day trips from Venice to lesser traveled places, to get content for my newsletter. (You can subscribe to the newsletter on my website, www.CorinnaCooke.com.) One night we arrived back late from a day trip, starving and exhausted. We had eaten near the apartment at a fabulous place on Fondamenta l'Osmarin a couple of nights prior and were tempted to go back again, but instead (for research's sake) decided to do something different. We turned a corner and found a place where I had eaten years ago, on Rio dei Greci. I couldn't rely on my usual guidelines for dining –none of the restaurants were busy again yet anywhere in town, tourists hadn't yet returned to Venice, and most Italians were watching the UEFA match. My usual "go where the Italians are" rule wasn't helpful. The greeter was Italian, so we sat down without looking at the menu first –such a rookie move on my part, but I figured we were far enough in Castello to be beyond the tourist traps.

Not so. Glasses of Prosecco appeared and we sat talking and sipping, each thinking the other had ordered them, going over work stuff before opening our menus –at which point my heart sank. The first thing I saw was spaghetti carbonara, a Roman dish. Followed by a series of generic Olive Garden style options that had exactly nothing to do with Venetian cooking. We would have left the restaurant at that point, except that we had realized the Prosecco was complementary and we would have no doubt been charged €15 per glass had we left. So, we decided to stay and each order something simple. I ordered pappardelle (my favorite type of pasta –in *Tuscany*) with seafood and Jennifer ordered a mushroom risotto. These were the two items on the menu closest resembling Venetian cooking. How bad could it be?

Bad. I can't even describe how bad it was. Had this been my first time in Venice, I would have thought Venetian food was ghastly, which is why I'm telling you this story. Instead of fresh pasta cooked *al dente*, this was flaccid, overcooked box pasta. Instead of fresh from the lagoon, the seafood had that nasty chewiness to it that screams *from frozen*. The risotto was awful, the mushrooms from a can.

This is why I tell you to **only dine at Italian-owned and Italian-run eateries** when in Venice (or anywhere in Italy). Italians have an extra chromosome that instinctively alerts them to when pasta is perfectly done. No self-respecting Venetian restaurant would use frozen seafood or canned mushrooms and Venetians definitely wouldn't screw up a risotto! There is a massive difference between a real Venetian restaurant and one owned by a foreign investor, staffed with cheap labor. I felt so badly for the greeter girl, who was the only Italian in the establishment. She kept sidling past whispering, "I'm so sorry!" The boss (dragon) lady kept prowling past our table with her hands behind her back, shooting venomous darts at the greeter if she came anywhere near us. It was like a parody of your most horrendous restaurant experience. We bumped into the greeter in the street the following day and got the full scoop. She had lost her job during Covid and that had been the only work she could get.

On every trip to Venice, I come across more Chinese-owned bars and eateries. Leave these places to the mass tourism folks –to people who maybe care less about food or are just looking for something they recognize. Meanwhile you and I will seek out and support locally owned businesses. Let our travel dollars flow into the local economy, instead of the mushroom canning company and the frozen seafood conglomerate. This way our travel dollars will support local fishermen and farmers.

How to Identify a Good, Locally Owned Restaurant

These rules apply anywhere in Italy:

1. Read the menu before you sit down and walk away if it is in multiple languages (more than three).
2. Avoid any joint with pictures of the food on the menu or in the window.
3. Look for local dishes on the menu.
4. Only eat where Italians eat.

Had I stopped in at any of the million or so *cicchetti* bars between the train station and the upper reaches of Castello, my crostini-sated belly would have stopped me from making such a stupid mistake. So, now I have a fifth restaurant rule for Venice:

> 5. Don't go to a restaurant super hungry. Stop along the way for cicchetti first.

So let me tell you about cicchetti.

10.
Cicchetti

If I could live in one city and do every single thing I do there, I would choose Venice. You can't turn your head without seeing something amazing.

–Nile Rodgers

Cicchetti/Cichetti/Cicheti –the spelling varies but the pronunciation stays the same *–chi-KET-tee.* In Venice, this is a food activity you *must* get intimately acquainted with. It could be argued (by me) that eating cicchetti is the quintessential Venetian experience, especially if you do it right. It combines all my favorite things –aperitivo hour (in this case it is also an all-day thing), delectable nibbles that satiate but don't overfill you, a slice of history, a cultural experience, and lots of socializing. What could be more fabulous?

What are Cicchetti?

Cicchetti are finger food sized morsels of local delicacies, enjoyed in one hand with a glass of wine in the other. Most of the time, cicchetti are eaten in standing room only bars called *bacari.* (Some do have seating so you can enjoy cicchetti seated too.) The selection of these little foods can run the gamut from bite-sized sandwiches (*panini* or *tramezzini*) to *crostini* (a perpetual favorite) crispy *polpette* (those crumbed meatballs I mentioned) skewered fish, deep fried sardines – you name it. There are endless options, some served hot, many served cold. There are plenty of seafood options, but also meat, vegetable and vegetarian choices. Choices are fresh and seasonal, so you will see an ever-changing variety through the year, and in many cases, through the day.

Some bacari serve cicchetti all day long, constantly changing their offerings. What you snacked on an hour ago may have been replaced with new options when you go back. Some serve cicchetti from early morning, others only at aperitivo time. They are the perfect mid-morning snack, and the ideal lunch bite. They get you over the hump between lunch and dinner, especially if a day of sightseeing is leaving you peckish. And they are the ultimate Venetian aperitivo snack. Around 6pm you'll find a continuous stream of fresh cicchetti options flowing from the kitchen. Some bars offer as few as eight options, while the glass cases of another will have a seemingly endless array of plates with colorful toothpick-skewered bites.

Don't get involved with choosing ingredients. Many of the combinations won't necessarily make sense to you. But your brain doesn't need to figure out what's going on here –your tastebuds do. If the bar is busy and I'm by myself, I'll just point to a couple of choices. When it's quiet, I'll chat to the bartender, get his recommendations, order far too much, and eat it all anyway. If I'm with Venetian friends, I'll let them choose. If I'm on a cicchetti walking tour I will eat whatever my guide Monica recommends.**

The bottom line is I'll always try something new and I've always loved whatever I've ordered, but at an average price of €1 per item, it wouldn't matter if I didn't like something. Don't shy away from the fried goods. Venetians fry foods in a magical, light, crispy way that enhances the food and doesn't weigh it down in a greasy, heavy batter. In fact, plenty of *fritto misto* seafood options can be found on a skewer in a cicchetti case.

** I sincerely recommend taking a cicchetti walking tour in Venice. I have included my foodie walking tour guide in my Venice Guides PDF, which you can download at www.glamitaliabooks.com/Venice-Private-Guides

What to Drink

Rather than a spritz or a Prosecco, order *un ombra* with your cicchetti. This is *a shadow* or little glass of wine. The ombra started centuries ago in Piazza San Marco, the main meeting place in town. Socializing in the sunshine was thirsty work, so local wine sellers set up mobile stalls, moving them to stay in the Campanile's shade. The little glass of wine became called an ombra or a shadow.

Some bacari have extensive wine lists. Some have wine specials on a chalk board. All will have a tremendous house red and a house white. If it's not busy, I'll ask the bartender (a great way to get into conversation with someone new). If left to my own devices, I'll order a house white or house red. They're always good and often only cost a couple of euros. If you're traveling on a budget, you can get two cicchetti and an ombra of house wine for around €5.

At this time of day, people from all walks of life, from every conceivable income bracket, stand shoulder to shoulder in a bacaro, enjoying the same *repast* as you. Going from one bacaro to another for a quick bite and just enough wine to wash it down, is a gorgeous way to experience the city and an inexpensive way to socialize, partaking in the local life and enjoying another facet of Venice.

Must-try Cicchetti

It's easy to get lost looking at the options in the glass case. You're not likely to see anything written in English, so keep an eye out for these.

Baccala'Mantecato is a creamy codfish mousse, served on rounds of sliced bread (crostini). To. Die. For.

Acciughe are anchovies and show up often in cicchetti. You may find a piece on half a hard-boiled egg or wrapped around a pickled onion (*cipollina con l'acciugha*). These anchovies aren't the salty brown things we get at home. They're fabulous. Chances are you'll have wolfed down a bunch of them before realizing you're eating anchovies!

Folpetto is baby octopus.

Polpetta are little fried meatballs.

Nervetti are beef or veal cartilage, served with vinegar and pepper.

Sarda Fritta are fried sardines and ***Sarde in Saor*** is one of Venice's most famous dishes, a sweet and sour sardine. It is unbelievably good!

Calamari fritti is self-explanatory, but try any fried seafood cicchetti, even if you don't recognize what you're eating!

Calamari Ripieni is stuffed squid.

Fiori di Zucca are zucchini flowers stuffed with a piece of anchovy and melted cheese. They are superb.

Crostini options are infinite. There are endless varieties and every bacaro seems to have their own creation.

Where to Find the Best Cicchetti in Venice (by Sestiere)

When asked for cicchetti/bacaro recommendations, I invariably name the last place I went to. Or say, "find one that is full of Italians". To me, it's all about the experience of great food and lovely wine, trying to balance everything while standing up, squished amongst Venetians, amid a hubbub of Italian voices. Listen closely and you'll hear both Italian and the local dialect, Veneziano, which is an entire language unto itself. (I speak Italian relatively well but have absolutely no clue what is being said in Veneziano.)

Over the years (decades), I have dropped in on countless bacari around town and had amazing cicchetti. If you're trying to decide whether it's worth stopping at a particular bacari, ask yourself:

1. Are there lots of Italians eating here?
2. Do the faces behind the bar look Italian?

You can probably find your own great local bacari, but I know it's helpful to have specific places to keep an eye out for, so here are some of my favorites, in no particular order. These places have great food, wine, and atmosphere. (My Cicchetti Walking Tour guide has another series of bacari she will take you to.)

Insider Tip: Don't be whipping out €50 bills for €5 of cicchetti. Bring your small coins and small denomination notes instead.

Santa Croce

Al Rivetta

This is a typical old-school, family run business. Low on frills, the food is great and very inexpensive. Another trattoria has the same name, so check the address first to make sure you've found the right place.

Address: Calle Sechera 637a
Hours: 11am—10pm
Vaporetto Stop: Ple Roma
What's Nearby: The train station and Piazzale Roma, San Simeon Piccolo and the Frari.

Cantina Arnaldi

This place is tremendous. The focus is on traditional Venetian cuisine made from locally sourced ingredients. The wines are local too. Outside peak hours, this is a great place to sit and enjoy the cicchetti and wine. The staff are super friendly and will take the time to tell you the stories behind their foods and wine.

Cantina Arnaldi is a little off the beaten track and definitely off the mass tourism radar, and a perfect stop when visiting the Frari, San Pantalon and the Scuola San Rocco.

Address: Salizada san Pantalon 35
Hours: 11am—12am, closed Wednesdays
Vaporetto Stop: San Toma' or Ca' Rezzonico
What's Nearby: The Frari, Scuola San Rocco and San Pantalon.

San Polo

The smallest sestiere is bursting with wonderful places to have an aperitivo. San Polo is the perfect patch to take *un giro di ombre*, or what, at one point in my life, we called "bacari-hopping" –bouncing around a few bacari for a snack and a mini glass of wine. Both your tummy and your tastebuds want you to come to San Polo.

Do Mori

Put this on your must-see list. Do Mori is the oldest bacaro in Venice. They've retained the old wooden countertop; copper pots hang from the ceiling. It feels old and you'll feel transported back in time here. I absolutely love it.

Address: Calle Do Mori 429
Hours: 8am—7.30pm, closed on Sundays
Vaporetto Stop: Rialto Mercato
What's Nearby: Rialto Market, Rialto Bridge, Caffe del Doge.

Cantina Do Spade

Up the romance of Venice by sipping a little wine and enjoying a bite at the same place Casanova brought his conquests for a little pre-loving sustenance. In the mid-1700s he would meet his lovers on the Rialto Bridge and dine with them here. By then, Cantina Do Spade was nearly 300 years old. This 15th century bacaro' was even mentioned in the 1566 consensus.

Tucked behind the fish market, expect excellent seafood cicchetti (obviously) along with other traditional options. Grab your wine and plate of nibbles, and secure the corner of a barrel outside to prop them on.

Address: Calle del Scaleter 859
Hours: 10am—10pm daily
Vaporetto Stop: Rialto Market
What's Nearby: Rialto Market, Rialto Bridge, Caffe del Doge.

All'Arco

All'Arco is tiny –more of a hole in the wall than a bar, and perpetually mad-busy, so don't plan on scoring one of the three tables inside. All' Arco is wildly popular with Venetians and tourists alike, because of the truly fantastic, mouthwatering seafood cicchetti. It's easy to find, just look for the crowds outside wolfing down plates of cicchetti in the street. By force of the sheer volume of food sold each hour of each day, everything is super fresh. Locals come for the excellent food, budget travelers come for the crazy low prices. I show up because it's a great place.

Address: Campo San Polo 436
Hours: 8am—2.30/3pm
Vaporetto Stop: Rialto Market
What's Nearby: Rialto Market, Rialto Bridge, Caffe del Doge.

Al Merca'

Tiny yet mighty, Al Merca', which literally means "on the market", is just a storefront on Campo Bella Vienna, between the Rialto Market and the Rialto Bridge. With no indoor area and no tables, this bacaro with working class roots sells a vast selection of unbelievably good mini panini (sandwiches) served on a napkin, and has a huge wine list. The staff are super friendly and will interact with you even though this bacaro gets super busy. It is absolutely terrific value for money –a hand-sized panino runs €1,50 and wines start at €2 per glass.

Address: Campo Bella Vienna 213
Hours: 10am—2.30pm, 6pm—8pm
Vaporetto Stop: Rialto Mercato
What's Nearby: Rialto Bridge, Rialto Market.

Dorsoduro

I adore this neighborhood. I almost always confuse the point where San Polo melts into Dorsoduro (if I get it right it's a fluke) but unless you're the mailman, I don't think it matters. Make sure you allow plenty of time to explore this area and eat lots of cicchetti along the way.

Cantine del Vino Gia Schiavi

Here you'll find fantastic cicchetti in a standing room only environment. This is another historic venue pairing wonderful wine with an excellent selection of finger foods. The crostini have endless toppings and at €1,20 each you can satiate your hunger without breaking the bank. There's a reason you find Cantine del Vino gia Schiavi on every best of list since the beginning of best-of lists –it's that good! Schiavi is both a wine shop and a wine bar, so you can take home a bottle of something fabulous too.

Address: Fondamenta Nani, 992
Hours: 8.30am—8.30pm, closed Sunday
Vaporetto Stop: Accademia or Zattere –it's midway between the two
What's Nearby: Accademia, the Zattere, the Peggy Guggenheim.

Osteria Al Squero

Just along the fondamenta from Schiavi. Al Squero is another gem. At lunchtime they cover every inch of counter with crostini, topped with every Venetian favorite. I always choose seafood options, but they have meat as well. The average price is €1,50 per item. Sit on the wall outside and enjoy the view, watch the gondolas being worked on at the *squero* (gondola workshop) opposite.

Address: Fondamenta Nani 943
Hours: 10am—8.30 pm, closed Sundays
Vaporetto Stop: Zattere
What's Nearby: The Zattere, Accademia, Santa Maria della Salute, the Peggy Guggenheim, the Dogane.

Al Bocon DiVino

Al Bocon DiVino has tables and chairs outside. You'll pay extra to sit here, the same way you pay extra to sit down for coffee all over Italy, but it's worth it.

Come here for old-school, traditional Venetian food. You'll see all the familiar food options here, but along with their must-try fried *fiori di zucca* this is a great chance to become acquainted with some appetizers that are too tricky to maneuver while standing. Order a platter of cicchetti to share. Their presentation is lovely.

Al Bocon DiVino is in a giant piazza, which is the nightlife hotspot of Venice. It is a joy to sit outside here on long summer evenings, enjoying the wines of the Veneto and great local food while watching the young folk socialize Italian-style, far from the tourist hubs of the city.

Address: Campo Santa Margherita 2978
Hours: 9am—9pm
Vaporetto Stop: Ca' Rezzonico
What's Nearby: Ca' Rezzonico, Ca' Foscari, San Pantalon, the Frari.

Castello

Crossing the Grand Canal, we will start at the top of this side of Venice. I love Castello. You feel a million miles away from the tourist crush, yet really are only a 5-minute walk from the bulk of the action. There is a ton going on up this end, but it doesn't feel frantic.

SALVMERIA

Salvmeria is a full-service restaurant with 20 tables inside and 24 outside, but you can drop in just for a glass of wine and cicchetti.

It used to be a grocery store and salumeria/butcher shop/deli. The original sign is still above the door, from a time when the U was replaced with a V. (It's pronounced *Sal-u-meria*, not *Salv-meria*). The building was vacant for more than 30 years when chef Giorgio Consolo turned it into an open-kitchen osteria. It is very contemporary but has a glorious selection of non-sandwichy, old-school cicchetti. The ingredients are a combination of zero kilometer (sourced from the immediate area) and imported from the deep south. The menu changes based on what was available each morning. You can go back over and over and be completely enchanted every time. I come here for dinner whenever I'm in Venice. It's a fantastic restaurant and a great place to stop for cicchetti.

Salvmeria has an excellent selection of wines by the glass too. The food is outstanding and there is no cover charge to sit here.

Address: Via Garibaldi 1769
Hours: 11am—11pm
Vaporetto Stop: Arsenale
What's Nearby: The Arsenale, the Biennale, the Museo Storico Navale and the little island of San Pietro.

El Refolo

This is a tavern-type bar with tons of locals, and a few travelers in-the-know. The food is delicious, ranging from little gourmet sandwiches to platters of meats and cheeses, to more traditional cicchetti, all served on wooden boards. You can sit outside and watch local life go by while enjoying a drink and chatting with the friendly staff.

Address: Via Garibaldi 1580
Hours: All day until midnight
Vaporetto Stop: Arsenale
What's Nearby: Arsenale, the Biennale, Museo Storico Navale, San Pietro Island, San Zaccaria.

San Marco

The next neighborhood along the Grand Canal is the busiest. The following are only four of the many wonderful places in San Marco.

Bacarando Corte dell' Orso

Pop in for a drink, swing by for cicchetti, or dine at their full-service restaurant. The current business is more than 30 years old, but there has been a restaurant on this premises for more than a century. Bacarando has a contemporary bar and a huge following of regulars who swing by for a chic cocktail. Order a platter of cicchetti to share, grab a table and soak it all in. The food is wonderful, the vibe is cool and there is live music at night.

Address: San Marco 5495
Hours: Noon—midnight, daily

Vaporetto Stop: Rialto
What's Nearby: Rialto Bridge on the San Marco side, close to the Fondaco dei Tedeschi.

Bacaro da Fiore

I always swing by da Fiore after visiting the Grassi museum. There is also a restaurant with the same name. For appetizers, head to the far end of the campo, turn left on the calle of the shoemakers. (Further along the calle there's a shoe etched into the wall, telling people this was Shoemaker Street.)

World renowned, da Fiore is always busy. It is 100% authentic Venetian food and is loved by locals and travelers alike. You just can't go wrong here. Although I've never met crostini I didn't want to eat, I love all the non-sandwichy options here. There is always more to choose from than you could ever try.

Address: Calle de le Botteghe 3461 (around the corner from Campo Santo Stefano)
Hours: 8.30am—midnight
Vaporetto Stop: San Samuele or cross the bridge at Accademia.
What's Nearby: The Accademia Bridge, Piazza San Marco, Campo Santo Stefano.

I Rusteghi

In Vino, Venetias. If you are serious about wine, this is the place for you. With over 875 bottles to choose from, this is a favorite bar for a next level wine experience and sensational cicchetti. Owner Giovanni d'Este is a fourth generation sommelier, so wine is hardwired into his DNA. He'll open any bottle for you to buy a glass –he takes it that seriously. I Rusteghi is situated in a quiet Venetian courtyard, so even though you are close to the hustle and bustle, you are also completely away from it.

Address: Corte del Tentor, 5513
Hours: 11am—3pm then 6.30pm—11.30pm
Vaporetto Stop: Rialto
What's Nearby: Rialto Bridge, the Marco Polo house, the Miracoli church.

Sepa

Sepa is a new cicchetti bar with a fresh, modern vibe. There is something for every conceivable dietary restriction, with vegetarian, vegan and gluten free options. The atmosphere, food and wine are wonderful. Try the risotto of the day if you find yourself needing a little more sustenance.

Address: Calle della Bissa, 5482
Hours: 11am—10pm
Vaporetto Stop: Rialto Bridge
What's Nearby: Rialto Bridge, the Miracoli church, Campo SS Giovanni e Paolo.

Cannaregio

Cannaregio has so much going on! It has a buzzing nightlife and is home to endless ghost stories. The Jewish ghetto is here, the big shopping street Strada Nova runs through it, it's busy and it's fantastic. There's never a dull moment in Cannaregio and there are loads of places for remarkably good cicchetti. My Cicchetti Walking Tour guide (who is a food writer and cicchetti specialist) conducts almost all of her tours within a few short blocks in Cannaregio.

Al Timon

Gorgeous rows of cicchetti line the windows here, luring you into this die hard favorite of Venetians and travelers alike. Al Timon has more meat options, but also great seafood. My favorites are grilled polenta bites topped with fried fish bites and the *baccala montecato.* There is seating inside but order your cicchetti and sit either at an outside table or on the wall along the rio della Misericordia. If you don't fall in love with the visual, your heart is probably made of stone. Outdoors at Al Timon looks like every dream you've ever had of Venice. I love it.

Address: Fondamenta Ormesini 2754
Hours: 5pm—11pm
Vaporetto Stop: Guglie
What's Nearby: Torrefazione Cannaregio, the Jewish Ghetto. Madonna dell' Orto and Tintoretto's house.

Il Paradiso Perduto

And now for something completely different...

My son is a jazz musician so I love coming here. It's shabby and gritty with exposed brick walls and floor tiles that don't quite work together, adding to the atmosphere. People come here for heaping platters of fried and grilled seafood, cheap beer and wine, and jazz. Live music starts some time around 9pm and goes until closing. Expect a huge assortment of cicchetti. If you want great food, live music and a bohemian vibe, you'll love Il Paradiso Perduto (Paradise Lost).

Address: della Misericordia 2540
Hours: Noon—11pm, closed Tuesday and Wednesday
Vaporetto Stop: Madonna dell'Orto, Fondamente Nove or S. Marcuola
What's Nearby: The Gesuiti church, Casino degli Spiriti (haunted house), Madonna dell'Orto, Campo SS Giovanni e Paolo.

Alla Vedova

Trattoria Ca' d'Oro Alla Vedova is one of the most famous bacari in Venice. The name has a split meaning, *Ca' d'Oro* is "the magnificent palace" (and the Vaporetto stop) and *alla vedova* means "at the widow's place". It's a reference to the restaurant or business owned by a husband and wife team, where he died and she kept running it.

Alla Vedova has a spare interior, a small menu and smaller wine list. But everything here is outstanding, and it's always packed. *Packed.* But hustle your fine self on up to the bar and order some cicchetti. The big thing here, so righteous that Michelin called them "legendary", are the fried meatballs. Some food critics say they're the best in the world. It's probably a crime to be in the know, and not try them. It is also a full-service restaurant serving Venetian specialties. There are few options, but everything here is incredible, so arrive hungry.

Address: Ramo Ca' d'Oro 3912
Hours: 11.30—2.30 then 6.30pm—10.30pm, closed on Thursdays
Vaporetto Stop: Ca' d'Oro
What's Nearby: Ca' d' Oro, Ponte Chiodo, Chiessa dell' Abbazia della Misericordia.

Vino Vero

"No Spritz –We Love Wine!" And they absolutely do. This beloved wine bar is on the fringes of Cannaregio just in front of the San Marziale church. Sit outdoors on the rio della Misericordia, enjoy the view and toast yourself for finding this treasure, largely unknown to tourists.

"True Wine" carries an extensive list of organic and bio dynamic wines. They're mainly from small boutique producers, sold by the glass and the bottle. Wine geeks love this place. Don't be surprised to see well-dressed internationals in the mix.

Vino Vero offers high-end cicchetti, including whole wheat crostini covered in delicious toppings, made fresh every hour. Vino Vero has one of the most extensive and chic selections of crostini in the entire city.

Choose your cicchetti and then ask the barman which wine he recommends. When it's not busy, this creates an opportunity to chat with a local, and guarantees a killer pairing.

Address: Fondamenta Misericordia, 2497
Hours: 12pm—12am, except Mondays when it is open 6pm—midnight
Vaporetto Stops: Madonna dell' Orto, Fondamenta Nove, S. Marcuola .
What's Nearby: Casino degli Spiriti, Chiesa Abbazia della Misericordia, Tintoretto's house, Madonna dell' Orto.

Don't Fear the Anchovies …

Anchovies show up everywhere in Venetian cuisine. But before you panic at the thought, know that these aren't the hideous salty, brown things we get at home. Venetian anchovies are fantastic. If you find cicchetti with anchovy, try it. If you don't like it, you are only out €1, but chances are you'll love it.

11.
The Best Coffee in Venice

Why, this Satan's drink is so delicious that it would be a pity to let the infidels have exclusive use of it!

–Pope Clement VIII

Did you know Venice introduced coffee to Europe and the western world? When you sip your steaming cup in Venice, you take part in the history of coffee, *in situ.*

The History of Coffee in Venice

In 1591, Prospero Alpini, a doctor working for the Venetian Consul in Cairo, published the first scientific mention of the medical use of African coffee beans. This magic potion instantly revived anyone feeling lethargic or lacking energy. Thereafter coffee beans became a cure-all for everything from headaches to consumption to gout.

From Ethiopia, coffee traveled to the Ottoman Empire. Realizing the business potential of this rich, energizing drink, the Ottomans expanded the farming of coffee beans to Yemen. Venice, the center of the merchant trade world, was the obvious place through which to route the new business. Venice gave us coffee.

When it arrived in the floating city, this drink of the Muslims was considered sinful. There were calls for Pope Clement VIII to denounce and ban its consumption. In a moment since called "the baptism of coffee", old Clement decided to try a cup before issuing his verdict. He famously said, "Why, this Satan's drink is so delicious that it would be a pity to let the infidels have exclusive use of it!"

With the Pope's approval, Italian coffee culture was born, and soon this once-medicinal drink became a popular social drink.

In 1638, the first coffee house opened under the porticoes of Piazza San Marco. A century later, the senate had to restrict the number of coffee shops allowed in the city. By 1758, there were 206 coffee houses in Venice, 34 of them in Piazza San Marco! Known for good food and a comfortable atmosphere, coffee houses became the chic places to be.

At the time, they prepared coffee Turkish-style. Roasted beans were ground with a mortar and pestle, then boiled with sugar and spices. It took several minutes to make each cup.

On 29 December 1720, a new coffee shop opened under the arcades of the Procuratie Nuove in Piazza San Marco. It became a favorite for artists, intellectuals, scientists, and nobles. Even the city's most famous lover, Giacomo Casanova, hung out here. Floriano Francesconi named his coffee house Alla Venezia Trionfante (Triumphant Venice). Before long, it affectionately became known as *Florian's Place*. Celebrating its 300th birthday in 2020, Caffe Florian is the oldest working coffee shop in the world. Florian broke social boundaries by allowing women to hang out there too. In 1767 the Republic banned women from coffee houses, except the times of the year when masks were allowed, but Venetian noblewomen and courtesans ignored the new law. Some frequented coffee houses for romantic hook ups, plenty just enjoyed the pleasure of coffee and *bussola'*, the traditional Venetian cookie.

Coffee houses were places where people from all walks of life could congregate. The cross section of society and different ways of thinking made them hotbeds for new ideas. Here you could exchange thoughts about politics, commerce, science, and garner a huge amount of knowledge, all for the price of a coffee! Unlike the rowdy establishments serving alcohol, coffee houses were quieter, and were a better venue for serious conversation. Caffe Florian set the precedent for coffee houses, and the role they would play even today.

What is Espresso?

Espresso is not a type of bean or roasting method. It is a brewing method. The word comes from the Italian *esprimer*, which means "to express or press out". Highly pressurized hot (but not boiling) water is forced over finely ground, tamped coffee, producing a rich, robustly flavored, very concentrated drink. Espresso is considered the purest form of coffee, as the quick process wreaks the least amount of damage to the grounds. Slower coffee methods use coarser grounds and hotter water.

The first espresso machine was invented by an Italian, Angelo Moriondo, in Turin in 1884.

Coffee in Venice

One of the sad consequences of mass tourism is the diminishing quality of products. Unlike the refined Italian coffee palate, the average tourist has a McDonald's/Starbucks mass-market preference. Consequently, in the touristy areas, you won't always find real Italian coffee. If the clientele doesn't appreciate the complexity of your blend, why bother making it? For travelers, this means you have to be a little more discerning and seek the coffee shops (bars) that the locals patronize. If a coffee shop is full of tourists, just keep walking.

One of my favorite books set in Venice is Barry Frangipane's hilarious memoir, *The Venice Experiment: A Year of Trial and Error Living Abroad.* Returning for a visit later, Barry and his wife discovered that the coffee shop they'd visited daily during their year living in Venice was now Chinese-owned. The delicious Venetian coffee, the locals they chatted with, and the *experience* of being there, had been replaced with mass market coffee and mass tourism ambience. Tragic.

Venice still has world renowned, completely fabulous coffee houses. While here, visit at least one of the following places. A couple on my list are pastry shops that also serve coffee. The bars/pastry shops on this list are all really popular with Venetians. All serve exemplary, real coffee. All are Venetian-owned.

How to Order Coffee

A coffee shop in Italy is called a bar. From there we get the word *barista* –the person making the coffee in the bar.

There are two prices at any bar. It is less expensive to stand at the counter to drink coffee, while sitting at a table is a slightly higher price. Outside of the prime tourist areas, you should expect to pay around €1 for *un caffe* (espresso) and €2 for a cappuccino.

In *Glam Italia! How To Travel Italy,* I break down the different coffee drinks you can order in the average Italian bar, as well as how to do it –it's quite different to Starbucks. Coffee in Italy is espresso-based, and they don't do American-style drip coffee.

Where to Go for the Best Coffee in Venice

1. Torrefazione Cannaregio

In 2018 (ish) Torrefazione moved from Strada Nuova to the current location on Fondamenta Ormesini, just outside the Jewish Ghetto. The new location is perfect, catering to the steady flow of Venetians and travelers. You'll have no trouble finding it, thanks to the awning outside.

The interior is beautiful, with mahogany shelves behind the counter holding a wide array of coffees. Torrefazione means "roastery", and yes they roast their own blends which you can consume on site or purchase to take home, ground or as whole beans.

The coffee at Torrefazione is outstanding. The menu has hybrids of Italian coffee drinks with some internationals –you'll see *flat whites* and *iced Americanos* alongside traditional espresso options. A cappuccino costs €2.50 while a macchiato costs €1.

Address: Fondemanta dei Ormesini 2804, Cannaregio
What's Nearby: The Jewish Ghetto, the Church of Madonna dell' Orto, the Casino degli Spiriti.

2. Caffe del Doge

This is hands-down my favorite. If fantastic coffee matters to you, add this to your must-do list.

Despite being in the heart of tourist-central, just 2 minutes from the Rialto Bridge, Caffe del Doge is the best insider secret and a *must* for coffee lovers. This non-descript coffee house in a quiet little calle is coffee heaven. The building used to be the roastery, but that side of the business has since moved to Padua. Caffe del Doge uses its own artisan roasted coffee beans, sourced from all over the world. They have a vast variety of coffees here. There is something for everyone, from the aficionado to the purist to the regular coffee lover. (I just order from the menu board.)

Although it's an iconic place to stop for a coffee, Caffe del Doge is an unpretentious, laid-back place to hang out at a table and enjoy a cappuccino. You'll fall in love with their richly roasted espresso and can buy packages of coffee to bring home. Providing they're not madly busy, the dedicated staff will happily talk coffee with you and make fantastic recommendations.

The clientele are exclusively Venetian coffee lovers and travelers in-the-know. Not sure what to order? Try a *cappuccino Veneziano* with fresh chocolate shavings on top. Most days when I'm in Venice I wander over here for a second breakfast (after my first at Rosa Salva, near my apartment).

Caffe del Doge has a second location in Cannaregio, not far from the train station (Rio Tera S. Leonardo 1403).

Address: Calle Cinque, 609, Rialto.
What's Nearby: The Rialto Bridge and the Rialto fish market.

3. Il Caffe Rosso (Il Caffe')

This iconic, bohemian coffee house has a cool history. Easily identifiable by its red frontage, Il Rosso (or Il Caffe') has been at the heart of the bar scene in Campo Santa Margherita since the late 1800s. Il Rosso shares a history with the bar opposite, Osteria al

Capon. The two famously were hangouts for political idealists of opposing beliefs, who loudly debated and argued politics across the campo all evening long.

With loads of seating outside, Il Rosso is a great place to enjoy bustling Venetian nights, to kick back with a coffee in the morning or a sandwich at lunchtime. The people-watching here is great any time of the day –you'll see a mix of students, aging Venetians and a few lost tourists.

This is a no-nonsense, old-fashioned cafe/bar that makes *really* good coffee. Be sure to check out the old-school coffee maker. It is one of the oldest I've seen. Expect good food at student-friendly prices. They're well known for their *tremazzini* (sandwiches), most of which cost €2 or less. It is a brilliant spot for travelers on a budget. I would rather spend three hours hanging out here watching Venetian life in the campo than deal with the tourist masses from Rialto to Piazza San Marco any day of the week. And I often do.

Address: Dorsoduro 2963 (Campo Santa Margherita)
Hours: Open every day from 7am until 1 am.
What's Nearby: Ca' Foscari (the University) the Frari, Ca' Rezzonico, the Ponte dei Pugni.

4. Pasticceria Tonolo

The most famous pastry shop in Venice, Tonolo opened in 1886 and is adored by locals. The pastry case is enormous with all kinds of tremendous goodies on offer, with an average price of €1,20. There are normally tons of students inside, filling themselves up on inexpensive yet fabulous food. During *carnevale* this is the best places to buy *frittelle*. If you see frittelle in the cabinet, buy them! The round, sugar-coated *crema*, *zabaglione*, or *mele* filled delights are not to be missed.

Tonolo has no tables, so take your coffee at the bar or lean against a counter along the back. The coffee is great and comes in pretty blue and white china cups. You can also pick up pastries to go.

Address: Calle San Pantalon 3764, Dorsoduro
Hours: Open every day except Wednesday, from 7am—1pm then 3pm—8.45pm
What's Nearby: This is a 1-minute walk from Ca' Fosscari (University).

5. Caffe Girani

My landlady introduced me to this one. It's her favorite coffee, and she always has a fresh package in my apartment for me when I arrive. We often walk over there together to pick me up some coffee to take home to the US. If we are going to meet up during the day for virtually any reason (like when I send her a WhatsApp with a question about a museum, or when she sends me a WhatsApp to say she has a story to tell me), her next text is always "Let's meet at Girani." *Ci vediamo a Girani.* Though we actually meet at the bar next door to the roastery.

Girani is the oldest coffee roaster in Venice. Giuseppe Girani, the legendary coach of the Venice football team, was introduced to the art of coffee in his wife's hometown of Trieste. From the beginning, his eponymous coffee business was about creating the highest quality coffee.

Girani quickly became the first choice of all the luxury hotels and cafes in the city. When Giuseppe died in 1951, his daughter Gigiola took over, maintaining her father's traditions, placing quality above all else.

Girani is neither a cafe nor a bar. It is a roastery. The beans come from uncontaminated volcanic soils in Cental America, and are roasted by hand on a very rare Vittoria machine. (I'm told this is the Ferrari of roasters.) Girani uses a low temperature process, which limits acidity and maximizes aroma. This is a full-bodied, beautiful coffee with no bitter bite and no burnt aftertaste. (Most companies use high temperature methods which limit acidity but bring out the bitterness in coffee.) It is the only business still roasting coffee in Venice –everyone else has moved production outside of the city.

Girani makes several unique blends, but my favorite is *Fassina.* Commissioned by Albano Fassina for his cafe on Calle Frezzeria, it is made with nine varieties of the most exemplary Arabica beans. Fassina instantly became an enormous hit and is very popular today. If you don't know which coffee to choose, you can't go wrong with Fassina. It also makes a wonderful gift to take home.

The staff are really helpful and happy to guide you to the perfect blend for your tastebuds. Sometimes you will even be lucky enough to meet and chat with the owner. Be sure to have someone at Girani teach you how to make the perfect cup of coffee. It's a game-changer.

Girani is still considered the highest quality coffee in Venice. Stop by the bar next door to taste Girani's coffee –they use Girani blends.

Address: Castello 3727
Hours: 8.30am—12.30pm, open weekdays
What's Nearby: Piazza San Marco (10 minutes), the Arsenale, Salvmeri.

6. Pasticceria Da Chiusso

This family run business not only makes an excellent cappuccino, but *good lord* –the pastries! Everything here is made on the premises, so this qualifies as shopping with local artisans. And if you're supporting local crafts people, the calories don't count, right? Everything here is wonderful.

Address: 306 Salizzada dei Greci, Castello
What's Nearby: San Zaccaria, San Francesco della Vigna, Paolo Brandolisio (Remeri).

7. Rosa Salva

Andrea Rosa started this business in 1870. It was a mobile catering service and the clientele were the owners of the luxurious villas along the Brenta River. In 1879, Andrea's son Antonio became a royal chef and an award winning pastry chef. Now they have locations by La Fenice Theater (Campo San Fantin 1965), Calle Fiubera 950, (San Marco), and my favorite in Campo SS Giovanni e Paolo. I go there every morning for breakfast. Their famous coffee is fabulous, and you just cannot beat sitting under the umbrellas in this gorgeous location, watching the world go by.

The backbone of the Rosa Salva business is their incredible pastries. If you're in Venice close to Christmas, Rosa Salva makes one of the best *panettone* anywhere. Be sure to have an espresso while you're there!

Address: Campo SS Giovanni e Paolo, Castello
What's Nearby: The hospital, Basilica SS Giovanni e Paolo, Libreria Aqua Alta, Campo Santa Maria Formosa.

8. Caffe Brasilia

Come here for excellent coffee and friendly service. It's a lovely little oasis to escape the tourist crush around the San Marco area. Caffe Brasilia is a hole-in-the-wall joint you'd probably miss if you weren't looking for it. They have a good snack/light lunch menu and fast wifi. It's a wonderful spot to sit under the umbrellas, upload to social media, and enjoy a great coffee.

I also get a kick out of the street name –Rio Terra' dei Assassini. I don't know whether stealthy assassins/murderers slipped along this former waterway or not, but it's something to think about while sipping your cappuccino.

Address: Rio Terra dei Assassini, San Marco
What's Nearby: Fortuny Museum, La Fenice,Piazza San Marco, Campo Santo Stefano.

9. Marchini Time

In the heart of the retail zone between Rialto and Piazza San Marco, the crowds spilling out of the doorway all day make this place easy to find. Marchini Time is famous for incredible pastries and outstanding espresso. The Vio family are known citywide for their beautiful cakes and pastries. They also have savory options available. Everything here is excellent.

You'll see a combination of locals and tourists here –the tourists because of the location, the locals because Italians live for outstanding coffee. Expect all the usual Venetian coffee options, but don't expect to sit –there are no tables or chairs. Either knock back your coffee at the bar Italian-style, or lean against the street-facing counter. I would stand on my head in the corner if I had to –the coffee here is that good. It's also why locals tolerate waiting, surrounded by tourists. Killer coffee is King in Italy.

Address: Calle de San Luca 4589, San Marco
What's Nearby: 4 minutes' walk from Rialto Bridge (less from the Rialto vaporetto stop). This place is in the heart of everything.

10. Caffe Florian

So here we are at the oldest cafe in the world. For 300 years, Florian has been a landmark, and is an important piece of Venetian history. The decor inside is *spectacular*. Sitting outside, listening to the musicians is one of the most iconic images of Venice. In the early morning, the piazza is less frenetic, but the musicians aren't playing, so if the piazza is packed with tourists, come back in the late afternoon when they're heading back to the ship or the train. In the evening, the musicians are playing, the light is exquisite, and there is no more beautiful place to be than right here. During the winter months, you can warm up inside with one of their world famous hot chocolates, or a coffee, while enjoying the art all around you. Florian's service is always outstanding.

Of course, the coffee is exemplary here. Frankly, it needs to be, because this will be the most expensive cup of coffee in your entire life. Before you order, make sure you are aware of the price and the extra fees you'll be charged for sitting at a table. If money is no issue, knock yourself out. But if you are on a budget, you don't want to be surprised by the fat bill you will definitely get here.

Instead of a cafe, think of Florian as a living museum *experience*, that comes with a coffee.

12.
Madly Chic Places to Have an Aperitivo in Venice

"You've got to see Venice," he began. "You've got to see a city of slender towers and white domes, sleeping in the water like a mass of water lilies. You've got to see dark waterways, mysterious threads of shadow, binding all these flowers of stone together."

— E. Temple Thurston

Look beyond the fanny-packed tourists and you'll see that Venice is a very elegant city. The average Venetian, be they rich or poor or anywhere in the middle, is beautifully put together. It's the whole *bella figura* thing. They dress stylishly and carry themselves with a sense of decorum. As evening falls, you'll see beautifully dressed Venetians heading out for an aperitivo, dinner or other evening entertainment. That means there are loads of really gorgeous, madly chic places to enjoy an evening in *La Serenissima* (Most Serene Republic of Venice). I'm going to acquaint you with just a few. These are definitely NOT places to show up wearing a fanny pack and clumpy sneakers. I always pack a dress to wear to a chic soiree. Bring something in travel fabrics that don't require ironing, look lovely with a pair of sandals, and will guarantee you entry to anywhere special. If you plan for something gorgeous to happen, it probably will. In fact, most of the time it does. Make an event out of it. Because why not?

The following is a list of madly chic places to have a drink in Venice. Dress up, feel fabulous and create yourself a magnificent, luxurious experience.

1. Belmond Hotel Cipriani

The Cipriani is a fabulous 5-star hotel on Giudecca. I dress up for it, then take the private Cipriani boat from the dock at San Marco across to the island. Right out of a movie, it feels ridiculously chic.

The Cipriani has bar service outdoors on the water, with a view, and a pool bar. The pool bar is the more glam of the two options. The clientele here are well heeled and beautifully dressed. You'll be sharing space with movie directors and international business titans, among the regular 5-star crowd.

The appetizers served here are sensational. The waiters are wonderful and have worked here forever. I always order the same drink –a passionfruit, St Germain, and Prosecco cocktail. According to the menu, this cocktail was invented here for George Clooney's wedding. I typically get the same server (I come here every time I come to Venice), who always greets me with, "*Welcome back, madam*" and a warm smile, followed by "*Will you be having a Nina's Passion this evening?*"

I don't bother looking at the cocktail menu anymore. Afterall, a drink that's good enough for Clooney is good enough for me. And it's delicious.

Address: Guidecca 10.

2. The Gritti Palace

This hotel on the Grand Canal offers three bar options, two of which I particularly enjoy.

The Gritti Terrace

The terrace bar is on the Grand Canal, opposite the Salute. It is a full-service restaurant, but you can also do a well-timed aperitivo. The well-timed part? Hitting the terrace in time for golden hour, blue hour or both. The view truly is iconic.

You may need a reservation –check first.

Bar Longhi

If you close your eyes and imagine the most iconic, Venetian-looking bar, Bar Longhi is what your mind would conjure up. The decoration of this space is swoon-worthy and frankly is fit for royalty. From the priceless Piero Longhi paintings to the Murano glass chandeliers and the Fortuny fabrics, it is a set designer's dream. Except it isn't a movie, its real life.

There are endless options on the drinks menu, all of which are fabulous. If you're in the mood for something extra stylish, look to their martini menu. My favorite is a glorious concoction of gin, St Germain, lemon, basil, and orange bitters. I'm not a martini drinker, so I can make one martini last all evening. They've also made me the same drink with Prosecco instead of gin. Just sensational.

Sometimes I come here when I'm in town alone and want to do something special. The bartenders wear tuxedos, are wonderful conversationalists, and give the entire event a very James Bond feel.

Address: Campo Santa Maria del Giglio 2467.

3. Hotel Danieli

The Hotel Danieli comprises three palazzi. The main building is the beautiful Palazzo Dandolo, a 14th century palace, once the home of Doge Dandolo's family. Imagine what a Doge's family palazzo might look like, multiply that by 1000 and you have the Palazzo Dondolo. The central lobby, with its dramatic, high gold-leaf ceiling, Murano glass, gothic splendor and, of course, that magnificent staircase, might be one of the most photographed hotel lobbies in all of Europe.

Bar Dandolo

This award-winning bar in the heart of the hotel, spills out into the lobby. You sit steeped in history and sophistication amongst pink marble columns in sumptuous décor, while you sip classic cocktails ordered from white tuxedo'd waiters. In the evenings, there is live piano music. In the afternoons, you can sit in front of the original fireplace and enjoy a sensational afternoon tea service. It's just gorgeous. I love to make this into an event, be it winter or summer, afternoon or at night. After all, when was the last time you had a cocktail or tea in a 14th century Doge's palace?

Bar Terrazza Danieli

The rooftop terrace bar is a little less dressy, but definitely smart casual at a minimum. From up here, you have unobstructed views of San Giorgio Maggiore and a sensational panorama of Venice. This is a lovely bar to enjoy a *bellini* with delicious snacks, or maybe a glass of wine before you meander into the wonderful Restaurant Terrazza Danieli. It is quite expensive, but worth it.

Since 2021, a reservation is required here.

Address: Riva degli Schiavoni 4196, Castello
Vaporetto Stop: San Zaccaria.

4. Terrazza Panoramica at the Ca' Sagredo Hotel

Ca' Sagredo is absolutely swoon-worthy. As in, to die for. So much so, this 15th century palazzo has been designated a National Monument. The frescoes, art, marble staircase, and echoes of the lives that dwelled in this noble residence over the centuries–it's all just spectacular. The rooftop bar is gorgeous and has ridiculous views across Venice and over the Grand Canal. Expect sophisticated drinks and a divine, atmosphere.

Address: Campo Santa Sofia 4198
Website: www.casagredohotel.com
Vaporetto Stop: Ca' d'Oro.

5. The Bar at the Aman

First, let's talk about the Aman Hotel. Filled with museum quality treasures and frescoes painted by former resident Tiepolo, the Aman is part of the spectacular 16th century Palazzo Papadopoli. The top floor of the palazzo is still the home of Italian royalty, the Arrivabene Velenti Gonzaga family. (We'll talk about them in the **Shopping** chapter.) The hotel is ridiculously, achingly beautiful. Be sure to check out the Piano Nobile dining room if only for the decor and the views. Mind you, every room in the Aman Venice is exquisite. The palazzo won a heritage award for Italy's best renovation.

The Bar at the Aman is a warm and inviting. It pays homage to Lord Byron, another former resident of the palazzo. The bar is in the Red Room, a richly toned space facing the Grand Canal and a secret garden. Ideal for a brooding romantic like Byron, The Bar combines one of the most beautiful places to watch the sunset with Venice's most extensive collection of gin. Although there are plenty of other drinks on offer, you should try one of their gins. The bartenders here are "mixologists", a term I find pretentious anywhere else. If, like me, you're not a gin afficionado, they'll talk to you, figure you out and mix a bespoke cocktail you'll love. They are masters at designing cocktails, and all things to do with gin. This alone makes coming here an experience. They have a wonderful cocktail called the *Passionate*, made from gin, lychee, lemon and rose syrup, and I have also had a tremendous bespoke cocktail here that combined a citrus-infused gin with Prosecco and pea flower liqueur.

On balmy summer evenings, take your drink up to the terrace. You can also order the Aman's own cicchetti, bar snacks and light meals.

Address: Palazzo Papadopoli, Calle Tiepolo Baimonte 1364, San Polo
Website: www.aman.com
Vaporetto Stop: S. Silvestro.

6. Settimo Cielo Rooftop Bar

Until 2019, this rooftop bar was reserved exclusively for guests of the Hotel Bauer Palazzo. At the time of writing this book, it is open to all. The Settimo Cielo Rooftop Bar is the highest terrace in Venice, and the views are sensational. Open from 6pm to midnight this is a lovely spot for a cocktail and/or dinner at the accompanying restaurant run by Michelin Star Chef Cristiano Tomei.

Address: San Marco 1459
Website: www.bauervenezia.com
Vaporetto Stop: San Marco.

7. Terrazza Bar at H10 Palazzo Canova

The H10 Palazzo Canova Hotel is in a renovated 19th century building on the Grand Canal, just a few meters from the Rialto Bridge. The rooftop bar has two different areas –a covered, indoor bar and a modern terrace bar with amazing views. This one isn't as dressy as some of the other bars on my list (think smart casual) and the terrace furniture is average, but the views are tremendous, including a superb view of the Rialto Bridge. This is a glorious spot to be during sunset/golden hour/blue hour.

The Terrazza Bar is open to the public on summer evenings.

Address: Riva del Vin 744, San Polo
Website: www.h10hotels.com
Vaporetto Stop: S. Silvestro.

8. Skyline

The Skyline is at the top of the Hilton Molino Stucky on Giudecca. This one is all about the view. It encompasses all of Venice.

The cocktail menu is 48 pages long and features interesting seasonal ingredients like rosemary, basil and thyme. There is some theater here too –order a Smokey Old Fashioned and they'll smoke it for you on the spot. The crowd is predominantly well dressed, wealthy European hip young things.

The hotel entrance from the fondamenta feels a bit like walking into a Holiday Inn. Don't be put off though –the Skyline Bar is chic, smart and stylish.

In 2021, a reservation was required due to Covid restrictions. Check ahead and make a reservation if required.

Address: Hilton Molino Stucky, Giudecca 810
Vaporetto Stop: Palanca.

13.
Seven Great Places to Get Gelato in Venice

Venice never quite seems real, but rather an ornate film set suspended on the water.

–Frida Giannini

I have two rules when it comes to gelato in Italy:

1. Only ever buy artisan gelato.
2. Don't buy flavors you can get at home.

There are two types of gelato:

The first is artisanal. It is made fresh on site each day, using only seasonal local ingredients and sometimes specialty ingredients (like Sicilian pistachios). It doesn't need to be frozen because artisan gelato is made to be consumed the same day. It has no preservatives, colorants or chemicals, and is not loaded with sugar.

The second type of gelato is industrial. It is made in factories and shipped in, full of preservatives and food coloring. Industrial gelato sometimes comes in powdered form and is whipped up in the store. There is a huge difference between them, from texture to flavor to aftertaste. The crazy thing is, they cost the same. Artisan gelato shops are everywhere and are easy to find. Leave the factory-made gelato to the mass tourists. You, my friend, are coming with me to get the good stuff.

How to Spot Industrial Gelato

As I've already said, cities with over-tourism have an abundance of tourist eateries, designed to fill the bellies of the undiscerning. The same applies to gelato shops. You'll see tourist gelato shops, churning out industrial gelato to people who don't know and don't care. (However, you've made it this far through my book, so clearly you're looking for a more authentic experience.) Industrial gelato joints are easy to spot. They're on busy streets and near big tourist sites. Their gelato case is full of brightly colored, whipped up mounds of confection.

High vs Low

Industrial gelato sits up high, all puffed and fluffy. (Look along the case and you'll see the flavors piled high, even on a hot day, in direct sunlight. Adding chemicals is the only way to make gelato fluff up high.) Whip your heart out, but no matter how hard you try, you can't whip artisanal gelato's fresh ingredients to any height at all. If it sits low in the pan and generally has a lid on it, that is the first sign you've stumbled onto the good stuff.

Vibrant Color Palette

With no chemical colorants, artisan gelato colors are muted. Instead of hot pink, artisan strawberry gelato has a creamy pinkish hue. Mint has a whitish tone, not bright green. The super popular (and my favorite) pistachio is a greyish green. If you see bright colors, it's industrial gelato.

Flavor Profiles

Industrial gelato comes in very mainstream flavors. Flavors you'd find in any supermarket freezer section, or stateside ice cream chain. Artisan gelato tastes completely different and has some expected flavors. It sometimes features really interesting, complex, and totally inspired flavor profiles –for example, fennel and almond, white peaches and sage, raspberry and rosemary, white chocolate with basil, ricotta with almonds and figs.

Before you get freaked out and run for the chocolate chip at the factory shop, know that:

1. Stracciatella is vanilla + chocolate, with chocolate shavings instead of chips.
2. There will always be simple flavors that you know.
3. They'll let you taste a few before you order.

I recommend trying anything we foreigners would consider unusual. If it has rosemary, basil, sage, bergamot, lavender, or anything you are not used to seeing at home, at least try it. Experience something a little different. You have a lifetime of rocky-road ahead of you at home. Live a little. At an average cost of €1,50 you're not going to break the bank by trying something different!

Gelato is diet food!

Well, sort of. Gelato has half the calories of ice cream. It's also creamier and denser, and you need less to feel totally satiated.

Buying Artisan Gelato

Even with a single scoop of gelato, your choice to buy from an artisan shop makes a difference. Every penny of your purchase goes back into the local economy. Local workers make it (not machines in a factory on the mainland), your purchase supports local farmers, and you're supporting local craftspeople, because gelato-makers are artisans.

If you're not sure where to go, ask a local Venetian –they will happily point you in the right direction.

Here are my top seven places to get great gelato in Venice.

1. Gelateria Nico

I came here for years before realizing they sold gelato! I was coming here for an afternoon spritz with a view across the Giudecca Canal toward the Redentore church.

Maurizio, who I have always called Nico, introduced me to "Select", the Venetian exchange for Aperol. Funnily enough, one is always delivered to my table minutes after I sit down, before I even place an order. (Some habits are too wonderful to ever change!) So, it was ages before I even noticed they sold gelato. And wouldn't you know it, it's one of the most famous gelato shops in all of Venice! Since opening in the 1920s, Nico has been a favorite spot of actors, writers and celebrities, including Angelina Jolie and Peggy Guggenheim, who've all enjoyed the relative peace here, the staggering view and the incredible gelato.

The most famous flavor here is the *gianduiotto*, a decadent Piedmontese hazelnut chocolate and cream that people walk clear across Venice for. Another incredible flavor (if in season) is the black cherry and cream.

Nico's serves gelato in huge hurricane glasses, so you can either sit inside or at any of their outdoor spaces and enjoy your gelato slowly, the way they intend it.

Address: Fondamenta Zattere al Ponte Lungo 922
Vaporetto Stop: Zattere
What's Nearby: Accademia, the Peggy Guggenheim, Santa Maria della Salute.

2. La Mela Verde

It is easy to walk right past this tiny, Granny Smith colored, hole in the wall gelateria. And I do mean *tiny* –it holds about five people at a time. Consider it an insider secret and be ready to taste some of the best gelato of your life. Made fresh daily using Italian whole milk, they only offer about 12 flavors each day. You cannot beat any of their fruit flavors –the white peach is a must-try. They also make an out-of-this-world Sicilian ricotta and pistachio gelato here.

Address: Fondamenta de l'Osmarin 4977A
Vaporetto Stop: San Zaccaria
What's Nearby: Basilica San Marco (5 minutes' walk) Campo Santa Maria Formosa, Palazzo Grimani.

3. Gelateria il Doge

This award-winning gelato shop is a chocolate lover's dream. Gelateria il Doge has two locations, the busier is in Campo Santa Margherita, the more relaxed is in Campiello San Toma'. They make 15 flavors per day, 8 of which are chocolate. Their signature flavor is *crema di Doge*, which is a candied orange and chocolate. My favorite is the spicy chocolate, made with black pepper. While I normally never order chocolate gelato, this is absolutely next level and not to be missed. (Assuming you enjoy spicy chocolate.) Another super popular flavor is the Himalayan pink salt and cocoa.

Address: Dorsoduro 3058A, Rio Terà Canal
Vaporetto Stop: Ca' Rezzonico
What's Nearby: Ca' Rezzonico,Ponte dei Pugni, Barca San Barnaba.

4. Gelato di Natura

A super popular gelato spot in Venice since 1982, there are now several branches of this shop in Venice and more on the mainland. Di Natura not only uses all natural ingredients but also ingredients that are IGT, IGP and DOP certified.

Their fig and ricotta gelato is beyond sensational. Their presentation is super pretty and very Instagrammable, so don't be surprised to find their confections all over social media. In fact, check out their own Instagram @gelatodinatura for photographic gastronomic inspiration!

While you're here, try the Venetian take on Japanese mochi, called *michi*. They stuff these little rice cakes with strawberry, coffee, green tea, vanilla or chocolate gelato and they are just wonderful.

Addresses: Campo Santi Apostoli in Cannaregio, Campo San Giacome dell' Orio in Santa Croce, San Marco 1164 (2 minutes' walk from Piazza San Marco), Gran Viale 5 on Lido, Riva Longa 27 on Murano.

5. Gelateria Alaska

Gelateria Alaska took its name from the milk store previously occupying this space. They're known for making seriously good gelato served in oversized scoops. You'll find all the usual flavors here but try the oddball savory flavors –they'll blow your mind! My personal favorites have included: arugula and orange, turmeric and ginger, and various other combinations involving celery –even artichoke flavored gelato. I always try whatever unusual flavors they have on the menu. It's inexpensive so were I to find one I didn't care for (not that it's ever happened), it wouldn't be a significant loss. If you feel you need to temper something that seems a little too outlandish, you cannot beat their pear gelato.

Address: Calle Larga dei Bari 1159, San Polo
Vaporetto Stop: Ferrovia (cross the Scalzi Bridge)
What's Nearby: The train station (over the bridge), the Scalzi Bridge, Natural History Museum.

6. Gelatoteco Suso

On the Calle della Bissa, you'll spot a line of people waiting to get inside this gelato emporium. There are more flavors on hand here than most gelato shops offer, largely because along with regular creamy cow's milk gelato, Suso also serves vegan and gluten free options. Spectacular flavors include bitter chocolate with mandarin, one called *manet,* which is a combo of pistachio and hazelnut with sea salt, and *nota' nera* which is dark raspberry with layered chocolate. You really are spoiled here with exotic flavors. If their mascarpone gelato with fig sauce and walnuts was the last thing you ate before you died, I'd say, *what a way to go*!

Address: Calle della Bissa 5453
Vaporetto Stop: Rialto
What's Nearby: Rialto Bridge, Marco Polo's house, the Church of Santa Maria dei Miracoli.

7. Venchi

Venchi is famous for chocolate. The brainchild of a boy from Turin, Silviano Venchi at age 20 saved up and bought two bronze cauldrons to experiment with making chocolate. He formed his company in 1878 and quickly became chocolate supplier to the royal house of Savoy. His was considered the most elegant chocolate shop in all of Piedmont.

The shop in Venice is one of 115 around the world. For the chocolate alone, this should be on your list of places to visit (you have to try the *nougatine*, a bonbon made of caramelized chopped hazelnuts covered in dark chocolate). You can buy fabulous gifts here. And while you're here, try the gelato. Venchi started making gelato in 2007, creating handcrafted delicacies using simple ingredients, local fruits, Piedmontese IGP hazelnuts and, of course, their own chocolate. Expect gelato versions of all their most popular flavors of chocolates, from the nougatine to p*istacchio di Bronte*. The raspberry is crazy good too.

Address: Calle dei Fabbri 989
Vaporetto Stop: Midway between Rialto and San Marco
What's Nearby: Scala Contarini del Bovolo, Piazza San Marco, Campo Manin.

14.
Interesting and Unusual Things to Look for in Venice

Venice is a combination of magic and pasta.

–Federico Fellini

Most tourists plod from one monument to the next, unaware of what they're missing. But historical cities are always full of quirky, fascinating things, hiding in plain sight.

Look for the following fascinating features as you explore Venice. Some are random things you wouldn't otherwise notice, others are cool places to visit. And of course, there's a story behind each one.

1. The Winged Lions of Venice

You'll see the winged lion of Venice everywhere you turn. *Everywhere.* He scowls menacingly, or gazes benignly right through you. He watches from columns, monuments, buildings, lampposts, and clock towers. You'll spot him in bronze and in stone, made from silver, gold, wood and glass. Tooled into leather, printed on fabrics and scarves, corbels under rooflines in the shape of the lion's head, brass rings through his nose will be door knockers. He is *everywhere.* The winged lion of St Mark became the symbol of Venice when Mark became their patron saint in 828AD.

He can be found everywhere the Venetian Republic ruled, through northern Italy, the Adriatic and eastern Mediterranean. If his front paw is on an open book, they erected him during a time of peace. His foot on a closed book means it was a time of war. When I brought my (then) 10-year-old to Venice, he kept track of all the lions we saw. He documented whether the paw was on an open or closed book and took photos of them all. Every time I see a winged lion, I automatically check the foot on the book! If traveling with children, tasking them with spotting, documenting and counting lions can keep them entertained for hours.

2. The Lions' Mouths

'These were the terrible Lions' Mouths. These were the throats down which went the anonymous accusation thrust in secretly in the dead of night by an enemy, that doomed many an innocent man to walk the Bridge of Sighs and descend into the dungeon which none entered and hoped to see the sun again.' – Mark Twain, *Innocents Abroad.*

Think of these as Renaissance era tip-off lines, where citizens of the Republic could rat one another out, sending them to the inquisition.

The Council of Ten was a secret police-style special tribunal, created in 1310 to investigate crimes against the state. They grew over the centuries to include three Inquisitors of State. Their secret police investigated offenses considered criminal, immoral, political, or religious (and if they knocked on your door, you were toast). The Inquisitors' findings went to the Council of Ten, whose decision was final. There was no turning back. The Council's control slowly expanded to include finance and foreign matters, making them the most powerful governing body in the Republic. Everything happened in secret, making it seem tyrannical, but apparently it was efficient and effective. And terrifying.

Reporting a coworker/family member/neighbor/rival guaranteed that person a trip to the torture chamber. So, it had to be secret. The Council of Ten wanted the juice on what was happening, so they invented an anonymous tip system, the Lion's Mouths. Scattered across the city, these open-mouthed lion faces (and other scary faces) were mailboxes. The writer slipped an anonymous note through the open slot of the lion's mouth, feeling especially patriotic because the lion was the symbol of the Republic. Each state department had a separate mailbox, including the tax department, market fraud, and the various administrative offices. The citizens didn't need riots, demonstrations, or protests when they could register complaints so easily.

The boxes were also used for complaints against public officials abusing their power. This attached value to the word of the average Venetian, helping maintain social peace, while strengthening the power of the Republic.

The *bocche di leone* were also called the *bocche che parlano*, "the mouths that speak". Behind each mouth was a locked box, the keys held by special magistrates. After reading a letter the judge would burn it. Anyone could write a denunciation, and sometimes innocent people were accused out of envy and malice. In 1542 a new law was passed to protect them, thereafter complaints must be signed and have two witnesses.

The only denunciations not requiring witnesses or signatures were for conspiracies and crimes against the state. These were dangerous for the person tipping them off and too dangerous for the republic to ignore. If caught lying, the accuser was in dire trouble.

When the Republic fell in 1797, most Bocche di Leone were destroyed. But keep your eyes open and look for the ones that are still there. You can still find them in a few places around town:

- You'll find a Lion's Mouth at the Doge's Palace. This one was for complaints addressed directly to the magistrates. (The Doge's Palace was the seat of government and home of the courts.)
- On the wall of Santa Maria della Visitazione in Dorsoduro there's one used for complaints about garbage in the canals. It reads *denunciations relating to public health of the sestiere of Dorsoduro.*
- There's another *bocca* in the museum on Torcello, and on the wall of San Martino church in Castello.

3. Gobba Antibandito

(I'm not sure if this is their real name, but it's the one I'm going with.)

Recently, my guide Emanuele pointed to a big, curved stone angling toward the ground where two walls met at a right angle, and asked if he'd ever told me about them. Too steep to sit or stand on, and about 3 feet tall, the stone blocked the corner. I had never even noticed them before! The story, as Emanuele told it, went back to the time when Venice was the great merchant trading hub of the world. The city was full of merchants from everywhere, walking around with pockets full of money. Other than the occasional lantern, the streets were dark at night. Bandits would hide around blind corners, jump on their prey, rob them, and disappear into the night. The situation was remedied by installing these stone wedges into dark corners all over the city. Bandits couldn't sit or stand on them, they and could no longer hide in the corner either. Another theory is the stone shapes made it impossible for men to slink into street corners to urinate, as the angle of the stone would spray it back at them. The Venetian slang for them roughly translates into something like 'urinal'.

Once you notice your first one, you'll spot them everywhere. Just don't sit or lean against them –that urinal reference had to come from somewhere …

4. The Paterae of Venice

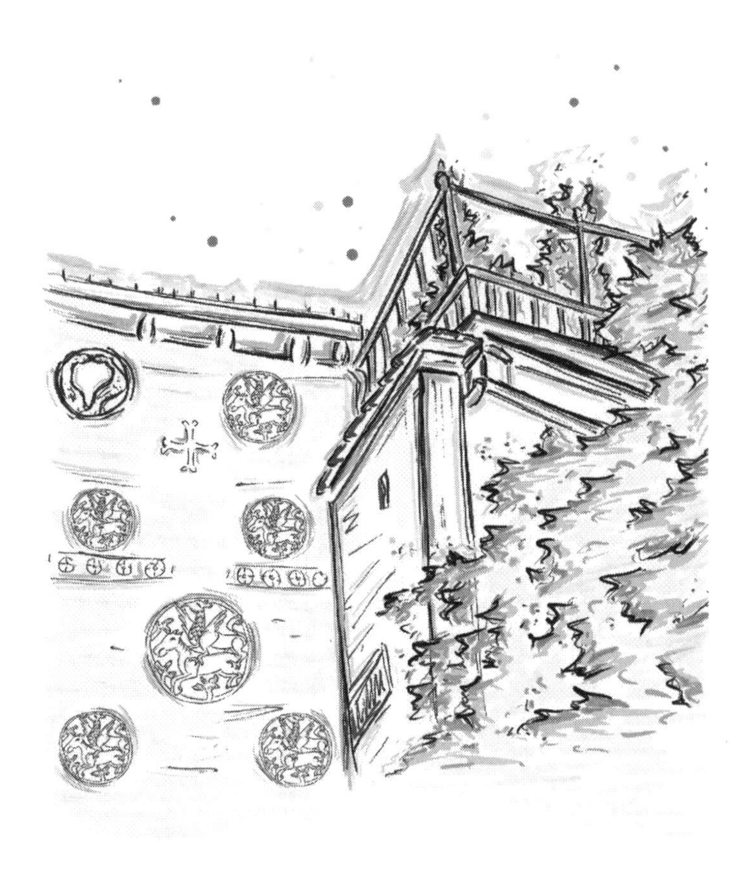

In Italy, you often see shields and family crests mounted onto exterior walls, so you might not notice *paterae* at first, or realize their significance.

The *patera* is a round bas relief made from white Istrian stone or marble. They measure 20—80cm in diameter (sometimes smaller) and are about 10cm deep. Paterae were decorative elements high on the walls of palaces and churches during the 10th to 12th centuries. Their job was to ward off evil spirits. Most depict animals fighting. Some show the animal's zodiac symbol, like Leo the lion. Some symbolize love, others are predatory.

The *paterae* (also spelled *patere*) from the tenth and eleventh centuries have smooth edges, while the twelfth century paterae has a scalloped or serrated edge. When a building was demolished, they were rescued and either moved elsewhere or inserted into the newer building. Many are not on their original building.

The Sant'Alipo portal of Basilica San Marco has paterae of the four evangelists, below the mosaics of St Mark. They are in a perfect line, with Luke (winged ox), Mark (winged lion) John (eagle) and Matthew (angel). The symbols of evangelists characteristically have wings.

You can see more evangelist paterae on a building in San Polo. Overlooking Calle Salviati where it intersects Calle del Ponto Storto, this time they float around the wall. Rather than presenting a united front against evil spirits, these paterae are freestyling.

I am intrigued by the concept of churches needing talismans to ward off evil spirits. The Church of Santa Maria dei Carmini in the Dorsoduro repurposed paterae in a 14th century rebuild, depicting animals at peace (peacocks drinking) and predators attacking their prey.

The biggest stash of paterae that I've found so far is on a wall near Santa Maria dei Miracoli. (address below). There are eleven of them, *plus* a cross. This family covered all the bases. They are all animals, starting with two birds making a heart, but then things get vengeful with eagles pecking hares, waders with twisted necks, a lion biting an animal, a dog biting a deer, dragons trapped aggressively in a circle –it's wild!

Once you've spotted your first paterae, you'll notice them everywhere. I love finding them!

Address: Cannaregio 5410, Sotoportego Widmann (the house with the 11 paterae).

5. Palazzo Mastelli del Cammello (House of the Mysterious Statues)

In 1112AD, the three Mastelli brothers owned the Palazzo Mastelli in Cannaregio. The brothers were turned to stone so they would remain there for all eternity (or at least until the building eventually falls down).

Rioba, Afani and Sandi Mastelli were merchants who traded in silks and spices. They tried to scam a Venetian woman by overcharging her for inferior quality fabric. Realizing what they were doing, she placed a curse on the money and when they touched it, they turned to stone. The petrified *Mori* (statues of the Mastelli brothers) stand against the wall in the campo, looking quite startled.

While you're here, notice the odd-looking fellow at the Ponte dei Mori bridge. This is Sior Antonio Rioba. Venetian folklore says rubbing his nose brings good luck in business. The original stone nose fell off in the 19th century and incongruously was replaced with a black iron one. On 30 April 2010, vandals stole Rioba's head, but the head was recovered on 3 May and the statue was restored.

Also, look for a bas relief on the facade of the palazzo of a man with a camel laden with goods. You can see it from the Rio della Madonna.

Address: Campo dei Mori 3381, Cannaregio
Vaporetto Stop: Madonna dell' Orto and Fondamente Nove
What's Nearby: Vino Vero, Chioda Bridge, the Jewish Ghetto, Casa Tintoretto.

6. The Pantegana

This quirky carving of the *pantegana* is neither the work of a great artist, nor a piece of modern graffiti. All we know about it is that it appeared in 1644.

From Campo San Felice in Cannaregio, take the Calle del Traghetto to Fondamenta Traghetto on the Grand Canal. On your right, look for a column in the *sotoportego* (covered walkway) of the palazzo on the corner. Look up and you'll see an enormous rat (*pantegana*) with a grotesque, long tail carved into the column.

The wooden dock was once a traghetto station. During inclement weather, the traghetto boatmen (*barcaroli*) would shelter under the sotoportego, and must have seen some sizeable rats floating by. One was so huge they deemed it worthy of carving into the Istrian marble. (Bubonic plague had raged through Venice 14 years prior, so maybe this enormous rat gave the sailors the willies.) Not only was the pantegana enormous enough to be immortalized in stone, they also dated the carving in Roman numerals above it, 1644.

Address: Cannaregio 3694
Vaporetto Stop: Ca' d'Oro
What's Nearby: Ca' d 'Oro, the Chioda bridge, Campo dei Mori.

7. The Half Palace of Venice

On the north side of the Grand Canal, look for Palazzo Flangini, a baroque style palace built between 1664 and 1682. Or at least half of it was. There are many stories about the half palace, including my favorite –how it was inherited by two brothers who became so estranged they had their palazzo cut in half. According to that story, one brother then demolished the other brother's half.

Unfortunately, the stories aren't true. There was only ever half a palace built. Palazzo Flangini is completely asymmetrical, and it looks like they intended it to be double the size. You'll notice the front door is all the way over to the left. Whether the family ran out of money, or they were unable to buy the little red brick house leaning against it, we'll never know. I'm convinced they ran out of money. The left-side facade looks like it was hurriedly closed up, displaying none of the opulence of the right-side wall. The columns on the left corner of the noble floors have been cut in half.

The last family member to own the palazzo, Cardinal Luigi (Ludovico) Flangini, died in 1804.

Your best view of Palazzo Flangini is from the left side of the vaporetto as it pulls into the Riva di Biasio stop.

Address: Campo San Geremia 252, Cannaregio
Vaporetto Stop: between Ferrovia and S. Marcuola.

8. The Secret Door Under the Bridge

If you've read my book *Glam Italia! 101 Fabulous Things to Do in Florence*, you'll already know how much I love secret, hidden doorways in old buildings. It's fun to speculate on the clandestine goings on happening here across the centuries, who snuck in, and who was sneaking out.

Unless you know it's there, you'll walk right past this one. The Feltrina Bridge connects Santa Maria del Giglio church and the walkway to Calle Zaguri. The hidden doorway is below the bridge. This was the old water door for the church. Boatmen delivered goods to this doorway, to be unloaded by someone inside the church. (Secret church doorways would come in handy for Casanova and all the randy priests interfering with the city's young nuns.)

The bridge above it, completely hides this door. From midnight runs to pirate contraband, this was the perfect hidden door for nefarious activities.

Address: Feltrina Bridge, San Marco
Vaporetto Stop: Giglio
What's Nearby: Piazza San Marco, Santa Maria del Giglio, Campo Santo Stefano.

9. La Scala Contarini del Bovolo

In the heart of the San Marco neighborhood, you'll be close to this place more often than you realize.

This palazzo looks significantly different to all the others in Venice. The building is beautiful, with 15th century red *coota* bricks offset by white Istrian stone arches and balustrades on every floor. The beautiful interior winding staircase in an external tower was added to the building in 1499. Ornate and spiraling upward, they nicknamed it *del Bovolo* (of the snail), a moniker that not only stuck to the palazzo but to that branch of the noble Contarini family.

It must have seemed incredibly modern, as there was and still is nothing else like it in all of Venice. The staircase ends in a beautiful belvedere with views stretching out across the city. The 80 steps are narrow and steep but are open to the public and definitely worth climbing.

The tower is only 85 feet tall, but from outside it appears to soar far higher. This is a Renaissance-era architectural trick. The arches decrease in height with each floor. The top floor arches are half the height of the bottom arches, which creates the illusion of much greater height.

Your €7 ticket lets you access part of the palazzo and an art exhibition space with a limited-yet-fabulous art collection that includes a Tintoretto.

Address: Corte Contarina 4303, San Marco
Vaporetto Stop: Midway between Rialto and San Marco
What's Nearby: La Fenice, Piazza San Marco, Campo Santo Stefano.

10. The Old Pharmacies of Venice

The Venetian Republic was famous for its advanced healthcare system. They were the first to have Public Health Officers, and created Europe's first plague hospitals, the *lazzaretti*. During the plagues Venice isolated the sick, dead and dying on plague islands to curb the spread of infection.

One important advancement of the Venetian health system was the city's apothecaries, now known as pharmacies. Some of the old pharmacies are still visible today, their beautiful centuries-old wooden fixtures cared for and preserved. Some wonderful examples include:

- The 17th century **All'Ercole d'Oro** (The Golden Hercules) near Campo Santa Fosca. It is now a perfume store called The Merchant of Venice, but the original baroque wooden carvings, shelves and cabinets are all still there.

- **The Merchant of Venice** shop (not the same place as the perfume store above) in Campo San Fantin was a 19th century pharmacy, built in the popular Gothic Revival style. It has life-sized statues that are allegories of the sciences.

- Near the main entrance to the beautiful **hospital of Venice** there's a door with a *farmacia* sign above it. This was the hospital's 19th century pharmacy and is now a museum. Full of cool old pots and jars and tools used by the pharmacists of yore, it also has a collection of relics from the hospital's pathology department.

- The most famous pharmacy is the **Farmacia Ai do San Marchi** inside Ca' Rezzonico. This 18th century pharmacy was originally in Campo San Stin. In 1908 a French antique dealer purchased the interior and donated it to the city. They moved the entire pharmacy to the Ca' Rezzonico museum, rebuilding it identically, including all the wooden shelves and desks, the jars and pots used to store all the medicines and the glass tools used to make them.

The Old Signs

Many current pharmacies kept their historical predecessors' names and the old signs on the exterior walls. In Campo San Polo, look for **Farmacia Burati Alla Colonna e Mezza** (At the One and a Half Columns). The exterior wall has a bas relief of two columns, one of them cut in half. It was originally called *Alle Due Colonne* (At the Two Columns), but another pharmacy across town had the same name. So in the 16th century, they cut one column in half, forever renaming the San Polo pharmacy *Alla Colonna e Mezza*! The bas relief is just a small, random thing, but fun to spot as you explore San Polo.

The Golden Head

If you've been to Venice, you've probably passed this iconic piece of Venetian medical history, completely unaware that it was looking down at you.

On Salizada Pio X in San Marco, 20 meters from the Rialto Bridge, look up to your left and you'll see a golden head above the shops. Etched into the wall just below it are the words *Theriaca Andromachi*. This is all that remains of one of the most famous pharmacies in historical Venice, the Farmacia Alla Testa d'Oro. At a time when most people couldn't read, the golden head made the pharmacy easy to find.

Venetian pharmacies were famous for a powerful cure-all called *Theriaca d' Andromaco*. Theriaca comes from the Greek word "theroin ", which means "wild beast". Emperor Nero's medicine man, Andromaco, perfected this magic potion, effective against the poisonous bites of various beasts. Along with viper meat, there were approximately 60 other ingredients, including exotic herbs and spices from far-away lands, brought to Venice on merchant ships. Because of this, Venetian theriaca was the very best in the world, and the theriaca from Alla Testa d'Oro was considered the best in all of Venice. Although the recipe was kept secret, theriaca had to be made in public, in an enormous cauldron placed outside the pharmacy, and it took several days to make a single batch. Because theriaca from Alla Testa d'Oro was the best of the best, the Republic regulators allowed them to make their version of the recipe three times per year, while the other pharmacies could make theirs only once each year.

Alla Testa d'Oro began making theriaca in 1603 and was the only pharmacy still making it in the 20th century. In the 1940s, when new regulations banned the use of psychotropic drugs and opium, theriaca could no longer be made.

Outside some of the historical pharmacies in Venice you can still see the round rings left by the heavy cauldrons that would sit outside once each year for approximately 300 years. Yet another random little detail to keep an eye out for in Venice.

11. The Flooded Crypt of San Zaccaria

The church of San Zaccaria is a beautifully ornate 15th century combination of Gothic and Renaissance styles. It's worth visiting for its own beauty but is more exciting when you know what lies below.

A 9th century doge built the first church on this site, roughly 600 years before the church that stands there today. The crypt of San Zaccaria is a lovely-yet-haunted looking burial basement, home to the tombs of eight doges from the time of the *original* church. It has columns and vaulted ceilings, tombs, *and water*. This subterranean level of San Zaccaria is permanently flooded. The standing water acts like a mirror pool, extending the length of the columns while making the arched ceilings appear lower. The tombs seem to rise out of the water yet are also reflected back upon themselves. It is sacred, spooky, beautiful, haunting and very, *very* cool.

Address: Campo San Zaccaria 4693
Vaporetto Stop: San Zaccaria
What's Nearby: Piazza San Marco, the Bridge of Sighs, Doge's Palace.

12. The Calle del Paradiso

Calle del Paradiso is one of Venice's best preserved and most picturesque medieval streets. It got its name (Paradise Street) from the lavish way they decorated it for feasts and holidays, and particularly for Good Friday. There are several features to look for here:

- The calle is in a perpetual state of semi-dusk. On both sides of the street, the second floor of the houses forms an uninterrupted line, the upper floors stretching out over the pavement level. A series of massive wooden beams (*barbicani)* support this wider second floor, keeping the street level in constant shade.

- The architecture has both Byzantine and Gothic influences. The oldest parts of the houses are from the 13th century, while the newer houses were built in the 16th century.

- Calle del Paradiso is an interesting play on light and shade. The far end of the street where it meets the Ponte del Paradiso erupts into sunshine and bright light. On summer days, your eyes need a moment to adjust. Near the bridge a triangular arch joins the two houses at the end. The pointy top of the arch directs the eye up to the blue Venetian sky.

- In 1993—1994 UNESCO organized a restoration project to clean, protect and strengthen the decaying old Istrian stone arch.

- From the street side, look for the *Madonna of Mercy*, with a devout couple kneeling at her feet in prayer. From the bridge side, the Madonna can be seen to be opening her cloak, protecting a single praying figure.

- At the bottom corners of the arch, look for faded coats of arms belonging to two of Venice's most powerful families, the Foscari and the Mocenigo. The arch was built to celebrate the 1491 marriage of Pellegrina of Michiel Foscari and Alvise Mocenigo dalle Zogie, a wealthy merchant, ambassador and politican. But why is it here, when both families had huge palazzi along the Grand Canal? Well, Pellegrina's dowry was so massive that Alvise bought all 26 houses on Calle del Paradiso, including the Ca' Foscari Mocenigo dalle Zogie, Pellegrina's childhood home. This is the beautiful palazzo on the right side of the arch if you're looking at it from the bridge.

Address: Calle del Paradiso, Castello.
Vaporetto Stop: Midway between Ospedale and San Zaccaria
What's Nearby: Libreria Acqua Alta, Palazzo Grimani Museum, Campo SS Giovanni e Paolo.

13. The Blue Door of Castello

This is great for anyone who wants to photograph fantastic doorways or who wants an intriguing Instagram Venice photo.

Tucked away beside Calle del Paradiso is the Calle de Mezzo. One block from the Fondamenta San Severo is a long, narrow alleyway called Ruga Giuffa. At what looks like a dead end to the alley, you can see a magnificent blue gothic doorway. It is not a doorway to a magnificent palazzo –nor really to anywhere.

This stranded gothic doorway is at least 600 years old, has survived inquisitions and wars and peace. No doubt it will still stand firm long after we leave this mortal coil. The perfect gothic arch meets the walls of the alleyway on either side, and frames a brilliant blue door, weathered by time. One floor above ground level is a second gothic arched blue window. The alleyway is barely wider than your wingspan. It's visually stunning.

As with many things in Venice, the dead-end alleyway is all smoke and mirrors –just before the end it cuts to the left with an almost hidden *sotoportego*, spiriting you away to somewhere new.

Address: Calle de Mezzo 79, Castello
Vaporetto Stop: San Zaccaria
What's Nearby: Campo Santa Maria Formosa, Palazzo Grimini, Libreria Acqua Alta.

14. Libraria Acqua Alta

I love quirky bookstores like Atlantis Books in Santorini, Shakespeare's in Paris, and the quirkiest of them all –Libreria Acqua Alta in Venice. It's one of the most Instagrammed places in Venice, but still should be on your must-see list.

What do you do with a ground floor bookshop in a city that floods four times per year? Owner Luigi Frizzo had a brilliant idea –why not store his books inside abandoned bathtubs and a full-sized gondola?

Libreria Acqua Alta is overloaded with books. Books are stacked on every surface, reaching from the bathtubs to the ceiling. They have every kind of book you can imagine. This self-proclaimed "most beautiful bookstore in the world" has multiple rooms, all crammed with books, maps, magazines and all manner of paper things. It's heaven. When I'm in Venice during the offseason, I can spend all morning in here flicking through the books, discovering things I had no idea I was even interested in. (Hilariously, a sign marked "Fire Escape" is merely a doorway dumping you into the canal below.)

You see the occasional cat stretched out on a stack of books inside, napping on a shelf or meandering through the aisles. Luigi agreed to take a cat to help a friend. One cat turned into three, and now who even know how many cats hang out here during the day? I'm sure neighborhood cats drop in to visit their friends and socialize.

Luigi petitioned to have the wall behind the bookstore removed, so patrons could enjoy the gorgeous view. After being repeatedly turned down, he came up with another of his fabulously quirky, whimsical ideas. With no market anymore for encyclopedias, he used sets of the huge tomes to make a literary staircase to the top of the wall. Customers can climb the stairs to look at the view. More encyclopedias turned the nondescript fence into a wall of books. Floods, rains and punishing sunshine have hardened it, making it safe to climb on. It really is just tremendous! Clever and unbelievably photogenic, this is possibly one of the most photographed staircases on the internet.

Libreria Acqua Alta gets quite a few tourists, mostly those who've come to Castello specifically to see it. I always tell my travelers to be mindful of Venetians who are here *actually buying books*, which tourists typically aren't. I also suggest if taking photos here, that you buy something. A fridge magnet or a bookmark –anything really. Spend a euro for the fun of being able to photograph the most unconventional bookshop in the world.

Address: Calle Lunga Santa Maria Formosa 5176B
Vaporetto Stop: Ospedale and San Zaccaria
What's Nearby: Palazzo Grimani Museum, Campo SS Giovanni e Paolo, Rosa Salva.

The Perfect Souvenir

While you're there, look for *Venetian Legends and Ghost Stories* by Alberto Toso Fei. This book is six inches tall, is not heavy to carry around all day, and makes a fantastic gift or souvenir. If you're spending a few nights in Venice, it's fun to read the ghost stories, then check out the places they happened in. There are copies of it published in multiple languages.

15. Colleoni Statue

The story of a man, his ego, his horse, and (believe it or not) his testicles.

For four decades from 1430, Bartolomeo Colleoni was a captain/general in the Venetian military. (Actually, he was a warlord and a *condottiero*, a romantic term for a mercenary.) He pioneered putting artillery on carriages in battle, effectively making him the creator of field artillery. Colleoni amassed a fortune, of which he bequeathed 216,000 gold and silver ducats to Venice. But with a condition–they must erect a bronze equestrian monument in his honor in Piazza San Marco. Or perhaps he said *in front of San Marco*? However, the Republic forbade personal commemorative monuments –even Doges couldn't have statues to themselves in the piazza. But it was an enormous sum of money … So, the senate devised a clever solution. Florentine master Andrea del Verrocchio created the spectacular bronze statue of Colleoni looking masterful on his horse. Then, instead of in the *Piazza* San Marco, they erected it outside the *Scuola* San Marco in Campo SS Giovanni e Paolo.

But there's more to the story. Not only was Colleoni a legendary warlord, he was also a legend of the *palle* (balls). He proudly had a condition called *orchitis*, which gave him three testicles. Look to the base of the statue. You'll see what looks like a set of three commas, or excited quotation marks, depending how you look at them. These represent Colleoni's *coglioni*. Looking at him all resplendent on his horse, you have to wonder where all that extra anatomy went? I would imagine being in possession of three testicles would complicate the simple act of walking, but where do you put everything when you're riding a horse??

My favorite breakfast spot, Rosa Salva, is in this lovely campo. Stop here for refreshments while you check out old Colleoni and his *palle*.

Address: Campo SS Giovanni e Paolo
Vaporetto Stop: Ospedale, Fondamente Nove
What's Nearby: Rosa Salva, the hospital, Basilica SS Giovanni e Paolo.

16. Sotoportego di Corte Nova

I walk through this *sotoportego* multiple times per day when I'm in Venice –it's right by my apartment in Castello. A sotoportego (in Venetian dialect, or *sottoportego* in Italian) is a passageway through the ground floor of a building, like a little underpass. This 17th century sotoportego connects Calle Zorzi to Corte Nova, hence the name.

Legends permeate this little underpass, starting with the plague of 1630. According to legend, the black plague swooped through Venice in terrible, deadly waves, sparing only the people living on Corte Nova, where a resident named Giovanna had painted a sacred image of the Virgin Mary, who, in turn, protected them. On the ground in the middle of the underpass, a red marble slab marks the point at which the plague was stopped from entering the Corte, under the gaze of the painting of the Virgin. Even now, residents consider stepping on the red stone a portent of bad luck.

They also attribute other miracles to the sotoportego. The residents of Corte Nova were spared from the cholera outbreaks of 1849 and 1855, then in 1917 and 1918 from the Austrian bombs during World War I. An inscription above the north entry to the underpass commemorates these events.

This underpass is also interesting because it is a mini votive chapel. In the late 17th century/early 18th century, the sotoportego was given a beautiful painted, gilded coffered ceiling and wood paneling. Four votive paintings depicting Venice overcoming the plague through divine intervention were added, as well as two small marble frames. One holds a canvas of St Lorenzo Giustinian with saints Rocco and Sebastian, the plague protectors. The second marble frame was for the painting of the Virgin. (Giovanna's original was lost or stolen, so residents of Corte Nova replaced it with a copy.)

Address: Cota Nova 380, Castello
Vaporetto Stop: Celestia
What's Nearby: San Francesco della Vigna, the Arsenale, Libreria Aqua Alta.

17. The Piraeus Lion

There are many lions in Venice, but chances are you've not yet heard of this one. This story involves a nine-foot-tall lion from ancient Greece, 1000-year-old Viking runes, and a man who became Doge.

The Piraeus Lion stands guard at the left side of the door of the Arsenale (the Venetian shipyard). This 4th century BC Greek marble lion originally guarded the port of Athens until Francesco Morosini, a famous Venetian Naval Commander, stole him during the seige of Athens in 1687.

Morosini was famous for stealing the lion and for destroying the Parthenon. The Ottomans occupied Athens at the time, and they used the Parthenon to store gunpowder. One of Morosini's cannon balls made a direct hit, turning one of the great wonders of the world into ruins. He returned to Venice a hero and was elected doge. He positioned the stolen lion at the entrance to the Arsenale, where it remains today.

In the 18th century, a visiting Swedish scholar noticed the strange decoration carved into the lion's shoulders. He identified them as 1000-year-old Viking runes! They think a Varangian mercenary scratched this graffiti into the lion in the 11th century, when Athens was part of the Byzantine Empire. The runes look like a ribbon but are in fact a cryptozoological lindworm –a headless serpentine dragon with an inscription carved inside. A thousand years of weather and wear have made the inscription indecipherable, the original message lost to time.

The poor lion has born witness to a lot in his lifetime. From the ancient Greeks to the Vikings, the Ottomans and the Byzantines, and then a trip across the sea from warm Greek sunshine to the cold fog of Venice. But still he stands, massive, proud and glorious.

Address: Campo de l' Arsenal, Castello
Vaporetto Stop: Arsenale
What's Nearby: Bepi Zolli, San Zaccaria, Caffe Girani, Salvmeria (cicchetti).

18. Bepi Zolli, the Faithful Soldier

An enormous bronze statue of Garibaldi, the hero of Italy's unification, stands in the Giardini della Biennale. Behind the statue, a bronze soldier stands guard, protecting Garibaldi. This is Giuseppe "Bepi" Zolli. (I love this story.)

Bepi joined Italy's war of independence in 1859 and became one of Garibaldi's redshirts. He proudly vowed to guard his hero until his dying day. As an old man, Bepi sat with the statue every day, guarding Garibaldi and vowing to watch over his hero from heaven too.

In 1921, Bepi died and was buried on the cemetery island of San Michele. Shortly after his death, a series of supernatural events occurred. A ghostly soldier in a red shirt tripped and tugged locals away from Garibaldi's statue. Residents created a committee to investigate, but when they reached the statue, a red shadow knocked them to the ground. A boy recognized the statue and called out, "Look! It's Bepi the Garibaldian!" So, with pressure from the locals, a second statue was erected behind the first, of Bepi Zolli proudly guarding his hero. Since Bepi's statue was erected, there have been no more ghostly sightings and nobody has been tripped or pulled away.

Address: Giardini della Bienniale
Vaporetto Stop: Giardini or Gairdini Biennale
What's Nearby: Arsenale, Salvmeria and San Zaccaria.

19. The Witch's Clock

On the quiet Calle della Toletta in Dorsoduro, look for a yellow/ochre house with a rusty old alarm clock hanging from an external pipe at the roof line. This clock is not the original one, but has been replaced three times over the years. According to local legend, a witch who dabbled in black magic once lived here. She used a clock to mark the time when invoices were due to be paid to her.

After she died, the house stayed empty for many years as no one wanted to live in a black magic house. Years later, a barber whose shop was close to the witch's house hung the alarm clock as a joke. When the clock was removed several years later, all kinds of disturbing events started happening. From sounds in the night, weird visions, objects disappearing without explanation, to accidents inside local homes. Residents hung a new alarm clock and the ghostly phenomena promptly stopped. A few years later, it was removed while the house was being restored, and the supernatural events started up again. So, residents of the calle hung the current clock, and it remains there to this day.

Address: Calle Seconda della Toletta, Dorsoduro
Vaporetto Stop: Accademia
What's Nearby: Accademia, the Peggy Guggenheim Collection, the Zattere.

20. La Barca San Barnaba

This is surely the most photographed vegetable stand in the Veneto. Located just below the Ponte dei Pugni, the Barca San Barnaba is a floating vegetable shop. Seasonal, locally grown vegetables line up on this colorful boat –nothing here has ripened in a truck driving across country. Venetians order their veges from the fondamenta next to the boat. Their purchases are then bagged and passed up to them. Behind the boat, a regular storefront sells fruit and a handful of Italian products, all part of the same business. The Tiozzo family started this business in 1947 and still run it today.

If you're staying in an apartment in Venice, it's especially fun to swing by and pick up ingredients for a salad. In fact, I guarantee this will be the most memorable vegetable buying experience you'll have for a while!

Address: Dorsoduro (docked at the Fondamenta Gherardni)
Hours: 7am—7pm Monday to Friday, 7am—5pm Saturdays
Vaporetto Stop: Ca' Rezzonico
What's Nearby: Ponte dei Pugni, Ca' Rezzonico, Campo Santa Margherita.

21. The General's Medallion

Close to San Pantalon church, mounted on the wall of a small *campiello*, is a *remarkable* 900+ year old marble bas relief medallion of a Byzantine emperor.

In 1256, a venetian general named Giovanni Tiepolo was leaving for Acre to fight the Genoese. Local nobles made fun of his military skills, telling him he had to bring back proof of his victory. Tiepolo returned with this huge medallion, torn from the palace the Genoese had garrisoned. He mounted it on the house of one of his detractors, where it has remained ever since.

Dumbarton Oaks has an almost identical medallion in their Byzantine collection in Washington DC. Theirs was part of

Prince Federico Leopold of Prussia's collection, purchased in the mid-19th century in Venice! The prevailing thought is that these medallions are of father and son Alexius I Comnenus and John II Comnenus, co-emperors of Byzantium from 1092 to 1118. They were possibly part of the booty stolen from Constantinople in 1204. Regardless, one is in a museum in the US while the other is on a wall in the glorious outdoor museum that is Venice.

Address: Campiello de ca' Angaran, Dorsoduro
Vaporetto Stop: San Toma'
What's Nearby: Tonnolo pastry shop, Chiesa San Pantalon, Scuola San Rocco, the Frari.

22. The House of the Five Heads

This house is another oddity with a lost history. Midway between the Scalzi Bridge and the Frari is the Rio delle Muneghete. Cross the Ponte Canal Bridge and walk along the Fondamenta Sacchere to a row of red brick buildings (opposite). Just before the next bridge, you will see the House of the Five Heads.

Around the water gate are five intricate Istrian stone heads, four female and one male. Nobody knows exactly where they are from. They were probably keystones from an ancient building somewhere, and for some unknown reason, were used to adorn this house. The faces are quite beautiful and look like they could be members of the same family. Inside the courtyard, another face looks down over the garden (not so handsome) along with at least one more on the internal exterior of the house.

The original name for this house has been lost. It is now a gorgeous vacation rental with its own private garden, named Casa delle Cinque Teste (House of the Five Heads).

Address: View this one from the Fondamenta Sacchere
What's Nearby: The Frari, San Pantalon, Scuola Grande di San Rocco.

23. Banksy in Venice

Secretive British artist Banksy caused a ruckus at the 2019 Biennale in Venice when he set up an unauthorized stand in Piazza San Marco. His stall displayed a nine-panel painting of a colossal cruise ship passing through Venice, towering over the buildings and gondolas in the water below. Below it was a sign saying, "Venice in Oil".

He was addressing the controversy surrounding cruise ships in the lagoon and the subsequent problems Venice suffers from mass tourism. Banksy always verifies his renegade projects by posting them on his Instagram account. If you scroll through, you'll find a tremendous video of this event. A cat looks up at the paintings, then a series of local Venetians check it out before the police make him (or his stand-in) leave. The hilarious caption reads: "Setting out my stall at the Venice Biennale. Despite being the largest and most prestigious art event in the world, for some reason, I've never been invited." (You can also find the video on Google.)

During the night of 10 May 2019, a permanent Banksy mural appeared on a run-down wall near the university in Dorsoduro. The mural is of a small child wearing a life vest, stoically holding up a pink flare. Banksy painted it flush with the water, so she gets partially (if not fully) submerged during *acqua alta*. The water creeping up the child's legs makes it even more poignant. The plight of immigrants, their clandestine water crossings to get to a new life, and the ports closed to them are hot button topics close to Banksy's heart. In 2015, he painted a mural of Steve Jobs at the refugee camp in Calais France. He said at the time, "We're often led to believe migration is a drain on the country's resources, but Steve Jobs was the son of a Syrian migrant. Apple is the world's most profitable company. It pays over $7 billion a year in taxes, and it only exists because they allowed in a young man from Homs."

Address: See the mural from the bridge between Calle della Chiesa and Campo San Pantalon.
Vaporetto Stop: San Toma'
What's nearby: Al Bocon di Vino, Ca' Foscari, San Pantalon, the Frari.

24. The Last Tango in Venice

Are you a fan of the Argentine Tango? Pre-Covid, on Venetian summer nights you could take part in (or watch) the Argentine Tango under the stars. I didn't see it in 2021, but hopefully they are back now.

There were several places to watch an open air *milonga*. The Tuesday Night Tango in Campo San Giacomo dell'Orio in Santa Croce was fantastic to drop in on. If it's happening while you're in Venice, arrive early to get situated with an aperitivo. On Wednesday nights in the summer, check out above the stairs of the church of Santa Maria della Salute. Sunday tangos were also held on the roof terrace at Palazzo Ca' Zanardi in Cannaregio.

Hopefully tango in Venice isn't a thing of the past. Should you find a *milonga* while in Venice, please shoot me a message on social media or on my website www.CorinnaCooke.com

15.
The Blue Hour

If anything can rival Venice in its beauty, it must be its reflection at sunset in the Grand Canal.

–Peggy Guggenheim

Nothing in this world can match the beauty of the light in Venice, especially on balmy summer nights. It still overwhelms me after all these years. This alone is reason to stay a few nights in Venice.

The Blue Hour

As sunset ends, there is a spectacular light you need to be prepared for. This is the Blue Hour, and be warned, *it will take your breath away.* Locate yourself somewhere with a view of the Grand Canal, with a tripod or a spritz.

The Blue Hour happens shortly after sunset, and again in the morning, moments before sunrise. In technical terms, it's when the sun is between -4 degrees and -6 degrees below the horizon, just before sunrise and immediately after sunset. The sky turns a deep, intense blue, saturated with color. Not a single flat shade either – multiple shades of blue all melding into one another.

Nowhere in the world gets a Blue Hour quite like Venice. It's all about the amount of water surrounding and running through the floating city and the way the blue light bounces off the water. To make it even more intense, blue light turns pale buildings (like Santa Maria della Salute) the most radiant, ethereal white imaginable. White is the divine color, the color of God. When blue hour bathed the *mendicant* (plague) churches, the people of Venice must have felt like he was right there with them. Today we see the combination of blue light against white buildings more as man's work than God's work, majestically amplified by artificial lights in the windows and along the canal. It is so dramatic!

Few places in the world are as photogenic as Venice, but this is the time of day when you catch the city at its most magical. On your first night in Venice, I suggest getting yourself to a bar or a bridge with a view along the Grand Canal toward the Salute. You will want to experience it from a different spot every night you're here. I like to be in the middle of the Accademia bridge, looking toward Salute, or in any of the rooftop bars. You will find waterways all over Venice that become otherworldly in the Blue Hour light.

The Blue Hour only lasts about 30 minutes, twice a day.

The Golden Hour

The Golden Hour is, the last 30 minutes before sunset and after sunrise, and is the other best time of day for photography. It is easily the most beautiful light to be photographed in. While the harsh light of day can wash your skin out and make any fine lines and wrinkles stand out, the Golden Hour light is soft and beautiful. Your skin tone will look gorgeous as it takes on a soft golden hue, blurring imperfections. As a makeup artist, I consider Golden Hour the perfect time to get your most stunning photos. Put on your lipstick, fluff your hair, hold your tummy in and turn your face to the light. Or hold your profile to the light –that looks gorgeous too.

The Golden Hour is also a beautiful time to photograph buildings. In the mornings I stay around Castello (the easternmost point of the city), or along the Riva. From there you can see the sun rising over the lagoon. As you head along the Grand Canal towards Piazzale Roma, watch the palaces light up with the morning sun.

I can't imagine how audacious (and spectacular) Ca' d'Oro must have looked when the morning sun hit its golden walls, bouncing rays across the canal. If I'm on the Grand Canal as the evening golden hour starts, I face the other direction, watching the golden light beaming to the east. Piazza San Marco is *stunning* in the evening Golden Hour and the Blue Hour. The cruise passengers are back on their boats, the day trippers have left. The crowd has thinned, and you are left with breathtaking beauty.

In the **Coffee** chapter, I talk about Caffe Florian, one of the most irrepressibly glamorous (and expensive) places to sit outdoors with a glass of Prosecco. Because Florian comes with a sturdy price tag, you need to make an experience out of it. *This is the time to have a drink.* The musicians serenade you, and the piazza looks so beautiful you could be in a dream. I promise you will never forget how gorgeous it all looks as the Golden Hour morphs into the Blue Hour. This will become your dream-sequence memory of Venice.

You can enjoy the Golden and Blue Hours from all over the city. One time, crossing Ponte Lion on my way home at the end of Blue Hour, I met a Venetian fellow packing up his camera. He had been shooting Rio San Lorenzo in the blue light. I talked to him for a while, mostly picking up photography tips. He showed me some photos in his camera, telling me *he does this every night*! He goes somewhere different in the city, sets up his tripod, and captures the insane beauty of Venice's Blue Hour. The photos were beautiful, from all parts of the city.

I think it's a crime to come all the way to Venice and not experience the Blue Hour. Yet another reason to plan on staying in Venice for a few days.

16.
Gondolas

If a couple in a gondola kiss as they pass under each bridge, they will remain in love forever.

–Venetian Folklore

The gondola is the most recognizable symbol of Venice, and the gondoliers as iconic as the vehicles they propel through the waterways of this spectacular city. They represent a luxurious lifestyle from a glamorous era. To hear them sing, call out approaching a blind corner –or my favorite, to watch a gondolier's leg gently push away from an ancient palazzo like a dream sequence in water-bound ballet –is to truly experience Venice.

Every gondola is handcrafted in Venice. There's no fiberglass hull produced in a factory on some mainland, no parts made on the cheap in China. One of ten separate local artisans built the elegant black boat gliding past you, each working their specific part of a trade that dates back 1000 years.

Nowadays, other than the occasional wedding or funeral, gondolas are mainly used to entertain tourists, transporting them along predetermined routes through the canals and waterways. Before dismissing it as too touristy, know that without tourists, gondolas and gondoliers, and all the artisans working with them, would disappear into the pages of history. Therefore, this is a touristy pastime that I fully endorse and support.

The History of the Gondola

Gondolas were first documented in 1094AD. The flat-bottomed boats were perfect for navigating the lagoon, the shifting sandbars, and the narrow waterways. Oarsmen stood as they rowed, providing an essential visual advantage in these shallow waters. For centuries, *two* gondoliers, one standing at the front, his counterpart at the back, operated each gondola.

Traditionally, gondolas provided private transport for the wealthy. Every palazzo had a watergate, where gondolas could slip inside, allowing family to board and disembark from the internal dock, clear of any bad weather or prying eyes. A private cabin called a *felze* was centered on the gondola, keeping the traveler warm and dry and providing the perfect spot for Casanova-style trysts. You can still see gondolas with felzes in the Doge's Palace and Ca' Rezzonico, and at the *squeros* (the workshops where gondolas are constructed).

Initially, gondolas were painted in the family's colors, many of them bright and decorative. Then in 1562, Doge Girolamo Priuli ruled all gondolas must be painted black to make them look uniform. The only place your gondola could be decorated was inside the private cabin of the felze.

How a Gondola Works

Every gondola is an original piece of art.

The traditional shape originally required two oarsmen to keep the boat balanced and moving in a straight line, until Domenico Tramontin invented a boat that could be operated by a single gondolier. The broader, right side of the gondola pushes the boat to the left, while the narrower left side pushes it to the right. Gondolas have a flat bottom, the port side has a slightly higher wall and is 9 inches (23cm) wider than the starboard side where the gondolier stands. These elements, paired with the skill of the gondolier, make the gondola go straight, allowing it to be operated with just one oar.

A wiggly piece of wood extends from the right side of the gondola. This is the *forcola* (oarlock). It is traditionally made of walnut and has different notches to put the oar in. Each wooden forcola is custom made specifically for each gondolier, tailored to his height and weight. At the end of the day, the gondolier always takes his forcola home –he would never leave this crucial piece of equipment with the boat.

If you watch from a bridge (the best view) pay attention to where on the forcola the *rèmo* (oar) is placed. It might be low when the gondolier starts moving, in the top C-shaped notch for forward motion, in the next notch down when he reverses, and to stop the oar is braced against the body of the forcola. The gondolier expends the same amount of energy to transport himself and two passengers as we use to walk at the same speed. The design is genius. Compare that to trying to row a dinghy, which goes round in circles unless the two oars are in an exact equal rhythm and harmony.

Apart from two metal pieces, gondolas are made entirely from wood. The *fero* (also spelled *ferro* in Italian, meaning "iron") is the horsehead-like curving piece at the bow of the gondola. This serves as a counterweight to the gondolier who stands at the stern, and helps the flat-bottomed boat stay level in the water. It also helps keep the gondola free of dents and scrapes.

The fero has several interesting features: the top resembles the Doge's hat, and below the hat a curve symbolizes the Rialto Bridge. The hole in the middle is the San Marco basin. Then, six rectangles face forward, one for each sestiere: San Marco, San Polo, Santa Croce, Castello, Dorsoduro, Cannaregio. One rectangle points back toward the gondolier, representing Giudecca. The S-shaped swoop along the spine represents the Grand Canal. Once you know this, you can't miss noticing the fero on every gondola swishing past you.

At the stern, behind where the gondolier stands, you'll see another curled piece of metal called a *risso.* It represents a seahorse and is largely ornamental, but also stops dings at that end of the boat.

The Squero

The *squero* is the workshop where gondolas and other wooden boats are built, repaired, and maintained. There used to be more than 40, but only 5 remain today. In Dordosuro, there is **Tramontin** and **San Trovaso**; on Giudecca, there is **Roberto dei Rossi** and **Crea**; in Castello, there is **San Giuseppe**.

Traditionally they were near Fondamente Nove or the Zattere, because timber could easily be delivered to these locations on rafts. The houses on the squeros look like wooden huts from the mountains (*tabia'*). Many of the *squeroli* came from the Dolomites. Known for exceptional skill working with wood, they came to Venice to become boat makers. The houses they built look like the ones they'd left back home.

The work of a *squerolo* is kept secret. You might catch glimpses across the water, but you can't just walk in. My friend Luisella is a licensed local guide who does a special gondola-building tour and is one of the few people who can take you inside a squero. Her tour is fantastic. Her contact info is in my Venice Guides PDF (www.glamitaliabooks.com/Venice-Private-Guides).

The gondola with the felze inside the Doge's Palace was made at Tramontin, and it was Domenico Tramontin who invented the asymmetric shape of the single-gondolier gondola. The Tramontin squero opened in the 1800s and is now run by sisters Elena and Elisabetta Tramontin. Tramontin is the first and only female owned and run squero.

How a Gondola is Made

It takes six months to build a gondola from start to finish –two months to construct and four months to paint. Construction usually begins in winter. Gondolas are made from more than 280 separate wooden pieces, using eight different types of wood –elm for the frame, oak for the sides, mahogany on top, pine on the bottom, linden for the front and back, larch for the footrest, and cherry or walnut for decoration. The wood all comes from France. It is allowed to dry for 2—3 years before it can be used.

Each side of a gondola is made from a single piece of wood. They wet the wood, then use heat from a gas fire to bend it to the right shape. The stern of the gondola is custom made to fit the gondolier's weight (the heavier the gondolier, the steeper the angle). Legend says that when she marries, the wife of a gondolier knows his weight for life, as a gondola lasts at least 40 years. Gondolas are always exactly 11.1 meters long.

Painting of the gondola takes place in the spring and requires four months for the six coats of paint to dry. The entire gondola is painted black except for the bottom, which is red or green and uses a special product to protect it from algae. Every 50 days, the gondola will be brought to the squero to have algae removed from its bottom. Every

10—15 years, the bottom of the boat will need to be replaced. If he wants to keep working, after 40 years the gondolier will need an entirely new gondola built for him.

Ten additional artisans are needed for the creation of a gondola, all of whom belong to the El Felze Guild (association/union). They create the forcola, oar, fero, risso, wood carving, gold leaf detailing, all ornamentation, and the cushions and seats. Artisans from this guild are also required to make the gondolier uniforms –the *sartori* make the clothes, the *calegheri* make the shoes, and hats are made by the *bareteri.*

It's a costly business. A bare-bones gondola with no decoration starts around €40,000. Each gondolier buys and owns his own gondola.

The Uniform

It must be the most recognizable uniform in the world. (Outside of law enforcement and the military.) When gondolas became black, the gondolier uniform did too and stayed black until the end of WWII. Then it changed to black pants, special black shoes, a red or blue striped shirt, an optional straw hat with a ribbon, and a black or white uniform jacket.

The shirts may have been linked to the French Navy's uniform as a safety measure, making it easier to spot anyone who fell overboard. Who knows for sure?

Gondolier shirts are embroidered with the logo for the Gondolier's Association. You can purchase authentic gondolier shirts and other accessories at **Emilio Ceccato** at the foot of the Rialto Bridge (Campo San Polo 16/17). This is the only place to buy an authentic shirt. All others sold on the streets of Venice are fakes. When you buy an authentic Venetian gondolier's shirt, the Association puts those royalties back into projects to safeguard gondoliers and support the artisan trades of the gondola industry.

Even when not working, or with friends or family, the gondolier must always be in uniform when using his gondola.

The Gondoliers

It is one of the oldest trades in Venice, dating back 1100 years. Most gondoliers come from families with generations of member in the business. They learn to row at an early age.

Gondolier licenses are limited, and securing one is extremely difficult. Applicants must pass rowing and swimming tests before attending the Arte del Gondolier school for 12—18 months. In addition to gondoliering skills, there they also learn languages, local history and geography. The final exams are incredibly difficult. After passing the exams, the next step is to register with the Chamber of Commerce and become a substitute gondolier. They spend at least a year working on one of the five *traghetti* transporting people from side to side of the canal. If you take a traghetto, tip well –they have a career of huge expenses ahead of them.

The gondolier license is affixed to a specific gondola station. Gondoliers can't just go freewheeling around town like Uber drivers. Everything is carefully regulated, and these licenses are like gold. In the 16th century, there were 10,000 gondoliers, now there are 433. You can only become a licensed gondolier if someone else quits, so passing your exams doesn't automatically mean you've got a job. If no one retires that year, no new gondoliers get hired. If your father retires and you are licensed and have completed your year as a substitute, only then can he pass his license down to you.

Voga alla Veneta is the Venetian style of rowing, standing up and facing forward. Gondoliers compete in regattas during the year, and on 25 April take part in the Regata dei Gondolieri on the Grand Canal. There is also the Regata Storica and the Festa del Redentore.

The world of the gondolier is closed to almost all. And almost all gondolieri know each other.

Riding in a Gondola

Although it seems touristy and is definitely expensive, I still recommend taking a gondola ride while you're in Venice. It costs €80 for 30 minutes (or €120 for 30 minutes at sunset and into the evening), so you want to optimize your experience, and to help you do this, I have two pieces of advice:

1. Get off the beaten path

The cruise ship crowd tend to use the gondola stations immediately around Piazza San Marco and the other heavily trafficked areas. There the wait will be longer, and the gondoliers are exposed to the worst travelers all day long. (That doesn't mean *you* are the worst if you're on a cruise or a big bus tour, but it means you will probably get grouped in with those travelers by association.) These are the tourists who are just checking things off their list, could care less about the city, the history, and the cuisine. If you watch them, you'll see plenty treating the city with no respect, being rude to the locals and basically being the kind of tourist you don't want to be associated with. The gondolieri in these areas know they'll be giving nonstop tourist rides all day, regardless of the quality of their service, so they don't need to be chatty or especially friendly. Of course, I realize this is a massive generalization about both the gondolieri and mass-tourists, but in order to building *you* a dynamic experience I want you to take a slightly different approach.

The Bridge of Sighs and the Grand Canal

Don't get stuck on the idea of riding a gondola under the Bridge of Sighs, thinking it will be all romance and beauty. That is the bridge from the courthouse to the prison, and the "sigh" part is from the prisoner getting his last look at the outside world. It's not romantic. If you do attempt this, expect to get caught in a gondola-style traffic jam, with all the other gondolas who are also waiting to pass under the Bridge of Sighs. It will quickly chew up your €2,66 per minute.

Don't plan on taking a gondola ride along the Grand Canal either. This is the busiest street in town, full of vaporetti, water taxis, emergency boats (ambulances, fire boats and police), and delivery barges –the water is almost never (if ever) smooth. It's like riding a bicycle on a busy freeway. You'll have a much better ride if you go somewhere more chill.

Go to a smaller gondola station, away from the masses and, in my experience, the whole game changes. The frenetic stress that happens in long lines at Disneyland, heavy metal mosh pits and in heavily touristed areas of Venice, at once gets replaced with a chill, easygoing vibe. Here the gondolieri are chattier and smile more, and everyone –you included –feels more relaxed and therefore more open to experiencing the absolute enchantment of Venice as can only be seen from her waterways.

The further away you are from the major tourist attractions, the fewer gondolas you will be vying for waterway space with. It's like taking a leisurely drive in the countryside versus driving in rush hour traffic on the busiest street in town. Completely different experiences!

When it's done this way, the gondolieri are more likely to want to chat with you, to point out their favorite eateries as you glide across the water and tell you stories about the palazzi you're floating past. My tour travelers come back from their gondola experiences completely exhilarated, full of stories about the gondolier, his life, his family stories, his dinner recommendations, and thrilled by the pure magic of Venice.

Stroll the calli of Castello, Cannaregio and Dorsoduro and you will easily find ideal small gondola stations dotted around the neighborhoods.

2. Make it an event

My next piece of advice is to make your gondola ride into an event. Put money aside for it. Don't jam in as many people as you can to cheapen the experience. You'll see loads of gondolas full of people and I always think it's a real waste. Yes, they paid only €15 each and are gaming the system, but to what end? The two people in the principal seat can only see their friend's hairy legs, and they're missing out on the glory of the experience. The people sitting on the sides aren't getting the full view or the full magic either. So, on my tours I put only two people in a gondola. I know it sounds extravagant, but my travelers settle back into the velvet cushions and do it right. They enjoy the expansive view the gondola was designed for, and they enjoy the sound of the oar swishing through the water. (You'll never forget that sound.)

I usually use the small station at Campo Santa Maria Formosa, which works out well because I love this area and I can show my travelers lots of cool things before and after their ride. Rather than farming everyone out like the production line at a factory, here I can rotate them through two at a time, keeping the land-bound travelers entertained while the others are off flirting with their gondolier. I find the gondolieri at these smaller stations to often be chatty and fun. They interact with their customers, rather than being on their phones or talking only to each other. My clients come back thrilled with the experience. They've seen loads of new things and the gondolier has told them stories and explained what they're seeing. Everyone is happy.

You see gondolieri all over Venice, offering rides. Look for one with a smiley face and who makes eye contact. If he seems friendly, chat with him. Ask him where the ride goes and how long it takes. If you think this is the gondolier you want to hire, ask him his name and use it. I'll usually do whatever I was on my way to do, and then come back and say, "Hey Marco! I'm back for my ride. Do you have time to take me?" He recognizes that, A) I remembered his name, B) I specifically sought him out, and C) I am one of the good customers! It sets you up for a fun, chatty gondola ride.

Museo Storico Navale

At the Arsenale there's a somewhat secret museum called the Museo Storico Navale. It's secret in that few people come here. It has five floors of fascinating Venetian maritime history, but the third floor has a room devoted to gondolas. This exhibit includes Peggy Guggenheim's over-the-top gondola. Peggy was one of the last people to cruise around in a private gondola. Stories abound about her cruising the Grand Canal wearing crazy oversized sunglasses, with her little dogs along for the ride. There are photos to accompany the exhibit and also a full-sized gondola with a felze.

Address: It's a short walk along the Riva from the Doge's Palace.
Hours: The museum is only open in the mornings.
Vaporetto Stop: Arsenale.

Visit a Forcola Workshop

Forcole and *remi* (oars) are made by specialty artisans called *remèri.* There are only four remèri in Venice, each with workshops that you can visit. Here, you can watch a master at work and experience an ancient Venetian tradition, replete with the smell of freshly cut wood. Any souvenir or gift purchased from remèri is you supporting local artisans and keeping their cultural heritage alive.

Paolo Brandolisio

Paolo Brandolisio's workshop in Castello sells unique, handcrafted wooden jewelry (bangles and rings) as well as miniature handcrafted forcole. All of them would be fabulous souvenirs and gifts. He also makes souvenir miniature walnut forcole measuring about 20cm (7 inches). Or you can buy full-sized forcole to ship home as sculptures. This workshop is considered a hidden jewel in Venice.

Address: Calle Corte Rota 4725, Castello
Vaporetto Stop: Midway between Arsenale and Celestia
What's Nearby: Arsenale, San Zaccaria, Libraria Aqua Alta.

Le Forcole

Le Forcole is Salverio Pastor's workshop in Dorsoduro, near Santa Maria della Salute. Salverio also sells full-sized sculptures and scaled down replicas of forcole.

Address: Fondamenta Soranzo detta la Fornasa 341, Dorsoduro
Vaporetto Stop: Midway between Accademia and Zattere
What's Nearby: The Accademia, the Peggy Guggenheim, Santa Maria dell Salute.

Remi e Forcole

Franco Furlanetto's workshop Remi e Forcole is in the heart of San Polo. He has a fantastic shop with all kinds of handcrafted wooden items to bring home with you. You can buy small-scaled gondola to keep on a shelf or a forcola built to scale, and walnut keychains and bookmarks in the shape of forcole and *dolfini*. You'll find cool, unusual items here. You can also watch Franco at work crafting oars and oarlocks.

Address: San Polo 2768B
Website: www.ffurlanetto.com
Vaporetto Stop: Rialto Mercato or San Silvestro
What's Nearby: Rialto Bridge, Rialto Market, Caffe del Doge, Ponte delle Tette.

Il Forcolaio Matto (The Mad Forcolier)

The last remèro is Piero Dri at Il Forcolaio Matto (The Mad Forcolier) in Cannaregio. As with the other three, here you can watch him working on oars and forcole. Piero also makes smaller works of art that ship all over the world and pieces you can take home as souvenirs. He is also super personable, and his workshop is wonderful.

Address: Calle dell' Oca, 4231, Cannaregio
Vaporetto Stop: Ca' d'Oro
What's Nearby: Ca' d'Oro, Chioda Bridge, Vino Vero.

17.
Shopping in Venice

Venice is like eating an entire box of chocolate liqueurs in one go.

–Truman Capote

Every euro you spend in Venice has an impact. Either a positive impact by sending money into the local economy, or a negative impact by sending money offshore. Your choice to buy artisan gelato supports the local farmers growing the ingredients you're eating. Industrial gelato supports the chemical endeavors of factories far from Venice. Both cones of gelato cost the same.

It's the same with shopping. Choosing to buy goods crafted by Venetians (or from boutiques owned and run by Venetians) is a choice to support the local economy *and* local culture. Shopping at international high street chains, or at junk souvenir stands and shops, instead sends your money offshore to support international conglomerates and sweatshops.

One of the most devastating consequences of mass tourism has been replacing local businesses and craftspeople with mass market chains. Every year mass tourisms forces Venetians to move to the mainland. They can't compete with mass market conglomerates or the havoc they wreak on local communities.

Italy has a history of artisan excellence, dating back *millennia.* The country is known for its exemplary handcrafted goods, made using techniques passed down through the centuries. Venice has enormous artisan shopping options for clothing, jewelry, shoes, foods, glass, and much more. The choice to spend your money with these local merchants is essential to keep the craft alive and to stop Venice from becoming a giant

Walmart. You will get more pleasure from a locally made souvenir than from a $10 piece of junk made thousands of miles away.

In this chapter, I'll teach you on how to identify if something is authentic and artisanal, and then I'll suggest some really cool places to shop. Several of these places are part of the *experiential travel movement,* offering workshops for travelers to learn about their craft and history.

How to Know if Something is Artisanal

How do you know which shops are authentic and which are replicas? The following tips are things to watch out for.

Made in Italy

A *Made in Italy* label doesn't necessarily mean it was *made* in Italy. Any item with partial production on Italian soil can have a *Made in Italy* label. It can be as minor as gluing a feather on a mask. Look beyond the *Made in Italy* label for signs the item may not be legit.

Signs in the Window

We've established that if it's on a souvenir stand in Venice, there is zero chance it is authentic. Souvenir kiosks target the cruise ship/mass tourism crowds. You'll see identical outlets selling similar junk all over Venice (as you would in any cruise port city).

Before entering a shop, look for signs in the window. When you see signs for €1, or 50% discount, or even large SALE signs, assume it isn't an artisan store. Craftspeople seldom discount their goods to bargain basement prices. Unless it's sale season and all the shops have sale signs, you can be relatively certain you're in a tourist trap.

What Can You See?

Look in the window. Does it look like a dollar store inside? Is the shop full of merchandise? Are the shelves cluttered and over filled? Is the lighting bright and cheap? Are there multiples of the same items?

Artisans and legitimate Italian businesses normally take time and care when displaying products, both in the window and within the store. You seldom see ugly, harsh lighting. The entire aesthetic is pleasing to the eye and relevant to that type of establishment. Many artisans also have a workshop on the premises. Sometimes you can watch them working –then you know it's the real deal.

Some artisans have more than one shop or have a separate workshop. Francesca Cecamore of **Karta Ruga** is the head of the mask makers' association. Karta Ruga moved their main laboratory to the mainland after massive damage from the 2019 flood, followed by economic damage from the Covid pandemic. However, Francesca does still have part of the workshop on the premises.

Are multiple mediums vying for attention? A tourist trap typically has lots of different types of (cheap) items on offer, whereas an artisan store normally only sells their specialty. Be wary of a shop selling masks and beads and glass and paper products, all crammed in together. If it looks like a souvenir shop, it probably is. Keep walking.

How Unique are the Products?

This is another giveaway. Handcrafted products are seldom identical. If you see ten identical masks and no sign of a workshop, they're probably made in a factory. A craftsperson might make a handful of the same item, but you'll see tiny differences in each one. Factory-made products are made in large runs and are all identical. For example, mask makers create multiple masks from a single cast, where the mask is painted white, then decorated by hand. But even if it's the same face, the masks aren't identical.

Recently a friend wanted a mask from Karta Ruga. After choosing the style, she went back and forth amongst the three masks made of that face. They appeared the same, but looking closely at each hand painted mask, you could spot little differences. It was brilliant! And a very treasured purchase.

Who is Working in the Store?

Does the salesperson know an enormous amount about the merchandise, its production and its history? If not, this is a dead giveaway it's a tourist souvenir shop. Salespeople in real Venetian shops are exquisitely informed about everything associated with that artisan and the intricacies of their work. They happily tell you all about it too. My antennae go up if the salesperson isn't a fountain of knowledge. Artisans are married to their craft and they don't hire cheap labor to run their front of house. Instead, they hire people who share their sense of wonder. As long as the salesperson isn't busy juggling customers, watching for thieves and people potentially breaking items, you can expect them to tell you all about the artisan, their work and much more.

If they sense you are truly interested (not just looking for directions to the nearest toilet), they'll tell you stories about the craft and the production. Expect to come away with a deeper understanding of your purchase.

When we were shopping at Karta Ruga, Francesca told us a story about a collection of styled animal heads her father had crafted. They were whimsical and delightful, and the story behind them was so beautiful, we had to buy one. Now, every time my friend talks about her mask, she repeats the story of Francesca's father, the concept behind this collection, the process of making these masks –all of it. Every telling is joyful for the teller and the audience. And that's what it's all about –a purchase forever connected to the wonderful time you spent in Venice.

Chocolate

VizioVirtù

Chocolate lovers need to know about this place. If you want a decadent souvenir or a gift for someone you *really* love, you need to come here. VizioVirtù is an artisan chocolate atelier and store, owned, run and staffed by women. They only use the very best ingredients, including DOP Bronte pistachios from Sicily and PGI Hazelnuts from Piedmont. Frankly, this place is not to be missed.

I was introduced to VizioVirtù by my foodie tour guide Monica (who is in my Venice Private Guides pdf, www.glamitaliabooks.com/Venice-Private-Guides), and who has encyclopedic knowledge of everything to do with Venetian cuisine.

VizioVirtù offers multiple workshops from chocolate making to ice-cream making and more, as well as guided chocolate tasting events. (*Swoon!*) Check out their website and book your space.

Address: Calle del Forner 5988
Website: www.viziovirtu.com
Vaporetto Stop: Rialto, Rialto Bridge
What's Nearby: Rialto Bridge, Marco Polo's house, Santa Maria dei Miracoli.

Paper Goods

Until the mid-15th century, books were handmade. They were expensive, coveted and a symbol of extreme wealth. (For context, wealthy Cosimo de' Medici owned three books growing up.)

In the 1450s, Johann Gutenburg invented moveable type, which along with advances in printing, changed everything. Now books could be produced quickly, and distributed around the world. Venice was the gateway connecting the west to the east. It was an intellectual hub and a center for artisans, making it the perfect place to set up large-scale book making and the creation of paper products.

Book binding workshops popped up all over the city. Venetians were already highly skilled at working with gold leaf, leather and color pigments. By the late 15th century, there were more than 400 printing presses in Venice.

Before the printing press, most people were illiterate. Why and how could you learn to read if you had no access to reading materials? The printing press changed that. One machine could print hundreds, even thousands of books, pamphlets, and documents. Production was cheap so books became accessible to the masses. Learning to read exposed Venetians to new ideas, new ways of thinking, new opinions. If they could read, ordinary folk suddenly had access to information, creating the desire and the need for mass literacy.

Because they kept the pope at arm's length, Venice was the perfect place for independent thinkers, philosophers and people who thought, lived and acted outside the confines of the Catholicism. One interesting character was Aldus Manutius, founder of the Aldine Press. Manutius printed texts by Aristotle and Plato in Greek and

Latin, developing a typeface that became known as *italic.* He invented the shape and curve of letters we still read every day and think of as regular, standard type face. He also invented small, portable books called *libelli portatile*, that in time would eventually become modern paperbacks. Reading, as we know it, was invented in Venice.

When they realized leather bindings were discoloring and damaging the paper, book binders replaced the inside cover with hand colored paper. Soon leather was only used for the spine, and book covers were made from pretty, marbled paper.

By the mid-1700s, Venetian bookbinders were incorporating *carta marmorizzata*, or marbleized paper into their book making. They put colored oil pigments into a shallow tray of water, swirling them into patterns, using styluses, single hairs (animal I assume), tiny combs and thin brushes. A clean sheet of paper was briefly laid onto this pattern, then hung to dry. Some of the most recognizable patterns include peacock feathers, snails and *marmo pettinato*, which is a raked or combed marble looking effect. It is all quite fantastic.

An American textile designer friend of mine studied the craft in Florence. (I talk more about this in *Glam Italia! 101 Fabulous Things to Do in Florence.*) She makes beautiful fabrics using these techniques. A few years ago, I spotted a shop in Castello with a window full of marble papers, books and other paper goods. I only noticed because my friend had been posting pictures from her paper marbling classes in Florence. So I went inside and told the owner about my friend. Artisans can tell when you're genuinely interested in what they do. Rather than kicking me out and locking the door, she told me stories about the history of paper in Venice, showed me designs, and explained how it works. It was fascinating! Even more fun, I connected her to my artist friend, and they have become great buddies. So that's the first shop on my list.

ARZANART

Come here for marbled paper, cards, notebooks, albums and jewelry. This is a wonderful shop to purchase unique gifts and souvenirs. They sell paper in individual sheets, rolling it into travel-friendly cardboard tubes.

Azanart offers two-hour workshops for anyone 12 years and over. You can learn the craft and make your own papers to bring home too.

Address: Barbaria de le Tole, Calle del Cafetier 6479A, Castello
Vaporetto Stop: Celestia and San Zaccaria
What's Nearby: Libreria Aqua Alta, Campo SS Giovanni e Paolo, Palazzo Grimani.

GIANNI BASSO STAMPATORE

Gianni Basso uses traditional hand operated printing machines to make gift cards, business cards, personalized stationery and prints. This father and son business is part shop, part museum, and feels like you stepped back in time a century. It's fantastic!

In the **Lido** chapter, we discover the printing workshop of the Armenian monks on the island of San Lazzaro degli Armeni. When he was little, Gianni's grandfather brought him to watch the monks creating and printing books. The experience affected him so much, he later served an apprenticeship there. When the monks upgraded to modern printing systems, Gianni took the old manual presses, opened his own stamperia and still uses them to this day.

When you buy something from Gianni Basso Stampatore you are buying 500 years of history (the age of his printing press). Gianni has a celebrity clientele, including royalty, actors, writers, Nobel Laureates, fashion designers, and composers. Every shelf holds samples of beautiful paper goods and personalized stationery made for celebs including Ben Affleck, Hugh Grant and Marisa Tomei. Gianni only uses Fabriano paper, a 100% cotton paper that is chlorine-free and acid-free.

Address: Calle del Fumo 5306, Cannaregio
Vaporetto Stop: Fondamente Nove
What's Nearby: Campo SS Giovanni e Paolo, Libreria Aqua Alta, Chiesa Santa Maria Assunta dei Gesuiti.

ALBERTO VALESE EBRU

Alberto Valese Ebru is a darling little stationery shop selling gorgeous handmade wrapping paper, cards, notebooks and accessories in colorful Venetian designs. This is the work of a world-renowned master artisan, using a craft that dates back millenia.

During the Middle Ages, Turkish masters elevated paper marbling to a level of unparalleled excellence. The called it *ebru*, which in the extinct Turkish language of Chagatai meant "cloud". In the mid-18th century, several prominent Venetian bookbinders were using this beautiful ebru style of decorative paper. By the 20th century, ebru had almost disappeared. In the 1970s, Alberto Valese studied ebru in Turkey with a master artisan, then reintroduced it to the world. He is one of the world's preeminent and most sought-after masters of the craft.

Most paper shops you see around Venice sell machine-printed papers and note cards, and factory-bound books made God only knows where. At Alberto Valese, he makes everything by hand. And it is beautiful.

Address: Campo Santo Stefano 3471 (Workshop Salizada San Samuele 3351)
Vaporetto Stop: San Samuele or Sant' Angelo
What's Nearby: Accademia Bridge, Piazza San Marco, Palazzo Grassi.

Plum Plum Creations

Arianna Sauteriello is a very talented, young Venetian artist. She creates pieces you can imagine hanging in your home, along with cool postcards and bookmarks that you'll keep forever. Her work is beautiful, fresh and modern, and her unique combination of an old artform with a current day aesthetic is really exciting and unique.

Arianna uses a very old art form called etching. She etches modern, cool sketches of Venetian landmarks into a copper plate. The drawing is pressed onto special paper, and when the ink is dry, she hand-paints the colors. (I'm leaving out multiple steps.)

You can visit her workshop and watch the entire process. She also offers classes in etching and in linocuts, and she speaks excellent English. Her prints, postcards and greeting cards are not expensive, and make perfect gifts.

Her workshop is on Fondamenta Ormesini in Cannaregio, close to the Jewish Ghetto.

Address: Fondamenta dei Ormesini 2681, Cannaregio
Website: www.PlumPlumCreations.com

Hours: 11am—2pm, 5pm—8pm Monday to Saturday
Vaporetto Stop: Madonna dell' Orto, Guglie, or if coming from the Grand Canal, S. Marcuola
What's Nearby: The Jewish Ghetto, Torrefazione Cannaregio, Al Timon.

Furlane Slippers

Furlane (also *friulane*) are chic handmade shoes. Known as the quintessential Venetian slipper, or gondolier slipper, you'll see them in Vogue magazine and on the streets of the most glamorous cities in the world. Furlane are the hallmark of lowkey yet super fashionable Italian style. They make gorgeous souvenirs and gifts for women, men and children.

The History of Furlane

This iconic footwear dates back to the end of World War Two, when impoverished women in the Fruili region of Italy began making shoes from old bicycle tires and scraps of fabric. These slipper shoes were hugely popular with gondoliers, as the non-slip rubber sole gave them a firm grip without damaging the gleaming black varnish on their gondolas.

The original name *scarpez*, became *fruilana* (named for the region). In Venetian dialect this translated to *forlana* (plural = *furlane, fur-lah-neh*)

By the 1960s, furlane were wildly popular. They looked stylish but were super comfortable. Not only worn by gondolieri, they also graced the feet of the city's nobles and the chic, in-the-know crowd. The shoe became a cult favorite and an iconic symbol of La Serenissima.

The fabrics included luxe velvets, tapestry and heavy embroidery, and later, canvas and leather. Before long, there were over a thousand different fabric and color options. Furlane are still made by hand using the traditional blanket stitch.

Where To Buy Furlane

PIEDATERRE

This tiny shop in San Polo has a huge international following. Their furlane are tagged in images all over social media.

Address: San Polo 60 (1 minute from the Rialto Bridge)
Vaporetto Stop: Rialto Mercato or Rialto (cross the bridge)
What's Nearby: Rialto Bridge, Rialto Market, Caffe del Doge.

PARUTTO CALZATURE

Near Piedaterre, Parutto sells frulane at a substantially lower price point. They offer fewer styles and fabrics, but the shoes are wonderful.

Address: San Polo 390/391
Vaporetto Stop: Rialto Mercato
What's Nearby: Rialto Market.

TEOD' AMAR (SOLD AT NORMA'S)

Teod' Amar make incredible sheets, towels, bags, accessories and frulane, all made in Italy by artisan tailors. Their furlane are exquisite and come in an extensive selection of the most glorious fabrics, including embroidered fabrics that are *to die for*. Their slippers are definitely more expensive, but if you are looking for something really unique, you need to check this one out.

Teod' Amar is sold at Norma's, just off Campo Santo Stefano. Norma's is an outstanding shop, well off the tourist radar, full of truly sensational merchandise.

Address: Norma's, Calle de le Botteghe 2995—2996, San Marco
Vaporetto Stop: Either Sant' Angelo or San Samuele
What's Nearby: Campo Santo Stefano, the Accademia Bridge.

ViBi Venezia

This store is owned by two stylish sisters who are European *IT* girls *and* Italian royalty, Viola and Vera Arrivabene Valenti Gonzaga.**

When they were little, the girls' mother, Princess Bianca di Savoia Aosta, dressed them in furlane. They grew up running around Palazzo Papadopolis in these iconic slippers. With a love for furlane, paired with Made-in-Italy pride, the girls launched their business, ViBi Venezia, in 2014. Their uber chic brand sells in the most prestigious boutiques around the world.

The @VibiVenezia Instagram page shows you the girls' glamourous life, and endless ways to wear this shoe. You'll see other European IT girls, models, movie directors, designers and celebrities living their best lives in their ViBi Venezia furlane. You'll be inspired to pick up a pair of your own.

Address: Al Duca d'Aosta, San Marco 284 (in Piazza San Marco)
Vaporetto Stop: San Marco
What's Nearby: The Basilica San Marco, the Doge's Palace, Caffe Florian.

** The Arrivabene Valenti Gonzaga family still live on the top floor of the 16th century Palazzo Papadopolis. They leased the bottom floors to the luxurious Aman Venice hotel. In 1718, it was owned by Giambattista Tiepolo, the greatest decorative painter of the 18th century. Tiepolo frescoed the ceilings and built an incredible library, acquiring many treasures still present in the palace. In the 19th century, the Papadopoli family of Corfu bought the palace. One son married Venetian noble Maddelena Aldobrandolini. When Vera Papadopoli Aldobrandolini married Count Giberto Arrivabene, this beautiful palace was part of her dowry. Her grandson is Count Giberto Arrivabene Valenti Gonzaga, current owner of the palace, husband to Princess Bianca di Savoia Aosta, father to Viola and Vera, the owners of ViBi Venezia. To get an idea of the size and grandeur of the palazzo, when Count Giberto's father was young, 86 people lived in the palace, 6 family members and 80 staff. The Aman Hotel comprises 24 rooms and suites, and hosted George Clooney's wedding in 2014.

Bespoke Venetian Shoes

ATELIER SEGALIN DI DANIELA GHEZZO

Daniela Ghezzo makes one of a kind, custom shoes and boots for men and women. Almost everything is made to measure and stitched to order, which, of course, makes Daniela's shoes highly sought after by the bespoke shoe crowd. Master cobbler Antonio Segalin and his son Ronaldo opened this atelier in 1932. Daniela was Ronaldo's star apprentice and is now a master Venetian shoemaker.

Segalin was famous for outlandish styles, like their gondola-shaped shoe, but the backbone of Daniela's business is classically elegant, beautiful footwear designed to be worn with maximum comfort for many years to come. If you want an impeccable pair of shoes, with precision devoted to every millimeter, created just for you, you must visit Daniela. Even if just window shopping, make sure you check this one out.

A pair of bespoke shoes takes about a month to make (Daniela ships all over the world to her elite clientele) and costs between €650 and €1,800.

Address: Calle Fuseri 4365
Website: www.danielaghezzo.it
Vaporetto Stop: Midway between Rialto and San Marco
What's Nearby: La Scala Contarini del Bevolo, Piazza San Marco.

Woodcrafts

SIGNOR BLUM

Signor Blum is a female owned and run artisan shop and workshop, specializing in handcrafted wooden objects. Signor Blum uses poplar wood and nontoxic paints, so are environmentally friendly too. From jigsaw puzzles to decorative objects, panels with cool scenes of Venice, to magnets, this is a great place to find something unique and beautiful.

I adore this shop for children's gifts (including babies/toddlers) and for cool souvenirs and gifts for adults. They sell many cool items that are not expensive, including handmade wooden kitchen magnets for €6.

Address: Campo San Barnaba 2840, Dorsoduro
Website: www.signorblum.it
Vaporetto Stop: Ca' Rezzonico
What's Nearby: Ca' Rezzonico, Ponte dei Pugni, Barca San Barnaba, the Zattere.

Gondola Goods

What better souvenir of Venice than something connected to gondolas and gondoliers? See the **Gondolas** chapter for my list of where to buy authentic gondola goods.

Beads

THE IMPIRARESSA, MARISA CONVENTO

My landlady in Castello told me stories about the Impiraressa. For centuries, these women sat outside their homes in Castello, scooping glass beads the size of seeds onto multi-pronged fork-like things with thin threads attached. It was backbreaking, eyesight-destroying, tedious work that paid very little. A morning's work earned enough for a loaf of bread.

The *impiraressa* (threader) sat outside her home, with a curved bottomed wooden tray filled with a single color of miniature glass beads balanced across her legs. Her tool had between 12 and 40 fan shaped prongs (which seems a lot to me), which she scooped into the beads over and over, threading them onto long skeins of thread. These skeins of beautiful miniature glass beads were trading currency in some parts of the world, known as trade beads. By the mid-1800s, a half kilo of trade beads was worth around $500 ($10,000 in today's money). Clothiers and artisans wove beads into their clothing, adorning everything from gloves to hats and coats. They also used beads for embroidery, loom weaving and a variety of other crafts.

Marisa Convento is one of the most highly esteemed artisans in Venice and she creates little works of art from her massive collection of 19th century beads. Her necklaces, bracelets, earrings and glass coral branches make wonderful gifts and souvenirs. Venetian artisans consider them collectors' items. Marisa is frequently featured in major international publications including *Conde Nast Traveler*, *GQ*, and *Vanity Fair*. She is also on *Dream of Italy's* Venice episode. To quote Marisa from this episode (find it on YouTube, streaming services and the *Dream of Italy* website), "when you wear a Venetian glass bead you wear 1000 years of history."

Marisa sells her creations from her **Venetians Dreams** shop inside a collective called **Bottega Cini**. She also offers workshops where you can learn about the craft and the history of bead making in Venice.

Bottega Cini is a concept store created by three entities, all working to preserve Venetian history and craftsmanship: **The Merchant of Venice**, **The Vittorio Cini Archive Foundation** and the **Museyoum**.

Address: Marisa Convento/Venetian Dreams, Bottega Cini, Dorsoduro 862
Website: www.marisaconvento.it
Vaporetto Stop: Accademia
What's Nearby: Bar Foscarini, the Accademia, the Peggy Guggenheim.

Alessia Fuga

Alessia creates glass sculptures and sensational glass jewelry in her Murano workshop. She is ranked in the Top 40 International Beadmakers. Her designs are fresh and modern, while embracing the history of Murano.

You need to see this shop. Check out her website to see her cool pieces, and to see workshops offered for travelers of all ages.

Address: Rio Tera San Salvador 12
Website: www.alessiafuga.com
Vaporetto Stop: Murano Faro (the 4.1/4.2 vaporetto)
What's Nearby: Basilica dei Santi Maria e Donato, the Glass Museum (Museo del Vetro).

Marionettes

L'Isola di Pinocchio (Pinocchio's Island)

My cicchetti guide Monica introduced me to this treasure. It is a fabulous place to find something truly unique to bring home. Roberto Comin's puppeteer workshop is a delightful fantasy-land full of marionettes, tools, sculptures and books, hidden in an old palazzo. Each marionette and costume is a work of art.

Roberto began making wooden puppets and marionettes as a teenager. He still makes each marionette by hand, in the traditional way. The head and feet are crafted from a wood paste/wood pulp mixture. The bodies are made from wood. Each puppet is painted by hand. The exquisite costumes worn by the marionettes are handmade by Roberto's sister Manuella. She is a professional tailor and costume designer. Roberto has an extensive catalogue of characters. He also sometimes creates custom pieces. (The *Pirates of the Caribbean* crew commissioned a Captain Jack Sparrow puppet one year for Johnny Depp's birthday.) Check out his website below to see his puppets and to identify his building in Campo S. Fosca.

L'Isola di Pinocchio is pure magic. When you ring the doorbell,

Roberto will greet you on the mezzanine floor of the palazzo, looking like a modern day Geppetto with his leather apron, curly hair and glasses worn low on his nose.

Address: Cannaregio 2417 (Campo S. Fosca)
Website: www.MarionettesInVenice.com
Vaporetto Stop: S. Marcuolo or Ca' d'Oro
What's Nearby: Ponte Chiodo, the Jewish Ghetto, Vino Vero.

Yarn

LELLABELLA

This is a rare jewel of a store that sells really gorgeous yarns –the finest, most high quality Italian yarns. Beautiful skeins and balls of colors ranging from dreamy to high fashion. They've been described as the most beautiful wools and silks in the world. And they're made in Italy.

The store is owned by a mother and daughter team (Lella and Monica) who not only run the store but also teach classes, both in person and over Skype. Here you can buy yarn and learn how to make it into something spectacular when you get home. They also make unique garments and ship both yarn and/or knitted pieces all over the world.

Lellabella is right in the middle of everywhere you're going to be in San Marco, roughly midway between Piazza San Marco and Rialto Bridge.

Address: Calle della Mandola 3718, San Marco
Vaporetto Stop: Rialto
What's Nearby: Scala Contarini del Bevolo, Teatro La Fenice, Campo Santo Stefano.

Hats

Giuliana Longo

This tiny shop is an absolute gem. Giuliana has been making beautiful hats in a multitude of fabrics, for decades. Big hats, small hats, waterproof hats, woolen hats, straw hats, fabric hats. Hats to shade you from the sun, hats to protect you from the rain. Hats to make you feel glamorous, hats to be functional. Berets, wedding hats, gondoliers' hats. Whatever your hat desires are, she's got it all here.

Most of the hats are handcrafted. Some of the hats are imported. Her Panama hats from Ecuador are without equal.

Giuliana is also the exclusive maker of authentic gondolier hats. She is the vice president of the El Felze association, the guild or union protecting the ancient crafts of the gondolier-makers and their clothing, everything from the *forcola* to the hat. Makers of gondolier hats are called the *bareteri.* Gondolier hats are straw with a colored band on the crown and the brim. The band on the summer hat matches the interior of the gondola. The winter hat is black. If you want to buy a gondolier hat in Venice, avoid the tacky souvenir stands and buy a real one from here. They are madly chic and built to last.

Address: Calle del Lovo 4813, San Marco
Vaporetto Stop: Rialto
What's Nearby: Rialto Bridge, Teatro Goldoni.

Fashion

Have you noticed how Italian women always look effortlessly chic? They understand the cut and quality of cloth, have a core wardrobe made of few key pieces, and accessorize with the exactly right sunglasses and handbag.

OTTICO FABBRICATORE

Ottico Fabbricatore is owned by a husband-and-wife team, optician Francesco Lincetto and designer Marianna Leardini. This is the place to get ultra-modern designer eyewear, styles you will not find outside of Italy. (Bring a copy of your prescription with you.)

Marianna designs gorgeous handbags in everything from calfskin to ostrich and has recently added a L'Oft space to this uber-stylish store for apparel.

The shop is visually stunning. The merchandise is glorious. Expect exquisitely cut staple items in cashmere and silk, stunning and unique handbags, and the coolest eyewear ever.

Address: Calle del Lovo 4773, San Marco
Vaporetto Stop: Rialto
What's Nearby: Rialto Bridge, the Golden Head, Teatro Goldoni, Giuliano Longo.

3856 (TRENTOTTOCINQUANTASEI)

3856 sells cool European niche brands and original designs of the owner Elvira Rubelli. Expect high quality clothing from workday pieces to weekend-wear, to all around daily favorites. Whether looking for wardrobe staples or something more whimsical, you can find it here. They have really lovely linen dresses in the summer, cashmere and mohair in the winter. The accessories are tremendous too.

When Elvira is in the store, don't be surprised if she styles you. She will pull items ideal for your shape and coloring and help you put together a perfect ensemble (I love this!).

Address: Dorsoduro 3749
Vaporetto Stop: San Toma'
What's Nearby: The Frari, San Pantalon, Campo Santa Margherita.

Banco Lotto #10

Imagine if all prison systems focused on rehabilitation rather than punishment. That's how they do it at the Women's Prison on Giudecca. (I'll talk about some of this in the **Giudecca** chapter, but Banco Lotto #10 is the clothing arm of this operation.) This is another example of your travel dollars really making an enormous difference to people's lives, while getting some sensational merchandise to take home.

In 2003, *Il Cerchio* (The Circle) created a program to teach female prisoners sewing and design. Using fabrics donated from Fortuny, Bevilaqua and Rubelli, they created a design studio, making fabulous dresses. Like *really* fabulous dresses! (And coats, jackets, skirts and bags.) They sell the clothing through this little shop. The proceeds go directly back into the program, funding education, further work and career training, and work experience for former inmates.

The clothing sold at Banco Lotto #10 is exceptional. The dresses are universally flattering styles, their fabrics are incredible (especially the

Fortuny silks), and the tailoring is outstanding. None of it is cheap, but the idea is to create pieces that are functional, flattering, and beautiful forever.

Il Cerchio chose clothing for this project because it's a fundamental part of society that will always be needed. They chose dresses as a starting point because quality dresses are a core part of the Venetian fashion ethos. Also, it allows room for creativity and individuality. The dresses in the store are classic, feminine and elegant. Any inmate who wants to, can learn to sew, and those who want to advance can work side by side with designers. With the design program, the women can be as creative as the choose. As they exit the system, these women re-join the outside world feeling a part of the local social fabric and with marketable skills.

Named for the former lottery ticket shop that occupied this space, Banco Lotto #10 is a must for anyone who loves beautiful, unique, well-tailored clothing.

Address: Salizada San Antonin 3478, Castello
Vaporetto Stop: San Zaccaria
What's Nearby: 5 minutes' walk from San Zaccaria and Piazza San Marco.

L'Armadio di Coco

This one is for serious *vintage fashion* shoppers. It is not a secondhand clothes store.

L'Armadio di Coco (Coco's Closet) is a carefully curated collection for fashion addicts. You'll find the biggest designer names here. Come for significant fashion moments from the likes of Chanel,

Prada, Dolce & Gabbana and YSL. Expect to find clothing, designer handbags and accessories in excellent condition. Nothing here is cheap, but everything here is fabulous.

They now have two locations, both in San Marco.

Address: Frezzeria 1797 and Campo Santa Maria del Giglio 2516A
Vaporetto Stop: Midway between San Marco and Rialto
What's Nearby: Rialto Bridge, Piazza San Marco, Scala Contarini del Bovolo.

Spices

ANTICA DROGHERIA MASCARI

In a city that made a fortune through the spice trade, this is the only surviving spice shop on a street named for them. (*Ruga dei Spezieri* is "the street of the Spice Merchants".) This magnificent, small food emporium is definitely worth a visit.

As the oldest food specialty store in Venice, visiting here is like stepping back in time to a different century. They display loose spices in brightly colored, medina-like piles, with handwritten prices, and retro-chic labels. The hundreds of spices lure you in with their exotic aromas.

Inside you also find truffles and teas, marmalades and balsamic vinegars, candies and biscuits, dried fruits and nuts, niche liqueurs and a selection of over 600 wines from some of the best vineyards in the country. Their candies and sugared nuts are kept behind the counter in old-fashioned jars.

They carry random, difficult to source ingredients here too.

Address: Riga dei Spezieri, San Polo 381
Vaporetto Stop: Rialto Mercato
What's Nearby: Rialto Market, Rialto Bridge, Cantina Do Mori, Bar All' Arco.

Brass and Bronze

FONDIERIA ARTISTICA VALESE

Fondieria Artistic Valese is the last remaining foundry in Venice. It follows the traditional processes and techniques for manufacturing brass and bronze.

The shop sells Venetian products, from winged lions to gondola ornaments, to figurines and other Venetian objets d'arte. They also sell housewares, from elaborate chandeliers to door knobs and cool old door knockers. Not only do they supply to travelers like you and me, they also create pieces of all sizes for hotels and museums around the world.

The foundry is in Cannaregio but the shop is 5 minutes' walk from Piazza San Marco.

Address: Calle Fiubera 793, San Marco
Website: www.valese.it
Vaporetto Stop: Midway between San Marco/San Zaccaria and Rialto
What's Nearby: Piazza San Marco, Harry's Bar.

Murano Glass

Approximately 70% of the "Murano" glass sold in the shops in San Marco is fake. Due to a loophole in the law (or a palm crossed with silver), much of the glass labeled Murano is not only NOT made in Murano, it's made in places like Indonesia. (I thought I must have that wrong, but a quick Google search confirmed it.)

So how do you buy authentic Murano glass? My best advice is to buzz over to Murano and walk around the glass factories. When you see the masters at work and step into their showrooms, you can be pretty certain you're looking at the real deal. There are around 60 glassmakers in Murano, each with their own specialty. Some work in art and sculpture (*vetro artistico*), some make glass paperweights, some make chandeliers, some make drinking glasses. The bottom line is if the glassworks is not on Murano, it is not Murano glass.

THE HISTORY OF MURANO GLASS

The most ancient glass came from Egypt, made in around 3500BC. Glassblowing, where a pipe is used to inflate and shape glass, started in Syria around the 1st century BC. The first record of glassmaking in Venice was in 846AD. During the Middle Ages, Venetian glass was so popular, it became a status symbol. The Royal Courts of Europe sought Venetian glassmakers, both to create glass for their palaces and to steal them away from Venice.

The glassmakers had brought a new source of wealth to Venice, but they had also brought the less appealing habit of burning down the neighborhood. –Steven Johnson

In 1291, glassmaking moved to Murano. This was for two reasons. The first mitigated the risk of a furnace burning the city to the ground. The second isolated the secrets of Venetian glass making. Venice was full of international merchants and it would be easy to steal the secrets of Venetian glass and replicate them elsewhere.

In the Middle Ages, Murano glass became a status symbol. To protect the secrets of Murano glass, they put massive penalties in place, punishing any glassmaker who might leave the island. Even now, many secrets of Murano glass stay within families and are passed from generation to generation.

The law about the furnaces lasted until the end of the Republic. In the 19th century, several furnaces in Cannaregio made mosaic glass. Today only one, Orsoni, is still around.

Unless it is manufactured on Murano, it is not Murano glass.

About Murano Glass

Murano glass uses sodium bicarbonate to lower the melting point (soda glass). Other glassmakers around the world use potassium carbonate (Bohemia glass) or lead oxide (English glass). Murano glassmakers have always been innovators, creating new techniques and ways of using glass. In the 15th century, Angelo Barovier revolutionized the industry when he created a perfectly transparent, colorless glass called *vetro cristallino*, or crystal glass. This was the first Murano classic glass –until then glass had never been clear.

Murano glass can be formed into very thin pieces. It is famous for *filigrana* glass (with threads of lattimo inside), *pulegosa* (air bubbles inside the glass) and also *lattimo*, a milky opaque white glass.

Not just for everyday useful products like vases and cups, Murano glass also became known as a decorative art. For centuries, it appeared in European palaces and the homes of noble families to impress their guests.

Now, although still expensive, Murano glass as an art form is affordable to regular folk too, and is found around the world in private homes. This connection with the art world gained strength in the 20th century with a glass manufacturer on Murano called Venini. Venini pioneered combining artisanal glassmaking with contemporary art design, hiring artists like Carlo Scarpa to design products.

How to Tell If It's Real

This is another reason to hire an officially licensed *local* private guide in Venice. When shopping with my tour groups, I can text guides I work with to ask if a shop is legit or not. Venetians are happy to help you find true artisans.

Some things you can look for:

- Is the store full of high end, expensive glass?
- Can this salesperson answer questions confidently, with no hesitation? Authentic Murano glass sellers know every conceivable thing about Murano glass and the people who make it.
- Are the pieces perfect? Authentic Murano glass has little imperfections. If all the pieces look identical and perfect, chances are a machine made them in a factory in China or Indonesia.
- Hand blown glass may not be entirely symmetrical, the bottom may have rough *pontil* marks where the piece was

taken off the stick, and there could be bubbles inside the glass. Remember, they make Murano glass with basic tools, using ancient techniques passed from fathers to sons. There is no modern technology involved and no conveyor belts in any glassworks on Murano.

- Can you see the signature of the glass master? They don't all have it, but it's a good idea to ask.
- Does it come with a certificate of authenticity? Genuine Murano glass should have one.
- Does the piece have a label with the name of the workshop? There are only around 60 glassworks on Murano and they all label everything they make.
- Beware of labels like: *Vetro Eseguito Secondo La Tecnica dei Maestri Di Murano*. This means, "made following the technique of Murano glass masters" and is 100% fake.
- Is the address of the factory/glassworks on Murano? If not on Murano, it's not Murano glass.
- Look for the symbol of the Murano Glass Consortium and a QR code on a sticker. You should also see Vetro Artistico® Murano on the label.

Murano glass is expensive. My best piece of advice is to get the details on the piece, grab a photo of the label with the manufacturer's name on it, then on your phone go online to the Corsortium (*Consorzio Promovetro Murano*) website and look it up here: **https://www.promovetro.com/en/**

Find your manufacturer on the website. I don't know of any glassmakers on the island who are not part of the Consortium. If it looks suspicious, call the workshop and ask them if they are selling glass at shop *XYZ*.

I'll tell you about two of my favorite Murano Glass shops and demonstrations in the **Murano** chapter.

Orsoni Mosaic Glass

You may not have heard the name before, but if you've been to the Basilica San Marco or the Sagrada Familia in Barcelona, you've seen the work of the Orsoni family. The Orsoni were Venice's most famous makers of glass mosaics. Angelo Orsoni was born in Murano in the mid-19th century. He worked in glass factories before finding a passion and superb skill making colored glass, crystal, and aventurine.

Giandomenico Facchina discovered Orsoni and then moved him to Venice to create *smalti*, the glass used to make mosaic art. When in 1888 Facchina moved to France, he gifted Orsoni the workshop and furnace, and then became his best client. The following year, Orsoni took his display panel of 1467 colors of smalti and gold mosaic tiles to the Great Exhibition in Paris. This was his springboard to international fame.

Over the following decades, the Orsoni name became associated with major international projects including the Ecole des Beaux Arts, Paris' Hotel de Ville, Sacre Coeur, and St Paul's Cathedral in London. In the Art Nouveau era, mosaics evolved from church art into the decorative and secular arts. Orsoni moved his workshop to the Fondamenta di Cannaregio, where it still is. He continued developing technical innovations in smalti and kept experimenting with color. He built a color library that exceeds 3000 colors, including more than 100 skin tones and 32 different shades of gold. Orsoni has *the* most exceptional range of colors, all of which are created using secret family recipes.

When he died in 1921, Angelo's son Giovanni took over. Giovanni made the mosaics on the spires of Gaudi's Sagrada Familia and those inside Rome's Altare della Patria. His sons took the business to all corners of the earth. Orsoni mosaic smalti are seen everywhere from Ankara to London, Belgium to Bangkok, the King's palaces in Saudi Arabia to the Grand Palace of the Royal Family of Thailand.

The showroom in Cannaregio has been renovated to show architects from all over the world how to integrate mosaics into modern buildings. In 2003 the business was acquired by the Trend Group.

Orsoni offers 3—5 day courses in mosaics, and you can visit the Orsoni mosaic showroom by appointment. (One of the guides on my list of Venice Private Guides takes small groups there for tours.)

Address: Cannaregio 1045
Vaporetto Stop: Guglie (from the #4.1, #4,2, #5.1 and #5.2 lines) or S. Marcuola from the #1, followed by a short walk.
What's Nearby: The Jewish Ghetto, Al Timon, Torrefazione Cannaregio.

Lace from Burano

Burano, the island with brightly colored houses and picturesque fishing boats, is also the lacemaking capital of Italy. For centuries, the island was famous for ladies stitching lace while their fishermen husbands took to the sea.

Today the streets are full of lace shops, selling everything from babies' gowns to tablecloths to small doilies and handkerchiefs. Much of the lace you'll find for sale here is neither made on Burano nor made by hand –plenty of it is factory-made in China.

Be aware, real Burano lace is very expensive. For souvenirs at more palatable prices, you can find gorgeous hybrid works sold in linen and lace shops all over Burano. Look for something 100% made in Italy.

The History

By the 1500s, Venetian needle lacemaking had risen to an art-form. Initially, (probably bored) noble women stitched lace behind the closed doors of their palazzo homes. There were two types of handmade lace –needle lace, made with a single thread and one needle, and bobbin lace, made using multiple threads wound on bobbins. By the 17th century, most of the lace made in Italy and across Europe was bobbin lace.

Lacemakers all over Europe struggled to emulate the distinctive stitchwork produced by the women of Burano. Their signature stitches and easily recognizable designs graced the royal courts and banquet halls of nobles. Burano lace was so coveted that the Sun King Louis XIV paid multiple Venetian lacemakers to move to France to teach their craft. Thereafter, the demand for Burano lace dwindled as it couldn't compete with the cheaper lace being manufactured in Europe, especially French and Flemish lace.

By the 20th century, mass-produced machine-made lace meant producing Burano handmade lace was no longer practical, and thereafter it would only exist as an art form.

Today

Wandering the little side streets of Burano, you still find groups of retired women sitting outside making lace in a circle. In some lace shops, you might spot an older woman stitching needle lace. They do this out of passion for the craft and to keep their heritage alive for another generation. You don't see many young ones making lace, but these older women all learned from their mothers and grandmothers, or at the Scuola di Merletti lacemaking school.

The Burano Lace Museum is an amazing place to learn more about the island's lacemaking history, where you can see examples of the lace, and find out what makes it so special. The museum also has a gift shop, and you can be sure that any lace you buy there is 100% authentic.

Address: Burano Lace Museum, Piazza Galuppi 187, Burano.

The Craft

Handmade lace (entirely made by hand) is rare. A small piece requires an extraordinary amount of time to stitch and will be expensive –at least 10 times more expensive than factory-made lace. A lacemaking machine can whip out a piece quickly, so you are likely to find hybrid pieces made using lacemaking machines and finished by hand.

Machine-made lace isn't all the same. Cheap versions have tight stitches, very close together, and feel quite stiff. Others are so well done you probably couldn't tell they're not made by hand. Be careful not to spend your money on an expensive factory-produced knock off made overseas. Google the shop before making an expensive purchase and ask endless questions of the salesperson.

If you want to find the real deal, here are some good places to look.

Dalla Lidia Meretti

This is the oldest lace shop in Burano. Lidia Meretti sells a vast selection of authentic, handmade, high quality Burano lace. Whether you are looking for housewares (tablecloths, runners, centerpieces, handkerchiefs) bed linens, nightgowns, clothing or baby clothes, this shop is an absolute win.

Address: Via Galuppi 215, Burano.

Martina Vidal Venezia

Come here for authentic Burano lace napkins, tablecloths, pillows, quilts, bathrobes, towels, clothing, lingerie, babywear and more. Martina's clientele includes royalty, sheiks, heads of state and celebrities. You can book ahead for a tour of her workshop and a glass of wine in her private garden. Who knows who you might rub shoulders with?

Address: Via San Mauro 307, Burano.

Merletti dalla Olga

This shop offers everything from large pieces like tablecloths to something as small as a bookmark. You can often meet Olga herself, and time permitting, she'll speak with you at length about the pieces she makes and the craft of Burano lacemaking.

Address: Piazza Galuppi 105, Burano.

Emilia Burano

This fabulous old-school linen and lace shop is an institution in Burano. This is the place to restock your linen closet with beautiful tablecloths and napkins, bed linens, and bath linens. They also sell luxurious nightwear, scarves and even ladies' handkerchiefs. Her luxurious bath towels are *to die for*. The store is glorious. There is also a small museum upstairs.

Address: Piazza Galuppi 205, Burano.

18.
Venetian Masks

Venice bewitches. Like many before me, I have been seduced by its art, architecture, poetry and beauty.

–Russell Norman

Venetian masks have a thousand years of history. They're rich in tradition and symbolism and evoke a sense of glamor and decadence. Made of papier mâché, hand painted then decorated with velvet, feathers, rhinestones and gold leaf, masks in Venice have always been wearable works of art, designed to create drama and mystery, and then seduce you.

Masks were the great social equalizer. In masks, the rich and poor could mingle together, even pursue clandestine trysts, all while avoiding social scrutiny. Venetian women used them as a vehicle with which to preserve their modesty and play games of seduction.

The mask is perhaps the most recognizable purchase you can make in Venice, and it is also the most ripped off item. So, let's learn a little about the history of the mask, the craft and skills involved, and why you should skip the cheapo Made in China knock offs and buy a real mask from a legitimate mask maker instead.

The History of the Mask

In 1094 Doge Vitale Falier made the first known reference to "public amusements", or what he called *Carnevale.* Documents from 1271 talk about a school that taught maskmaking, the tools, material and techniques used to make them.

By 1296, the Venetian Senate declared Carnevale a public holiday. Initially, it was supposed to only be for a day on Fat Tuesday or *Martedi Grasso* (which contracted to *Mardi Gras*), but before long, these public amusements ran from St Stephen's Day (26 December) until Ash Wednesday. For a time, mask wearing expanded from only during Carnevale to encompass most of the year. Different styles of masks developed and were adapted to daily life. In some social situations, masks were compulsory. For example, at one time married women were required to wear masks when they went to the theater.

By the 13th century, there were multiple mask makers in the city. Venetian mask makers were elevated to a subcategory of a guild called the Arte dei Depentori. This was the guild for decorative crafts, and included textile designers, painters, gold leaf artisans, playing card makers, sign makers and even embroiderers. Mask makers became known as the *mascareri*. On 10 April 1436, a new statute recognized it as an official craft, and the makers established a mask makers' guild of their own.

By the 18th century, Venice was in economic decline and the number of mask makers dwindled. In 1773 there were only 12 mask making workshops in Venice, about the same number as today (although there are 2000 places selling them). When the Republic fell in 1797, Carnevale was banned, and masks were no longer allowed in public life. The craft of mask making temporarily disappeared.

Rebirth

On 27 February 1979, 182 years later, a local radio station joined forces with the Scuola Grande di San Marco to resurrect the Carnevale party. Musicians played, word got out, and Venetians hit the streets and danced. A few artisans began making masks again, unsure if Carnevale would return. The masks were popular and the craft was reborn.

Beware the 'Handmade' Label

Plenty of outlets flog cheap plastic masks, or partially papier mâché masks. A loophole in Italian law allows a product to be labeled "handmade" if some part of it somewhere in the world was made by human hands. You will find that cheap plastic masks with a tiny bit of papier mâché or a piece of ribbon glued on are labeled "handmade".

Types of Masks

You will find two specific types of masks in Venice –Historical Venetian masks and Commedia dell'Arte masks.

Historical Venetian Masks

These were worn by citizens from the Middle Ages until the fall of the Republic. There are many, but the following are four main types, each with an interesting story.

The Bauta (also spelled *Bautta*) is the most traditional carnival mask. It was initially worn only by men, but by the 18th century, women were wearing them too. The bauta is a broad, square white face with a prominent nose and a triangular bottom jutting out, with enough room for the wearer to eat and drink. Worn with a *tabarro* (black cloak), a *zendale* (black hood) and a *tricorno* (three-cornered hat), the complete look is a little menacing.

The Moretta (also called the *Muta*) is a black oval mask worn only by women. Held in place by biting a button inside the mask, it prevented the wearer from speaking. This gave her an air of mystery and made it harder for men to figure out her identity. This was a mixed message eroticism –at the time, women wore dresses with deep plunging necklines revealing lots of cleavage yet erased their mouths and facial expressions with a black mask. They must have looked like boobs and a wig, with a black hole for a face.

The Gnaga is a half face, resembling a cat or sometimes a pig and was often worn by gay men. It comes with a crazy (but true!) story of transvestites, the bridge of the boobies (Ponte delle Tette), the street of boobs (Fondamenta delle Tette), prostitutes, and a 16th century sex-for-sale crisis …

Despite extreme punishment (hanging and burning in Piazza San Marco), homosexuality was rampant in Venice. Gay men had found a loophole in the law, which stated that wearing a mask meant *becoming* a mask. So, the wearer was essentially playing a role and therefore no masked person could be arrested. Men who wore a *gnaga* and a dress, who acted like a woman and were on the arm of a man, were *playing the role* of a woman. This created an opportunity for gay prostitution, which consequently, pushed the working girls of sexually liberated Venice into an economic recession. The gnagas were stealing their clientele. The story gets even crazier. In 1511, the female prostitutes complained to Bishop Antonio Contarini that their business was suffering, so the Republic allowed the working girls to advertise, by hanging out of windows half naked and shimmying their goods at men passing by –hence the names Ponte delle Tette and Fondamenta delle Tette!

The Colombina is a half-face mask covering the eyes, cheeks and nose (not to be confused with the Gnaga mask, which is specifically a cat or a pig with ears). It can be decorated in a variety of ways.

The Commedia dell'Arte Masks

These were the masks of the improv theater, or Commedia dell'Arte. This was an early form of professional theater that originated in Italy, before becoming popular all over Europe. A specific type of costume and corresponding mask defined each distinct character in the plays of the Commedia dell' Arte. There were four main character groups in these plays, and each had its own type of mask.

The Zanni were the servants. They included the clowns Arlecchino (Harlequin), Pulcinella, Pedrolino, Brighella and Scapino.

The Vecchi were the wealthy old men. Their masks were Il Pantalone and Il Dottore.

Il Capitano or **La Signora** (if female) were the self-imposed captains and showoffs.

The Innamorati were the young upper-class lovers.

The female lead was called the **Prima Donna**. Female actors didn't normally wear masks, and the female love interest never wore a mask. Another central female character was **the Cortesan**, who usually came with a servant.

You'll see plenty of masks inspired by the Commedia dell'Arte. All the characters were caricatures of specific social groups. In the plays, specific characters hailed from specific places, and were performed in the dialect or accent of that city. For example, Harlequin was always from Bergamot, Pantalone was always from Venice and Il Dottore was always from Bologna.

The Plague Doctor Mask

You also see the Plague Doctor mask everywhere, with its malevolent long beak. The Plague Doctor mask originated in neither Carnival nor Commedia dell'Arte. It was created for a specific job, somewhat like a 16th century form of PPE. Doctors literally wore the masks to treat plague sufferers. The beak of the mask had twin slits along the sides, and doctors filled the beak with aromatic herbs to hide the stench of the sick. They covered the eye holes with an early form of eyeglasses, and doctors wore a waxed canvas coat that sealed around the mask to try to prevent infection. Although initially altruistic, they soon became associated with the horrors of the plague islands and the pyres where the dead and dying were cremated. It must have been terrifying to be visited by one of these doctors at the time. It still looks ominous today.

At some point the Plague Doctor mask was adopted as a Carnivale mask and became part of a costume worn on Fat Tuesday.

The Craft

Venetian masks are either made from papier mâché (*cartapesta*) or leather.

Papier Mâché Masks

Traditionally, historical Venetian masks are papier mâché. It was lightweight enough so that the mask could be worn comfortably without pulling down on the face and obscuring vision.

The process of making these masks is fascinating to watch. The artisan hand-sculpts a clay model, then pours liquid plaster over it. Once it hardens, you have a reverse mask, or the negative. This becomes the mold to make the papier mâché mask. Once three layers of papier mâché have set and hardened, the mask is painted white. Then it is ready to be decorated. There are plenty of talented mask decorators, but few are gifted at making the molds. Artisans use each mold multiple times.

Artisans build their masks to be anatomically correct, so that they fit well, don't drop over the eyes and are easy for the wearer to feel comfortable in.

Traveling Shows

Traveling theater troupes or *compagnie* weren't popular with magistrates and the church. Performers were known to strip nearly naked, and their storylines were frequently lewd and overtly sexual. That, combined with their nomadic lifestyle, led to them being called *vagabondi* (which in English became "vagabond") and to this day still carries a negative connotation.

Leather Masks

Papier mâché masks weren't practical for the Commedia dell'Arte performers, especially the men who often sweated profusely while performing. They needed something more durable that would last for years without getting smashed while the *compagnie* or troupe of actors traveled all over Italy.

Leather was the perfect material for actors' masks. Although much more expensive, it was well worth the investment. Commedia masks were standard and never changed, and the leather adapted to the face of the wearer, lasting for years. For much of the time, the masks were painted black, which must have made maintenance and repair much easier.

It takes two days to make a leather mask. The leather is dampened, then molded onto a wooden form and secured with tiny brass nails. While the leather is still damp, they manipulate it into all the facial creases and features on the mold. Once the mask has dried into its shape, the leather is treated, tinted and glossed. It is painstaking and incredibly specialized work and it takes an enormous amount of time. That is partly why leather masks are super expensive. Leather masks cost around €200, while authentic, artisan-made papier mâché masks are closer to €75, or as low as €30 for a Colombina.

While you're in Venice, you must check out some leather masks just to see how incredible they are.

An Evolving Art Form

Master mask makers still use the original techniques and create the traditional masks, but have also evolved to make masks inspired by the modern age. You see masks of animals, personalities from pop culture and modern movements such as Steampunk. The consistent trait is they all are handmade. Authentic mask makers, the artisans, don't use factory-made masks or mask molds.

Most people don't think of the *bauta* as being the traditional Venetian mask, instead, they think of the more rococo, glittery, feathery masks we associate with Carnevale. Artisan mask shops are full of brightly colored and over the top options. It can be overwhelming, so start by identifying the historical Venetian masks and Commedia dell'Arte masks, look for the familiar face shapes and styles like the bauta, then work your way through the store. If they're not super busy, I like to engage the salesperson in conversation and find out the stories behind the masks, the artisans making them, and about that store specifically.

Artisan Mask Shops in Venice

The following are some of the artisan mask makers in Venice. Many offer workshops where you can either watch masks being made or take part in the process. These are the shops I direct my Glam Italia Tour travelers to, knowing that a mask from any of the stores below will be a 100% authentic Venetian mask.

Another great resource for finding authentic masks is Venezia Autentica (veneziaautentica.com), an organization that will point you to authentic Venetian craftspeople in every *métier* (trade).

Kartaruga/ Il Canovaccio

My go to shop is Kartaruga/ Il Canovaccio. This family business is one of the original mask makers. Since opening his business in 1980, Franco Cecamore has crafted around 3000 mask molds. Along with those he makes for his shop, he also makes molds and masks for movies and runway shows. This is one of a group of mask businesses contracted to create masks for films and runway shows.

Kartaruga is now run by Franco's daughter Francesca who is also the president of the mask maker's association. They previously had two locations (including their main workshop) in Venice, but the second location was so badly damaged in the *acqua alta* of 2019, they had to move most of the workshop part of the business to the mainland. They still have a fabulous store, where they offer workshops and demonstrations. You cannot go wrong here.

Address: Calle della Banda 5369, Castello
Website: www.kartaruga.com
Vaporetto Stop: Midway between Rialto and San Zaccaria

What's Nearby: Piazza San Marco, Campo Santa Maria Formosa, Libreria Acqua Alta.

CA' MACANA

Another of the oldest and most internationally renowned mask makers in Venice. They make historical Venetian masks, Commedia dell'Arte masks and a contemporary line of masks, and everything is handmade. They also work with major movie productions, runway shows, and international opera houses. Along with selling their creations, they offer workshops, mask making courses and demonstrations.

Address: Calle Cappeller 3215, Dorsoduro
Website: www.camacana.com
Vaporetto Stop: Ca' Rezzonico
What's Nearby: Ca' Rezzonico (3 minutes), Ponte dei Pugni, La Barca San Barnaba.

ATELIER FLAVIA

Since 1980, Atelier Flavia has been handcrafting traditional masks and making costumes. Their historical costumes are made from the finest silks and brocades, by the finest weavers, all of them local. You can buy masks here and rent or buy costumes. This place is a great resource if you're planning a trip for Carnevale. (Book your rental costume as far ahead as possible.) You can also rent costumes to wear while you have yourself a photoshoot in Venice.

Address: Corte Spechiera 6010, Castello
Website: www.VeniceAtelier.com
Vaporetto Stop: Rialto

What's Nearby: 3 minutes' walk from Rialto Bridge, 5 minutes from Campo Santa Maria Formosa, between Rialto Bridge and Campo SS Giovanni e Paolo.

Alberto Sarria

Alberto has been creating masks for the theater since 1986. From his atelier in San Polo, he and his daughter Sophia make all kinds of masks, of both papier mâché and leather, all made by hand using traditional Venetian techniques.

Address: Ruga Vecchia San Giovanni 777, San Polo
Website: www.masksvenice.com
Vaporetto Stop: Rialto Mercato or Rialto but cross bridge to the San Polo side
What's Nearby: Rialto Bridge, Bar All' Arco, Rialto Market.

Tragicomica

Mask master Gaultiero dall' Osto's shop Tragicomica is another institution in Venice. His selection of masks of every type is almost overwhelming, the detailing just astounding. Along with making masks for movies and international events, Gaultiero also creates entire costumes. Put this one on your must-see list.

Address: Rio tera' dei Nomboli 2800, San Polo
Website: www.tragicomica.it
Vaporetto Stop: San Toma'
What's Nearby: The Frari, Scuola san Rocco, Chiesa San Pantalon.

La Bottega dei Mascarei

There are two stores, both called La Bottega dei Mascarei, run by brothers Sergio and Massimo Boldrin. Here again, you will find authentic masks made by absolute masters. Not only do they make traditional Venetian masks and Commedia dell'Arte masks, but also sensational pieces inspired by Tiepolo's art, along with others reflecting the sun and the moon. Sergio also creates for film, fashion design and Shakespeare festivals around the world.

Address: Calle dei Saoneri 2720, San Polo / San Polo 80 at the Rialto Bridge
Vaporetto Stop: San Toma' / Rialto Marcato
What's Nearby: The Frari, San Pantalon, Scuola San Rocco/ Rialto Bridge, Rialto Market, Caffe del Doge.

L'Arlecchina

Marilisa dal Cason learned her craft in her teens, working with another master mask maker. Now she has her own shop where she specializes in handcrafted masks. Her work is sensational, her shop a feast for the eyes. You can find all the favorites here, as well as her unique and colorful mask designs.

Address: Ruga Vecchia, S. Giovanni 789
Vaporetto Stop: Rialto Mercato or Rialto (cross the bridge)
What's Nearby: Piedaterre, Caffe del Doge, Rialto Bridge, Rialto Market.

Rugadoro

Just when you think you've seen it all, artisan Sarah Zanarella takes mask making to a new level. The face shapes are the traditional forms, and of course she makes them all by hand, but the decoration is like nothing I've ever seen before. Her exquisite work with different textured fabrics and intriguing color combinations is really special. She also uses Murano glass, and rare and unusual feathers. These masks can be expensive but each one is a perfectly formed masterpiece.

Address: Ruga Rialto 1035, San Polo
Website: www.rugadoro.com
Vaporetto Stop: Rialto (cross the bridge), Rialto Mercato
What's Nearby: Bar dall'Arco, Rialto Bridge, Rialto Market.

La Pietra Filosofale (The Sorcerer's Stone)

No mask maker's list would be complete without Carlo Setti, the craftsman at La Pietra Filosofale. Carlo is one of the few artisans still making handcrafted leather masks. Not just the Commedia dell'Arte faces, which are remarkable on their own, but also real people's faces that are borderline eerie. Seeing is believing with these –they are dynamic! He starts by carving the face from a block of wood and has made a collection of famous musician masks that are just unreal, from Beethoven to Janis Joplin to John Lennon.

Rather than the traditional black painted leather masks, Carlo treats and tints his masks so they come to life with a glorious patina –the real people masks are freakishly accurate. Carlo is an absolute character. He is not a salesperson or a marketer, but if you're serious about bringing home something truly remarkable and very different, this is the place to come.

Address: Frezzaria 1735, San Marco
Vaporetto stop: Midway between San Marco and Rialto
What's Nearby: Piazza San Marco (3 minutes' walk), Campo Santo Stefano, Rialto Bridge.

Wearing a Mask

Most masks have large eye holes. If you are wearing a mask to an event or to Carnevale, it will look best if you use makeup to color the area around your eyes. Frequently black eye makeup is used to disappear the eye, so it doesn't distract from the detailing on the mask itself.

For several years, I taught a pro makeup artistry class (my other career is a makeup artist). It was a class for students wanting to pursue a career in film/TV/celebrity work. Years ago, a student told me she was taking my course to learn how to do makeup for Carnevale in Venice. She had been to Carnevale and had fallen in love with the city and the event. So, in a stroke of complete genius, she'd decided to learn how to do makeup and have it pay for her to spend an entire month in Venice each year, by getting women ready for Carnevale. Brilliant! Not all masks are worn all the time, and some masks only cover part of the face, so there were endless opportunities for someone creative, with a savvy business mind. I was so impressed with the audacity and brilliance of her plan! Her hotel even helped her fill time slots for makeup. Every year, she would spend 11 months planning and perfecting her own wigs and costumes that she would wear to Carnevale events after work each day. Then she would fly to Venice and make a small fortune getting women ready for balls and parties and other events of Carnevale. She did it year after year, saving up her vacation days and sick days, escaping her corporate career for a month at a time!

19.

Piazza San Marco

In Venice, if you didn't know where you were going, you usually ended up in the Piazza, and since this was always true, maybe it was where you were always going.

–Scott Stavrou

Piazza San Marco is one of the most sensational piazzas in all of Europe. Majestic, beautiful, and full of secrets, it is the heart of Venice –it is also ground zero for mass tourism, which means you'll need to use a little strategy when you visit here. By day the piazza is full of tourists, but in the evenings, with the day trippers gone, another dream-like piazza emerges. In summer, the nighttime beauty of the piazza is otherworldly. The combination of exquisite light, magnificent architecture, over a thousand years of history and the music floating through the air from Caffe Florian and Quadri makes it feel like a dream sequence. In the early mornings before the crowds arrive, the piazza will belong almost exclusively to you. To be honest, even when it's packed with tourists, I still come through here multiple times per day. Piazza San Marco is too beautiful to miss seeing as many times as you can.

There is an enormous amount to see in the piazza, and most tourists will miss the fantastic little details, so here are some cool things you may not know about Piazza San Marco. (This chapter is really long, but really worth it.)

Trivia

- Piazza San Marco, simply called "the piazza" by Venetians, is the only piazza in all of Venice. Every other public square is called a *campo.*

- The history of the piazza can be divided into four periods:

  1. In the 9th century, the piazza was a small square with gardens and trees and the vegetable gardens for the monastery of San Zaccaria.
  2. Until 1174, a mini canal called the *Rio Batario* separated the Doge's Palace from the original square. In 1174, they enlarged the piazza by filling it in.
  3. In 1267, they paved the square with herringbone-patterned bricks.
  4. In 1735, they replaced the bricks with natural stone pavers. A white pattern marked spaces for merchants to set up their stalls. The alignment of the pattern runs west to east, visually extending the length of the piazza, emphasizing the Basilica at the eastern end. The new design included raising the level of the piazza by approximately one meter to mitigate flooding and adding internal drains to send water back into the Grand Canal.

- At 90cm above sea level, Piazza San Marco is the lowest point in all of Venice, and is the first place to flood when the tide gets high. But flooding doesn't come from the embankment along the canal. Instead, water rises from directly beneath the piazza via the stormwater drains. Sometimes you'll notice puddles in the center of the piazza even when there has been no rain. This is high tide water coming up from underneath. Look for the octagonal white drains along the pavement in the center of the piazza.

- You can eat at the cafes bordering the square, but walking around eating, or sitting on the piazza to eat is strictly forbidden and can result in a €200 fine. **

** It is also forbidden to sit on monuments, bridges, fondamente, embankments, the sides of canals and waterways, steps, and high-water walkways/ramps, anywhere in Venice and plenty of tourists learn this the hard way. In 2019, a pair of backpackers using a portable stove to brew coffee on the Rialto Bridge steps were fined €950 and asked to leave Venice. (What were they thinking? A coffee at Caffe del Doge, a 2-minute walk from there, costs €1,20.)

Interesting Finds in the Piazza

1. Procuratie Vecchie

A beautiful 16th century arcade called the Procuratie Vecchie runs the length of the north side of the piazza (the side with the clock tower and Quadri). Originally built as offices and homes for high-ranking state officials, the lower level is now shops and restaurants, while offices and the Michelin Star Quadri restaurant occupy the upper floors.

2. Procuratie Nuove

The south side of the piazza has a matching arcade, built after 1582 and thus named the Procuratie Nuove (new). The ground floor has more restaurants and shops, most famously the beautiful Caffe

Florian which opened in 1720 (I talk about Florian in the **Coffee** chapter). During Austrian rule, Venetians took their business to Florian while the much-hated Austrians sipped coffee across the piazza at Quadri.

The upper floors of the Procuratie Nuove house the Correr Museum, bracketed at the west end by the Ala Napoleonic, and at the east end by the gorgeous Biblioteca Marciana.

3. Museo Correr

Looking around Piazza San Marco, you'll notice something odd. There is no church. The basilica wasn't a church for the people; it was the private chapel of the doge. Almost every campo in Venice has its own little church, so what happened here? Napoleon happened here.

Pre-Napoleon's arrival, a beautiful Jacopo Sansovino church stood opposite the basilica. Built in the 6th century, the church of San Geminiano had several rebuilds over the next 1000 years. The final renovation was ornate, richly decorated and considered an important example of Venetian Renaissance architecture. In 1805, Venice became the second city of Napoleon's newly created Kingdom of Italy. His stepson Eugene ruled Milan, while the little guy made himself king. Napoleon turned the Procuratie Nuove and the Marciana Library into his Venetian palace, but he also wanted a party room with a grand staircase opening onto Piazza San Marco. So, he demolished San Geminiano to build a new wing in its place. Eugene awarded the project to architect Giovanni Antonio Antolini (who, believe it or not, wanted to demolish both of the Procuratie –the two long arcades that line the piazza! Can you even imagine? Clearly Eugene was an idiot). Eventually the project was passed to Giuseppe

Maria Soli and Lorenzo Santi who replaced the church with the Ala Napoleonica, blending with the other two sides of the piazza and making all three coherent and harmonious. The Ala Napoleonic was completed in 1836, and although Napoleon and Eugene never saw it, it has kept their name. The only sign of San Geminiano is on the pavement under the arches of the Ala Napoleonic. Look for a cream rectangle set into the checkerboard tiles. Inside is a picture of the old church.

The Ala Napoleonica now houses the amazing Museo Correr. The Correr Museum is a fantastic crash course in Venetian history. It gets crowded here during the tourist season, so visit first thing in the morning or at the end of the afternoon, before or after the day trippers fill it up.

4. Grancaffè Quadri

Between the Museo Correr and the basilica, you'll find the other most famous coffeehouse in the piazza, Caffè Quadri. Since 1775 like Florian, Quadri has been a legendary historical landmark in Venice. Everyone from Proust to Brangelina has enjoyed their coffees under its mirrored walls, with one of the world's most dynamic views.

The awe-inspiring Quadri restaurant is directly above the Grancaffè and has been open to the public since 1844.

The Alajmo family took over Quadri in 2011 and within one year, it not only gained international acclaim but also its own Michelin star. The menu is purely Venetian and Italian, using a contemporary spin with ingredients sourced from the lagoon. In 2018, the Alajmo brothers gave it a Philippe Starck revamp, revitalizing it while preserving its 18th century allure. They contracted local Venetian artisans to restore the establishment to its original beauty and even made a documentary about the process.

Everything about the experience of Quadri is sensational. Throughout the day and long into the evening, you can enjoy their musicians playing on the stage outside. I love wandering through the piazza at night, getting swallowed up in the music, the Venetian night sky and the insane beauty of the piazza. There's nothing quite like it. The lights and the music spilling out of Caffè Quadri and Florian have to be one of the most iconic experiences of Venice –you'll be able to close your eyes and relive it forever.

5. Clock Tower Museum

The city's 500-year-old clock is a marvel of 15th century engineering and ingenuity. Commissioned by Doge Agostino Barbarigo in 1493 to symbolize the city's power and control, it not only had to be beautiful but also had to be accurate. The Torre dell' Orologio, also known as the Moor's Clock Tower, displays the time, the phase of the moon and the current sign of the zodiac.

This gorgeous clock tower has five sections:

1. At the top, two bronze figures, hinged at the waist, bend and strike the bell on the hour. Originally intended to be giants, the weather turned the bronze black, and Venetians nicknamed them "The Moors".

2. Below them the winged lion of Venice stands on an open book, in front of a beautiful blue background covered in golden stars.

3. Below this level a semi-circular gallery has copper statues of the Virgin and Child, flanked by big blue panels. The left panel displays the hour in Roman numerals while the right shows the minutes in Arabic numerals (at 5-minute intervals). On Epiphany and Ascension Day, the Moors are joined each hour by carved figures of the Three Magi. They emerge from the left panel and move in procession around the semicircle, bowing to the Virgin Mary as they pass her, before disappearing back inside the right panel.

4. Level two has the magnificent blue and gold clock face inside a circle of marble, engraved with the 24 hours of the day in Roman numerals. (They built this giant clock face high enough to be seen from the canal by approaching ships and boats.) A gold pointer with an image of the sun moves to show the hour. Inside this, a circle of golden zodiac signs moves around the clock's face, showing the position of the sun in the zodiac on a background of blue enamel. These are the original golden zodiac symbols from the 1490s. Inside the circle of zodiac signs, the moon slowly revolves around the earth showing its phases, surrounded by stars. If this section were the only part of the clock tower, it would still be absolutely amazing. You have to wonder how they figured all of this out 500 years ago?

5. Below the clock, a two-story high archway straddles a street called the *Merceria* as it leaves Piazza San Marco. This stretch of the Merceria is called the Merceria dell' Orologico.

When the clock was revealed to the Doge on 1 February 1499, legend says he was so overwhelmed by its beauty, he had the clockmakers blinded so they could never replicate it. In reality, the two mechanics became its caretakers. This began the tradition of clock keepers living inside the tower with their families. Other than the eardrum shattering noise, it would have been a tremendous deal.

You can take a tour inside the clock and see its inner workings, the living quarters and the huge spinning drums that make the hours and minutes work. The guide also takes you up to the Moors. The original bell is still there, cast in 1497 and signed by the bell maker.

Make sure you are in front of the tower when the clock strikes the hour to see the Moors bang the bell. It is just fantastic.

6. The Red Lions of San Marco

On the north (left) side of the basilica, there's a small *piazzetta* with two red lion sculptures. I'm especially partial to these lions because when I had no earthly clue how to get home from Bar Foscarini, Paolo told me to walk between the lions and follow the way back. To this day, every time I see them, I hear Paolo's voice telling me, "Walk between the lions."

Although they *look* as old as the ancient statues surrounding the basilica, these red Cottanello marble lions were made in Venice in 1722.

Basilica San Marco

I am going to give you a brief overview of the Basilica San Marco but be aware there is more here than you can possibly absorb in a single visit. Having visited the church both on my own and multiple times with a guide, I sincerely recommend going with a private guide or taking a small walking tour. Pre-Covid, along with sharing their encyclopedic knowledge and love of this incredible place, licensed guides could walk you in through the guides' entrance. However, at the time of writing this book, the rules have changed. Now, you must buy a ticket at the booth opposite in the *loggetta*, and they have restricted the number of people allowed in at a time. For now, the guides' entrance is closed, but as things move forward, I hope it will reopen.

History of Basilica San Marco

The first church on this site was built around 830AD. The construction of the current gorgeous Italo-Byzantine style basilica began around 1063AD. For 1000 years, this was the private church of the Doge. San Marco became the cathedral of Venice in 1807. For the 400 years prior, San Pietro di Castello was the city's cathedral.

The basilica forms the shape of the Greek cross, with a dome over each arm and a massive dome over the central point where the four arms meet. These domes are in the style of old Constantinople, with a ring of windows around the base. The windows not only let in light, but they also create the illusion that the dome is soaring upward. Without them, the domes would look heavy and dark.

Venice had no saint of its own, or at least no *relics* of its own. The original patron saint was a lesser-known Greek one, Saint Theodore. Doge Giustiniano Partecipazio realized that procuring the relics of a major saint would be great for business, luring streams of pilgrims and tons of cash, and the remains of one of the four apostles would up the ante even more. So, in 828, he had his men steal the relics of St Mark from Alexandria in Egypt. He built the first St Mark's Basilica to house these relics.

How did they successfully smuggle sacred, valuable relics out of Egypt? The thieves hid the bones under layers of pork, knowing the Muslim guards wouldn't touch pork and would therefore let them pass without inspection. While sailing home, a massive storm almost drowned the thieves and their sacred cargo. As they were about to sink, a vision of St Mark told the captain to lower the sails. The ship was saved and returned safely to Venice. (You'll see the story of this miracle at sea retold in the 13th century mosaics above the left door as you enter the basilica –see my description below.)

In the 11th century, construction began on what is the current basilica. You might notice the architecture is quite unusual. Venice is physically closer to the Byzantine realm than to Rome, and the city was the center of international trade –it had residents who traveled extensively and hosted merchants from all over the world. This exposed the citizens to cultures most Italians (and Europeans) had never seen before. The Venetian Republic was closely linked to the Byzantine Empire and, amongst other things, was strongly influenced by its architecture. Rather than mirroring the other churches and cathedrals in Europe and in Italy, this basilica looks more like the Hagia Sofia in Istanbul. It must have seemed so wild to Venice's visitors throughout the centuries!

A Story Told from East to West

There is so much to see on the facade alone, it can feel mind-boggling, so let's just look at a handful of specific details, starting with the story of the mosaics on the lunettes of the lower half of the basilica (the two arches on either side of the main entrance).

These mosaics tell the story of the relics of St Mark the Evangelist being taken from Egypt and brought to the basilica. They tell it from right to left, the *geographical direction* of the story.

The lunette on the far right (closest to the Doge's Palace –and Egypt) is my favorite. It shows the relics of St Mark being stolen by two Venetian merchants, Bono from Malamocco and Rustico from Torcello. These are the two fellows to the left of the basket, holding up the lid. Bono and Rustico hid the bones below fruits, vegetables and, most notably, pork. To the right of the basket, we see the turban-wearing Egyptian customs officers. The one in front wearing red and green pulls away in disgust, while (my favorite) the fellow in blue, pinches his nose with his right hand while holding up his left as if saying "Stop!"

The second lunette on the right shows the relics arriving in Venice. The ship is to the left, with the two merchants and the relics wrapped in a white sheet.

In the third lunette, to the left of the main door, St Mark lies under a vibrant blue blanket, while Doge Giustiniano Partecipazio, resplendent in gold, welcomes him with open arms. The Doge is surrounded by nobles all in awe and adoration of St Mark.

The fourth and final lunette, positioned furthest from Egypt, is the most ancient of the mosaics. Created in the 13th century with a bright golden background (24 carat gold leaf), St Mark the Evangelist is carried into the basilica built especially for him. Above are two fellows in the center with curled staffs, St Mark lies in what appears to be his coffin, his head elevated as if looking out at the people of Venice, or as if his halo is preventing him from lying flat –you decide.

A Glorious Plundering

Just like the relics of St Mark, most of the basilica's treasures were plundered from other countries, many from the crusades, particularly the 4th crusade which ended with the April 1204 conquest of

Constantinople (Istanbul). At the time Constantinople was the largest Christian city in the world. Doge Dandolo joined forces with the crusaders of another holy war, using the opportunity to settle debts the Turks had with Venice. The sack of Constantinople was horrific. The crusaders' absolute brutality catastrophically wounded relations between the Catholic and Orthodox churches for centuries. It also weakened Constantinople to the point where the Ottomans could step in and take over, ultimately collapsing Christianity in the east.

But on the bright side, Venice executed some brilliant plundering, starting with the bronze horses of the Hippodrome, known as the Triumphal Quadriga. The four horses were brought back to liven up the facade of the basilica. (It turned out to be lucky the Doge stole them, because the crusaders melted down all the ancient Greek bronzes they could get their hands on, including a giant bronze statue of Hercules from the 4th century BC.) Six centuries later, Napoleon took these bronze horses to Paris. They were returned to Venice in 1815. The originals are held in the museum inside the basilica –the ones outside are replicas.

In addition to the horses, Doge Dandolo stole lots of religious relics and works of art and brought it all back to Venice. The basilica became the new home of the Madonna Nicopeia, crosses, chalices, *patens* and the golden altarpiece enamels.

The Treasure of St Mark's

The treasure of St Mark's is a collection of 283 pieces of gold, silver, glass and other precious items. There is a lot of gold, along with chalices, Islamic bowls, and Byzantine enameled gold work mounted with precious stones. There are two icons of Archangel Michael and a collection of western art objects.

This is all that remained after Napoleon's looting of the Republic, although, to be fair, they had stolen it themselves. After the great impoverishment of 1797, the Venetians sold some of it (pearls and precious stones) to finance restoration of the basilica.

The treasure is divided into four sections: Antiquity and the early Middle Ages, Byzantine art including work by goldsmiths dating to around the year 1000 and the two Archangel Michaels, Islamic art from the 9th and 10th century, and Western Art. It can be found in the old rooms between the basilica and the Doge's Palace and is accessed through the door in the south transept with 13th century mosaics depicting two angels carrying the reliquary of the cross. The vestibule on the left leads to the sanctuary and on the right to the treasure. Look for eight niches in the walls with multiple reliquaries holding the relics of saints gathered from the Holy Land, Constantinople, and areas outside of the eastern Mediterranean.

Mosaics to Die For

The walls of the basilica are *covered* in golden mosaics. And I mean *covered* –it's like being inside an enormous pirate treasure chest. There are over 6000 square meters/85,000 square feet of mosaics inside the basilica.

The golden mosaics were completed over 8 centuries. You can come in and out of here all day long and it constantly looks different based on the light. If you're spending a few days in Venice, try to visit the basilica more than once, at different times of day. Light will flood in through a different set of dome windows, illuminating mosaics that were dark on your previous visit. The quality of the light throughout the year and across the day keeps changing from bright white midday light through soft apricots and golden hour light. These different colors of light impact the mosaics, making the various scenes look different too.

I have no idea how many times I've been inside the basilica in the past 30 years, yet every time the mosaics still take my breath away. No matter how spectacular you imagine they'll be, they are a thousand times more impressive, even when you've already seen them a hundred times. My guide Emanuele grew up here, has lived his entire life in Venice, and has been visiting the basilica since he was a baby. He *still* is completely wowed by the mosaics. Every time I come here, I learn something new and see something I never noticed before. (Once you've seen it, you'll understand this).

(You can download my PDF with local private guides at www.GlamItaliaBooks.com/Venice-Private-Guides.)

THEN THERE'S THAT FLOOR

The ceilings and mosaics of the basilica are so astounding, it's easy to miss the stupendous sight below you –the floor. If the only thing inside the basilica were the floors, you'd still come to see them. The 2099 square meter marble carpet shows the incredible wealth of the Republic. Not only could it afford grandeur on such an astronomic scale, but it could also hire the greatest artisans and mosaic masters of the time, no doubt from Byzantine Greece and Constantinople.

They made the floors of the Basilica San Marco from two types of mosaics: *opus sectile*, where marble pieces of different colors create geometric shapes and forms, and *opus tessellatum*, where marble or colored glass pieces make animal figures and flowers. (These styles and techniques date back to antiquity and are documented in the writings of Pliny.)

The patterns go beyond traditional religious themes. Look for animals including deer, doves, roosters, pigs, eagles and dogs. On the right side of the church near the altar of the Virgin Nicopeia, two roosters carry a stuffed fox between them on a stick. There are peacocks symbolizing immortal life, their 'thousand eyes' representing God knowing everything. Meanwhile, in front of the Chapel of St Isidore, a rhinoceros symbolically wards off disease.

Every time I walk through the basilica, I spot new patterns. There is so much to see here it's impossible to absorb it all. I'm always mesmerized by the way flood damage has made the floors roll like the movement of the ocean. This is a desperately unfortunate consequence of all the flooding the basilica has endured. Hopefully it can be remedied before it's too late.

Thousand-Year-Old Tombs

The oldest tomb in Basilica San Marco is 1000 years old and belongs to Doge Vitale Falier, who consecrated the basilica in 1096. It's incredible to imagine making such a mark on the world that your tomb is still in place 10 centuries later.

Counting Columns

Another random fascinating fact speaking to the vast size of the basilica, is its number of columns. Basilica San Marco has over 500 columns. Most are from the 6—11th centuries and of Byzantine origin. Look for Byzantine capitals but also random re-appropriated 3rd century capitals. Some columns were spoils from Constantinople and others date back to the Middle Ages. If the gold and the mosaics feel overwhelming, focus on the columns. It's hard to wrap your head around the volume of them.

Mary's Got a Gun

This is nutty, but true. On the left transept, look at the Romanesque bas reliefs. One of these is (I kid you not) a carved relief of the Madonna and Child –with a rifle! The Madonna and Child part is from the 13th century, while sailors who survived an Austrian bomb explosion in nearby Marghera added the rifle in 1849.

The Pala d'Oro

The Pala d'Oro is the high altar *retable* of the basilica. *Pala* comes from the latin word for cloth and *d'oro* means gold. They were used to cover or embellish the altar during a church service. Over time, the cloths were replaced by gold and silver.

Commissioned by Doge Ordelaffo Falier in 1102, it was delivered in 1105. Think of it as a huge altar screen, made of gold and studded with hundreds of gems, including 1300 pearls, 400 garnets, 300 sapphires, 300 emeralds, 100 amethysts, rubies and topaz. More impressive than the gems in the Tower of London, the Pala d'oro The Pala d'Oro of St Mark's has 250 enamels on sheet gold and is one of the most incredible examples of Byzantine genius in the world. It is more opulent than Britain's Crown Jewels. In the center of the piece, look for Christ holding open a book, the text is replaced by gems to show the magnificence of the word, while the Evangelists surround him. Below Christ, the Virgin prays, and on either side of her are Doge Ordelaffo Falier and Empress Irene.

The piece actually comprises two parts, the Palo d'Oro and the wooden container immediately behind it. Traditionally, the box only gets opened during specific church celebrations, otherwise they cover it with another altarpiece called a *ferial*, which is a painting on wood.

The original ferial, made in 1343—45 by Paolo Veneziano and his sons, is now in the church museum. The current one is from the early 15th century and can be seen from the back side of the retable.

Outside the Basilica

The Four Tetrarchs

On the southwest corner near the Doge's Palace, look for an unusual sculpture embedded into the wall. It doesn't blend in with anything else, yet you could easily walk right past it. Like everything in Piazza San Marco, it has a story.

This story begins in the 3rd century AD when the Roman Empire was in disarray. Between civil wars and the overexpansion of the empire, things were getting out of control, but then along came one of my favorite emperors, Diocletian. (You'll know all about him already if you've read *Glam Italia! 101 Fabulous Things to Do in Rome.*) Realizing the empire was far too huge for just one man to rule, Diocletian created a Tetrarchy. He divided the empire into two parts, east and west, each with an emperor and a junior emperor. This way there was always a *caesar* (junior emperor-in-training) guaranteeing stability and a smooth transition of power. Diocletian stayed in the east and Maximian ran the west. The two caesars were Galenius and Constantius. Had this system stayed in place, the Roman Empire would have lasted longer and might have skipped the dark ages.

The Tetrarchs is a sculpture of Diocletian, Maximian, Galenius and Constantius and made from purple *porphyry*, a rare and expensive stone from Egypt, exclusively reserved for emperors. Unlike traditional highly individualized and easily recognizable Roman and Greek sculptures of emperors, here there is no way of knowing who's who. To make them all equal with no one more powerful than the others, they removed all individuality. Two tetrarchs have beards, two are clean shaven. We can assume the bearded are the *augusti*, the older and wiser leaders Diocletian and Maximian, while the smooth cheeks belong to the junior emperors. All four have the same abstract facial features, bodies, clothes, and even the same odd body language, divided into two pairs symbolizing the senior and the junior of each side of the empire. The left hand of each tetrarch grips a sword with an eagle handle, while the right hand of both bearded emperors grips the left shoulder of his junior.

The junior emperor at the southeast angle appears to wear a white boot. During the sack of Constantinople in 1204 (the most barbaric looting and pillaging foray of the entire medieval era, which is *really* saying something), the Tetrarch sculpture was stolen from Constantinople and brought to Venice. While being plundered, the foot broke off. We can only assume that in 1204 the effort to get more purple porphyry proved too difficult or too expensive, so they jerry-rigged a white foot instead. (It looks crazy! Did they think we wouldn't notice, or didn't they care?) In the 1960s, archaeologists found the heel of the missing foot near the Bodrum Mosque in Istanbul. It is now in the Instanbul Archaeology Museum.

The Pillars of Acre

Next to the Tetrarchs along the south wall of the basilica are two square columns. Again, you could easily walk past them, but they really are very interesting. These have always been called the Pillars of Acre (Pilastri Acritani), assumed to be looted in 1258 from Acre after the Venetian victory over the Genovese. However, it turns out they too were part of the great plunder of 1204.

Byzantine princess Anicia Juliana commissioned the pillars in 524AD when she rebuilt the church of St Polyeuktos on a scale to rival the biblical Temple of Solomon.** Each pillar has elaborate carvings of vines growing from a vase and scrolls with bunches of grapes and flattened vine leaves. When archaeologists in Istanbul found the huge foundation of this church, it had pillars like these, thought to be from the lower level of the church. St Polyeuktos was only excavated in the 1990s, so when you consider how many centuries the pillars have stood here, this information is technically brand new.

** Three lily capitals on the southern and northern corners of the basilica were stolen from this same church in Constantinople.

The Stone of the Proclamation

Opposite the corner of the basilica, just beyond the pillars, look for a big circular stone made of red porphyry. This is the Pietra del Bando, the Stone of the Proclamation. From here they once read official proclamations to the people of Venice. In ancient Venice, the heads of traitors would be displayed here for three days and three nights, to warn citizens against betraying the Republic.

The Campanile

And off in the far distance, the gold on the wings of the angel atop the bell tower of San Marco flashed in the sun, bathing the entire city in its glistening benediction. –Donna Leon

Opposite the basilica is the tallest building in Venice, an imposing square bell tower called the *campanile* (*cam-pan-ee-leh*). At 98.6 meters, it is one of the tallest bell towers in all of Italy. This iconic structure with its golden angel on top has always been the first sight of Venice to anyone arriving by sea. Locally known as *il paron de casa*, which roughly translates to "the master of the house", it holds the bells of Basilica San Marco, and has its own interesting stories to tell.

Galileo used the campanile to study the sky, and on 21 August 1609, it was from here that he demonstrated his telescope to Doge Leonardo Donato and the Senate. It must have seemed magical. First, he showed them the tower of Saint Giustina in Padua, 35 miles away. Then towns like Treviso and Chioggia, before letting them watch parishioners walk into the church of San Giacomo on Murano, and finally galleons in the Adriatic, still hours away from being visible to the naked eye.

The original 10th century campanile was a watchtower, monitoring approaching ships, and a landmark guiding Venetian ships home safely. In the 12th century they added a belfry and a spire. For the first few centuries, the belfry was wood, covered in copper plates. Unfortunately, the spire was prone to lightning strikes that set the belfry on fire. After one of these fires in 1388, they covered the copper plates in gold leaf, making the belfry visible to sailors far away in the Adriatic Sea. After a devastating earthquake on 26 March 1511, they rebuilt the belfry in Istrian stone.

Above the band of four white arches, look for a brick attic with a gleaming white sculpted relief on each side. The east and west sides have allegorical figures representing Justice with the sword and the scales, with lions on either side. The north and south sides have the lion of St Mark, the symbol of the Venetian Republic. In 1513, a copper plated, gilded wooden statue of the archangel Gabriel was erected on top of the spire. The angel gleamed golden in the sunshine, and functioned as a weathervane, pivoting so Gabriel always faces into the wind.

THE BELLS

There are five bells in the bell tower, each with its own name and special purpose.

1. **The Marangona** is the biggest. Its name means "carpenter" in Venetian, but symbolised all the workers. The Marangona rang at sunrise and sunset, heralding the beginning and the end of the workday.
2. **The Maleficio** (the curse) is the smallest and was used to announce death sentences.
3. **La Nona** rang at the ninth hour.
4. **The Pregadi** (also called the Meza Terza) rang to summon the senators to the Doge's palace. (The Venetian Senate was formerly called the Consiglio dei Pregadi –the Council of the Invited.) It also rang in the evening to announce a meeting the following morning, or in the early afternoon to announce a meeting that evening.
5. **La Trottiera** rang to summon the magistrates.

Of the five bells, only the Marangona survived the collapse of 1902 (more info on the collapse of the campanile below).

One of the beautiful things about Venice is the ringing of the bells. The sound peals out across the canals and the lagoon, always in beautiful harmony. But while the ringing doesn't always make sense to visitors, it makes perfect sense to Venetians. We expect the number of chimes to reflect the hour, with maybe a single dong announcing the half hour, so it's confusing hearing unusual numbers of chimes at odd times of day.

The following is a rough guide to the schedule of the bells of the campanile (separate from the list above, and not including holy days and celebrations):

Dawn: The Meza Terza (also called the *pregadi*) rings 16 rounds of 18 strokes.

Sunrise: The Marangona rings its own series of 16 rounds of 18 strokes, historically signaling the opening of St Mark's Basilica, the Loggetta, and the gates of the Jewish Ghetto.

Sunrise + 30 minutes: Half an hour after sunrise, the Meza Terza rang to tell government workers, mechanical guild workers and the workers at the Arsenale that the workday had begun.

Sunrise + 2 Hours: The Marangona goes off again.

Midday: The ninth hour in the Venetian 24-hour clock, the Nona now rings 16 rounds of 18 strokes to announce the beginning of the lunch break.

Midday + 30 minutes: The Nona rings again, telling workers their break is over.

Sunset: Now the Marangona rings 15 sets of 16 strokes, telling government workers, mechanical guild workers and Arsenale workers their workday is over.

Sunset + 60 minutes: Meza Terza rings for 12 minutes telling night watchmen of St Mark's it's time for work.

Sunset + 84 minutes: After a 12-minute silence, Nona would ring for a new 12 minutes telling workers to take the letters to Rialto to be dispatched.

Sunset + 108 minutes: Now Marangona would ring again for 12 minutes, ending two hours after sunset.

Midnight: Marangona rings 16 rounds of 18 strokes.

Pay attention to the bells. They won't go off when you're expecting, frequently go off when you're not, and will pretty much *never* ring the number of times you are expecting. Try counting the number of chimes at midday and you'll see what I mean!

Noon and the Ninth Hour

Noon derives from the Latin word for nine. The Romans counted the hours of the day from sunrise, not midnight. Sunrise was around 6am, so the ninth hour was 3pm. Then in the 12th century the Christian church adopted the Jewish prayer schedule, with monks required to start the first prayers of the day at 3am. Therefore, midday became the ninth hour, which later became colloquialized to "noon".

THE LOGGETTA

The *loggetta* (covered walkway) at the base of the campanile was a place for nobles to gather when coming to the piazza on government business, and a place for the sentries protecting the entrance to the Doge's palace. It's easy to miss because there is so much to see in the piazzetta but be sure to stop and look.

Originally it was made of wood, but this proved problematic when pieces of masonry fell after storms and earthquakes. After a lightning strike caused more damage in 1537, they hired Jacopo Sansovino to rebuild it in stone.

The loggetta is only on the side of the tower facing the Doge's palace. Wooden retail spaces made up the other three sides, their rent earning revenue for the procurators of St Mark. They didn't remove the wooden stalls until 1873.

THE COLLAPSE OF THE CAMPANILE

On 14 July 1902, the campanile collapsed. In 1873, when the wooden stalls were removed from the loggetta, they discovered the terrible condition of the base and foundation of the campanile. The only restoration done was surface, cosmetic work. Then in 1902, while repairing the roof of the loggetta, they noticed the tower trembling as the workers hammered. Glass was inserted into the crevices to track the movement of the tower –by the next day, many pieces had broken. On 12 July, a large crack appeared on the northern face of the tower. Wooden barricades kept citizens back, to protect them from being hit by falling debris and mortar. All bell ringing stopped apart from the Marangona announcing the start and finish of the day. Two days later, things looked even worse. The piazza was evacuated at 9.30am, by 9.45 stones began falling and at 9.53 the entire tower collapsed.

The access ramps between the inner tower and the exterior tower fell one after the next from the top down, causing an implosion of sorts. This meant that although the tower came down, it didn't crash into the other buildings around it, limiting the damage. The loggetta was destroyed and a corner of the Marciana Library building was damaged, but the basilica remained unharmed. The only fatality was the custodian's cat.

"Dov'era, com'era" (where it was, as it was)

Immediately, money was raised both in Italy and internationally to rebuild the tower *where it was, as it was.* They salvaged bricks and fragments of bronze statues, carefully collecting and inventorying reliefs, columns, capitals and anything else that could be retrieved from the destroyed loggetta. Bricks that had turned into rubble were carted off on barges and dumped into the Adriatic. The original medieval pilings below the foundation were still in good condition and only needed a small amount of reinforcement.

The first two years of the rebuild focused on extending the foundation 3 meters on each side, which required driving 3076 pilings into the lagoon below. Then eight layers of Istrian stone blocks were layered on top of the pilings to create the new foundation. The new tower is a faithful replica, but inside, structural changes have improved weight distribution while reducing the overall weight. Instead of masonry, reinforced concrete beams secure the inner and outer shafts, and replace the old stone support for the spire.

The allegorical figures on the east and west sides of the belfry attic were restored from the fragments recovered from the ruins, but the winged lion of St Mark which had occupied the north and south sides had been irreparably damaged during Napoleon's destructive foray into Venice, so was completely remade. With the restored archangel Gabriel re-erected, the tower was inaugurated on 25 April 1912.

On the north side of the campanile look for a plaque showing how high the flood waters reached in 1966. I can only imagine how horrifying it must have been with gale force winds and waves crashing up the sides of the buildings.

From the top of the campanile, you get gorgeous views of Venice. The views over the upper parts of the basilica alone make it well worth seeing. In 1962 an elevator was installed, so rather than climbing hundreds of stairs you can shoot to the top in 30 seconds.

The Doge's Palace

The Palazzo Ducale (the Doge's Palace) is one of the most famous landmarks in the world. For four centuries, it was the most powerful piece of real estate in all of Europe.

This was the Doge's residence, and the seat of government. Built in Venetian Gothic style in 1340, it has been modified and expanded over the centuries. Positioned on the Grand Canal next to Basilica San Marco, its opulent lace-like exterior was one of the first sights merchants, foreign heads of state, diplomats and power players saw as they arrived in the wealthiest city in Europe.

Other European palaces and castles of the time were heavily fortified. Dominance was measured by soldiers patrolling the ramparts, and the thick block walls that made them impenetrable. Venice instead demonstrated her dominance with lavish displays of wealth and beauty.

Arriving in St Mark's Basin must have felt surreal, with the pink and white palace glittering in the sun that reflected off the water. The city was a melting pot of races and religions. Visitors were greeted by the view of luxurious buildings, the likes of which they'd never seen before, and by an exciting mix of peoples. Turban-wearing Middle Eastern men walked with caped Venetians. Asian faces engaged with Germanic blondes. Africans did business with Europeans. It must have felt like arriving at the center of the world. (And for a time, it was.)

BUILDING THE PALAZZO

Unlike in other cities in Italy, this was the only building in Venice allowed to be called a *palazzo*. Other palatial homes were called *Ca'*, short for *casa* (home). No matter how huge, how beautiful, how richly decorated they were, they had to take the lesser name.

For 1000 years, the Venetian Republic was politically more stable than anywhere in Europe. Protected from invasion by its geography –you couldn't exactly mount a stealth attack on a city in a lagoon on the Adriatic Sea. They'd see you coming for days. Because of this, Venetians were free to experiment architecturally, focusing on beauty instead of fortification. With no heavy, defensive requirements, they built a charmingly fresh and open palace, built on three levels, with pink Verona marble and white Istrian stone.

The exterior of the Doge's Palace is a gorgeous hybrid of Byzantine, Islamic and Gothic cultures, wrapped in Venetian Renaissance. At the ground level, a *loggia* (arcade) has pointed arches, above which a divinely ornamented, second-level balcony looks like lacework with its pretty balustrade and pointed arches topped with quatrefoils. The third floor features pink and white Byzantine patterned stone, punctuated with arched windows. Above them, a row of small, quatrefoil windows softens the trajectory to the Islamic influenced crenellated roofline. Unusual and magnificent today, it must have been mesmerizing during the Republic.

The palace comprises three main wings:

- The oldest (begun in 1340) faces the Grand Canal.
- The facade facing the piazza and piazzetta was added nearly 100 years later in 1424.
- The side wing with the Doge's apartments and government offices was built from 1482 to 1565.

Since its 1340 inception, the palace has experienced multiple rebuilds, additions and extensions. There were several fires over the centuries that not only destroyed great works of art but also the Doge's apartments (1483) and rooms like the Grand Council Chamber (1577).

Visit the Doge's Palace, either with a guide or at least with the audio guide from the ticket office. You'll learn how the Republic worked, how awe-inspiring it must have seemed to foreign dignitaries visiting Venice, and how hideous it was to be pronounced guilty and sent across the Bridge of Sighs and down into the prisons below.

There's an enormous amount to see at the Doge's Palace, so I've cherry picked a handful of my favorites.

1. The Chamber of the Great Council

As with the White House in the US, the Doge's Palace was not only a residence, it was also the place where official government business took place. The Republic was an oligarchy, ruled by a Great Council made up of a select group of nobles, who's elected leader was the Doge. The Great Council comprised all the males of the noble families over the age of 25, regardless of social stature, wealth or merit, so in its own weird way, the council had a diversity of sorts. (The system must have worked –the republic lasted 1000 years.)

The council held all other state authorities and departments accountable if they felt anyone was getting out of line or getting too powerful. They were the guardians of the laws and the maintainers of the political equilibrium. They needed a room to meet in, and because there were about 2000 of them, that room had to be massive.

At 53 meters long and 25 meters wide, the chamber of the Great Council was the largest, most sumptuous room in the palace, and one of the largest in Europe. Every Sunday the bells called the Council members here, with the Doge at the podium and his counselors sitting in the two rows of seats stretching the length of the room. It must have been quite something to see, this weekly convening of noblemen decked out in all their finery, doing the business of the Republic.

The first stages of the election of a new Doge also happened here. (At a later stage, the task moved to the Sala dello Scrutinio.) I love standing in the middle of this room imagining hundreds of years of deliberations happening right here, surrounded by art and the views over St Mark's Basin through the windows.

The Chamber suffered fire damage in 1577 but was restored by 1580, and literally *covered* with artwork by Palma il Giovane, Veronese, and Jacopo and Domenico Tintoretto. The walls tell stories of Venetian history, the ceilings of Venetian heroics.

The wall behind the Doge's throne holds the longest canvas painting in the entire world, Tintoretto's *Paradiso*, measuring 22 meters by 7 meters. Painted between 1588 and 1592 to replace a Guariento fresco destroyed by the great fire of 1577, it is breathtaking and gigantic.

Immediately below the ceiling is a frieze of portraits of the first 76 doges. Each holds a scroll highlighting their most important achievements, except one –Doge Marin Faliero who attempted a coup d'état in 1355. His portrait is covered by a simple black cloth. Faliero, a traitor to the Republic, was not only condemned to death but also to *damnatio memoriae* –the complete eradication of his memory and name.

This chamber is spectacular –you have to see it in person to comprehend just how magnificent it is. Even if you're not interested in art, you should stand in the middle of this massive room just to get a sense of how completely stupefying it must have seemed to anyone walking in here, which, of course, was the whole plan. The Chamber of the Great Council was a show of strength and an obscene display of wealth. But it is not the frivolous Vegas-like gilded wealth of Versailles. The wealth in this room is draped in power.

2. Scale dei Giganti (Staircase of Giants)

The Staircase of Giants was the official entrance to the Doge's Palace. Built between 1483 and 1491, it is named for the two giant statues flanking the top of the stairs, representing the Republic's dominion over land (Mars) and sea (Neptune). The staircase connects the courtyard with the inner loggia on the first floor, and among other things was where the coronation of the Doge took place. It was also where they beheaded Marino Falier (the Doge who tried to overthrow the Republic) on 17 April 1355. The Republic didn't mess around when it came to treason. The huge statues were also intended to diminish the height of the Doge, reminding him (after Marino Falier's attempted coup) that a doge was a regular man, equally punishable as everyone else.

3. Scala d'Oro (Golden Staircase)

Heading to the state rooms, you climb the 130 stairs of the beautiful Scala d'Oro, a staircase with walls and rounded ceilings adorned with white stucco and 24 carat gold leaf. The Scala d'Oro, named for its exquisite Roman-style white and gold stucco, starts at the top of the Staircase of the Giants. This would have been the route taken by important guests coming to see the Doge and it brought the visitor into the center of La Serenissima's power, the reception rooms of the Doge and those of the Senate and Collegio.

Other than high-ranking magistrates, the golden staircase was exclusively reserved for illustrious, important visitors, who must have been dazzled by such magnificence. From the majestic Staircase of the Giants and through the unparalleled splendor of the Scala d'Oro, this path was designed to impress kings and princes, ambassadors, and foreign ministers, while reminding them of the power and wealth wielded by the Republic. Remember, all the other heads of state were living in heavily fortified, bulky castles, not light, airy palaces of beauty like this one.

Like the Staircase of Giants, this project was also assigned to Jacopo Sansovino and was one of the last major works done to the Doge's Palace in the 16th century. The Scala d'Oro not only displayed beauty, wealth, and power, it also served to separate the Doge's residence from the workings of the government.

The first section of the staircase leads to the Doge's apartments while the second set of stairs goes to the heart of the palace. The staircase has two opposite but sensational views: one out over the Rio de la Canonica and the Bridge of Sighs, and the other across the glorious courtyard of the Doge's Palace.

Look at the decorative ceiling of the staircase. It is not just gold, stucco and bas reliefs, there are also frescoes inside stucco frames. The Giambattista Franco frescoes were designed to fit inside these frames and align perfectly with the vault-line of the ceiling. At the lower end of the staircase, the frescoes glorify the defense of Cyprus and Crete, while at the upper end they show the virtues by which a good Doge must live.

Notice how the side walls of the staircase are smooth and bare in contrasts with the stupendous ceiling to draw your eye upwards.

4. The Sculptures of the Golden Staircase

With so many details as you climb the staircase, it's easy to miss these four sculptures.

Two columns flank the staircase at its entrance, each with a sculpture on top. On the left, *Hercules Killing the Hydra* and, on the right, *Atlas Carrying the World*, both by Tiziano Aspetti.

Midway up the second flight of stairs, you'll see two more statues are on either side of the steps, this time by Francesco Segala. They are *Abundance* and *Charity*. Look at the gorgeous draping of fabric depicted in stone and maybe like me you'll wonder how on earth a sculptor can do this?

5. Museo dell' Opera

Over the centuries, the Doge's Palace has been restructured, repaired, and restored many times because of fires, structural problems, and sometimes for modernization. The organization responsible for this work was called the *Opera*. By the mid-1800s, the Doge's Palace was in a terrible state of decay. In 1876, a major renovation repaired the two facades and the capitals of the columns along the ground floor arcade and the upper loggia. These capitals had been masterpieces of 14th and 15th century Venetian sculpture. Forty-two of the original capitals were in particularly awful shape and were replaced with replicas.

The originals, along with sculptures from the two facades, have their own special area in the palace, the Museo dell' Opera (Museum of the Works). After careful restoration they are exhibited with their original columns, across the six rooms of the museum. The museum also has fragments of architectural works and decorative pieces from other parts of the palace, and pieces of statues. It's especially fascinating if you paid attention to the capitals along the exterior of the palace (see more on the capitals later in this chapter).

6. The Prisons

Every sestiere had its own prison for minor crimes (such as debt), but serious crimes landed you in the absolute horror movie of the prisons of the Doge's Palace. Initially, the palace prisons were the *Piombi* (the Leads) and the *Pozzi* (the Wells).

The Pozzi (the Wells)

The Pozzi were the worst place to serve your sentence. Down in the lowest floors of the palace, they routinely flooded during high tide, earning them their nickname. This flooding wasn't clean fresh sea water, it was filthy sewage-laden water that was accompanied by rats. It created a horrific stench that rose into the courtyard and inside the palace itself.

The cells of the Pozzi were on two floors, built in concentric circles with no exterior windows, they had no natural light and no circulating air. Prisoners couldn't tell if it was night or day. The ceilings were too low for the average man to stand up straight. The only furniture was a plank serving both as a bed and table, and a shelf with a slop bucket as a toilet. The worst offenders were kept here, plenty of whom didn't make it out alive. Many prisoners tried to leave some sign of their existence by carving graffiti into the wood and the stone, which is still visible today.

Prison Art

During 20th century restorations, a genuine work of art was discovered in Cell X. In a different setting it could have been a fresco cycle, but here in the Pozzi it was an etched cycle of graffiti created in the 16th century by Riccardo Perucolo, an imprisoned fresco artist from Conegliano.

On one wall is Virgin and Child surrounded by Saints Rocco, Sebastian and Benedict, on the opposite wall is Christ on the Cross with Saint Rocco holding a bell, accompanied by two pigs. He created the artworks by scratching into the fresh limestone with a nail, then going over it with a brush soaked in water and coal dust. Over the centuries, it was preserved under a thick layer of filth, dirt, and grime.

Riccardo was imprisoned for the crime of being a Lutheran. He didn't stay in the Pozzi for long –the terror of torture and the inhumane conditions made him confess quickly. He lived outside jail for 20 years as a pretend Catholic –but maintained his belief in the Protestant church, which ultimately got him burned at the stake in 1568.

The Piombi (the Leads)

The Piombi was another area for prisoners, this time for imprisoned nobles and people of social standing, as well as defrocked priests and political prisoners. Typically, these were people serving shorter sentences for lesser crimes. This area was called the Piombi and was named for its location on the top floor of the east wing of the palace, under the lead roof. There were only seven cells. The social status of the clientele afforded them certain privileges. Unlike the horrors of the Pozzi below the palace, these cells were dry and had natural light. They were also artificially illuminated at night. Prisoners up here had furniture, medical care, and could have food and wine delivered from outside. On the downside, the lead roof above the cells made them insufferably hot during the summer and icy cold in winter.

In the entire history of the prisons, there was only one successful jail break, achieved by Venice's most renowned Lothario, Giacomo Casanova. **

On 26 July 1755, Casanova was arrested for indignities to religion and common decency. On 12 September, without trial and without being told why he had been arrested, they sentenced him to five years under the Leads. He spent his first five months in solitary confinement with a pallet bed, a table, an armchair, some clothes and "millions of fleas". Then he had a variety of cell mates. While on an exercise walk in the prison garret, he found a piece of black marble and an iron bar, which he secreted back to his cell and hid in his armchair. During a spell without cellmates, he sharpened the iron bar against the stone, turning it into a spike. He started cutting a hole in the floor, planning to escape into the Inquisitor's chamber below during an upcoming holiday when the chamber would be empty. But three days before his grand escape, his plan was foiled when he was transferred into a bigger, brighter cell.

I'm skipping a bunch of the story here, but Casanova eventually befriended a wayward priest in the cell next door. He devised an escape plan that had Father Marino Balbi make a hole in the ceiling with Casanova's sharpened iron, and then make an escape hatch in the wooden ceiling above Casanova's cell. The two escaped into a crawl space below the lead tiles, then used the sharpened iron rod to pry open a space and escape onto the palace roof. It was a night blanketed in fog, which kept them hidden but also made the lead tiles slippery. Many things went wrong, including Casanova nearly falling to his death but holding onto the gutter and pulling himself back up, James Bond style. Ultimately, he found a dormer window in the roof, and lowered the priest to the floor below, using a rope they made from knotted sheets and blankets. He was stuck on the roof for another hour before finding a ladder to lower himself down. After catching a few hours' sleep (again I'm abbreviating the story), the two changed their clothes and alerted the custodian, telling him they'd been locked inside the palace after an event the night before. The custodian unlocked the palace door, and the two prisoners sauntered down the Staircase of Giants and to the piazzetta and freedom! They took a gondola to Mestre and then Casanova escaped to Paris where, amongst other things; he invented the lottery! Thirty years later, Casanova recounted this story in his book *The Story of My Flight*. The book was extremely popular and was translated into many languages.

** Beyond his sexual exploits, Casanova was a fascinating and brilliant character. I had no idea how interesting he was until I read Laurence Bergreen's excellent biography, *Casanova: The World of a Seductive Genius.*

The New Prison

By the mid-1500s, Venice needed a bigger prison, and so the New Prison was established. While the Pozzi and the Piombi and the courthouse were inside the Doge's Palace, the New Prison was located across the Bridge of Sighs. Once found guilty in court, the prisoner would be marched across the bridge and down into the New Prison.

This prison was the first freestanding state prison in Europe. They wanted a vast structure with better conditions than the previous prison, with natural light, air circulation and larger spaces. An imprisoned architect named Zaccaria Briani, had his life sentence reduced by three years for helping.

The new building had a central courtyard, allowing light to penetrate all four walls. It was two stories tall with the main facade opening onto the Riva degli Schiavoni. At first glance, it's hard to believe it's a prison. But if you look a little closer, you'll see that the gratings covering the window openings are a fascinating metal weave that, instead of being an addition to the building, was *built into it.* They were part of the initial construction, almost as if the walls were built onto and around them. There was no way to pull these grates out to escape. Cutting or unscrewing them was impossible. It was an ingenious way to build a maximum-security prison in a place of beauty, next to one of the most beautiful palaces in the world, without destroying the vista. The New Prison could hold 400 prisoners.

People associate the Bridge of Sighs with romance, but it was quite the opposite. The sighing was from the prisoner crossing the bridge, passing the windows, and having his last look at the world outside. From there it was all downhill (literally) to life in the new jail.

Your ticket to the Doge's Palace allows you to walk through the New Prison, which is both creepy and fascinating. You can take the same walk the prisoners made and explore the prison cells. Although considered humane at the time of construction, the cells were actually pretty horrific. I can't believe human beings were sentenced to spend time in this place.

7. The Capitals of the Doge's Palace

These are another incredible find that most tourists are completely oblivious to. But once you know about the capitals on the columns along the arcade of the Doge's Palace, it is impossible to un-see them.

The ground floor arcade along the exterior of the Doge's Palace looks like a series of arches held up by columns. Each column has a huge stone capital at the top, carved between 1340 and 1355. No two capitals are the same. In fact, there are 600 different carved images – it is a visual encyclopedia telling the story of Venice. More than just decoration, they broadcast the history, politics, and moral teachings of the Republic.

Every capital tells a story. There are animals, zodiac signs, angels, fruit, and human faces. The Republic wasn't beholden to the pope, so the story involves non-Catholic symbology mixed with virtues the Republic considered important, and (my favorites) the people of Venice. Once again you can see here how diverse the city was. The capitals show people of different cultures living here together – Asians, Turks and Moors, just as you would have seen walking through the calli of Venice during the Republic.

Each of the three corners represent a biblical scene. Beginning with the southwest corner, we have the beginning of human history, with the story of Adam and Eve. Adam eats the forbidden fruit in the presence of the Archangel Michael who guards the gates of paradise. (Archangel Michael also guards the Chamber of the Great Council immediately above.)

To your right, on the corner next to the Bridge of Sighs is *The Drunkenness of Noah*. Noah bends around the waterfront side of the palace, leaning against a vine and looking completely hammered, while his sons reach around the corner, covering their father's nakedness with a blanket. (Who knew Noah had a wild side?)

The third corner is next to the Basilica. Here we see *The Judgment of Solomon with the Archangel Gabriel.* It was added in 1435.

The capitals are numbered 1—36. Number 1 is the first capital by the Basilica end and number 36 is around the corner by our drunk friend Noah.

Rather than list each capital's story, I'll just point out my favorites:

- **Column 35**: Birds with their prey. This symbology is about virtue conquering vice. Here we see a bird eating a fish, and a stork eating a serpent.

- **Column 32:** Kings and Emperors. Look for Trajan with a sword symbolizing military power, then follow the sides of the capital through a line of kings to Nebuchadnezzar, with the fleur-de-lis scepter symbolizing good governance based on purity of the soul.

- **Column 31:** Latin Women. This is a series of intricate women's heads, their social status and age reflected in their hairstyles and headwear. Most look out at you with an expression somewhere between knowing and serene, but one of them, wearing a headpiece with the cloth covering her neck and chin, smiles at us. (I always wonder, who was she?)

- **Column 21:** People of the World. These unbelievably realistic heads represent people from around the world. It must have been cool to be a non-Venetian walking the streets and seeing yourself represented here. Not just obliquely, but created in stone, to be remembered for all time. My favorite heads are the Moor in his turban and the Mongolian/Tartar. Check out the ears on the head to the left of the Tartar – they're elf ears! Once you've spotted them, in becomes impossible to *not* notice them every time you go past! There are several capitals with an intriguing face on one side that I can't *un*-see. Over all the years I've been coming here, my eye still zeros in on them.

- **Column 29:** Monsters. Look for the capital with the young man playing a violin. His lower half is a fish. Next to him, a lute player has bear's claws poking out from under his robes. To the left of the violin player, there's a young man with a dragon's tail.

Personally, I love all the people ones. Even if you only look at the capitals with faces on them (there are several) it changes how you see the arcades and this whole stretch of the Doge's Palace.

8. The Pink Columns

From the piazzetta (the stretch between Piazza San Marco and the Grand Canal) look at the second floor of the loggia running the length of the Doge's Palace. Part way along, two columns don't match the others –they are pink, made of marble from Verona.

These columns hold an important place in Venetian history. The Doge would appear between them during big events in St Mark's Square. One of these was the Svolo del Turco, during Carnivale. An acrobat disguised as an angel would float down from the bell tower on a rope, landing between the pink columns where the Doge waited for him.

More ominously, it was also from between these pink columns that death sentences were announced to the crowd waiting below. If the accused was an aristocrat, they hung him between the pink columns and left him there for days as a warning to others. It was also the spot from which the Doge would watch public hangings. The gallows were erected between the columns of Saints Theodore and Mark, with a direct view to the clock tower.

The convicted would have a chance to be absolved, though. Facing the water, you'll see that the 4th column from the corner is out of alignment. If the convicted could walk around the circumference of the base without losing his balance, he would be pardoned. Very few were successful. Even doing a slow shuffle with your back pressed to the column, there is a point at which you lose your balance. I'm not sure if the new rules forbidding climbing on monuments include walking the base of this column, but there was a time when you could try it yourself.

Insider Tips for Visiting the Piazza San Marco

- **Time your visit.** Cruise passengers and day trippers head off by late afternoon. This is when the number of people trying to see the Doge's Palace thins out, making it an ideal time to visit. The museum is spectacular, so try visit it when it's not overcrowded. First thing in the morning is great too.

- **Check online first**. Since Covid, many museums have introduced limited, timed entry, so find out before you go. Also, be aware that there are multiple flights of stairs inside the Doge's Palace. If you have restricted mobility, check the access options online before booking.

- **Book a *skip the line* entrance**. If booking ahead, it is definitely worthwhile to pay a little extra (I think it's only about €5 more) to get priority entrance. This is one of the most visited museums in Europe, so getting away from the crowds and avoiding the lines is worth the extra few dollars.

- **Get the audio guide.** If you are visiting the museum without a human guide, get the audio guide. There is so much to see and you will miss out on too much without it.

- **Book a private guide.** Art lovers, if you can, book a private guide. You can combine the palace with other places too – one guide can show you all over Venice. For a PDF list of my favorite private guides in Venice go to www.GlamItaliaBooks.com/Venice-Private-Guides

- **Take the Secret Itineraries Tour and the Hidden Doge's Treasure Tour**. I love secret passages tours and the Doge's Palace offers two great ones. They are restricted to a maximum of 10 people and must be booked ahead online. Each is just over an hour long and you can stay in the palace for as long as you like afterwards.

- **Make the most of your ticket**. The museum ticket also lets you into the Museo Correr, Museo Archeologico Nazionale and Monumental Rooms of the Biblioteca Nazionale Marciana.

- **Visit visitmuve.it** for more info on the Doge's Palace, Museo Correr, Museo Archeologico and the Marciana. This is where you can get more details and book your tickets.

Biblioteca Marciana (Library of St Mark)

The last building I want to tell you about in the Piazza San Marco is the spectacular Biblioteca Marciana, which faces the Doge's Palace. Andrea Palladio, one of the most influential designers in the history of architecture, described the Biblioteca Marciana as "the richest and most ornate building since ancient times". In a town like Venice, that's *really* saying something.

In 1468, Cardinal Bessarion bequeathed his entire collection of 482 ancient Greek and 264 Latin manuscripts to the Republic of Venice, on the condition they be kept in a public library. Cardinal Bessarion had a passion for collecting and copying rare ancient manuscripts. He preserved the works of classical Greek writers and literature from Byzantium that would otherwise be lost to us. He chose Venice because of its connection to the Byzantine Empire and its large population of Greek refugees. This was one of the first public libraries and is one of the earliest still in existence in Italy. It also has one of the most important collections of classical texts *in the world.*

Construction began in 1537. Jacopo Sansovino had an immense understanding of classic Roman building design, which he put to use here. The ground floor was based on the Colosseum and the Teatro Marcello in Rome. Before the Biblioteca, rundown 13th century buildings had stood here. Some were storefronts, paying rent to the procurators of St Mark's, so the new building would need retail rental property on the ground floor, with the library to be located on the second floor.

On 18 December 1545 during construction, a heavy masonry vault collapsed. Sansovino attributed the disaster to a combination of workers removing wooden supports before the concrete had set properly, and a ship in the harbor firing its cannon, the resounding boom from which shook the building badly. Although he was the most renowned local architect of the time, he was blamed for the accident, and had to pay for the cost of the repairs! It took him 20 years to pay it off, and the Republic refused to pay him his stipend for 2 years.

Not only magnificent from the outside, the Biblioteca is also full of amazing art inside. This building is now mostly a museum. The library collection, reading rooms and offices have been moved to the adjoining building, the Zecca, formerly the mint of the Republic. The Biblioteca is the only government institution from the Republic still functioning today.

Let's Talk About the Art

Entering the Biblioteca, you pass through a room with ancient Roman statues and an intriguing ancient world map created in 1450 by Fra Mauro –before America had been discovered. The map shows circumnavigation of Africa, with an entirely different course for the Nile River, and (my favorite oddity) it's all upside down. South at the top, north at the bottom.

There's a magnificent Titian on the ceiling. The oil on canvas *Wisdom* is set inside an octagon and measures 177cm (5'8") across. Painted in 1560 when Titian was painting more symbolic and metaphorical works, *Wisdom* was the perfect subject for the entrance to a library.

The former library room was the original location for all of Cardinal Bessarion's manuscripts. It has a remarkable ceiling, with 21 tondos set into rich golden moldings. Seven different master painters from the time, including Veronese, Schiavone and Salviati, created the tondos. Veronese, Schiavone, Salviati, and Tintoretto adorned the walls with beautiful paintings of ancient philosophers.

The Biblioteca Marciana is a gorgeous building to visit, especially if you are interested in Venetian history and art. On the first Sunday of the month, entrance is free, and you enter from the Piazzetta and go up the monumental staircase with its spectacular ceiling. (Don't forget to look up!) The rest of the month you enter from the Correr Museum.

The Columns of San Marco

Before we move on, I want to draw to your attention to one final glorious detail –the giant granite and marble columns overlooking the lagoon –and tell you why locals won't walk between them. Mystery shrouds the arrival of these columns, but we believe them to be from Constantinople, a gift from the Byzantine emperor around 1127, in gratitude for Venetian help during the second crusade.

The Statues

Each column has a statue on top. A giant bronze winged lion faces east to the palace, linking the evangelist and the government of the Republic. His paws rest on an open book (added later in history). Restored numerous times over the millennia, the lion is made up of pieces of bronze, added at different times in history. Scientists dated his core to the end of the 4th or beginning of the 3rd centuries BC. His provenance is the ancient city of Tarsus in south-central Turkey, where he was part of a monument to the god Sandon, the god of war and weather. Sandon was traditionally depicted in human form, standing on the back of a winged lion, carrying either a sword or an axe. A monument to Sandon stood in Tarsus at least until the 3rd century AD. At some point in Venice, the winged lion became the symbol of St Mark the Evangelist.

Napoleon stole this lion and displayed him on a fountain in Paris' Place des Invalides. He was returned to Venice in 1815. However, while being removed from the fountain, whether by sabotage or accident, the rope broke and the lion crashed to the ground, breaking into 20 pieces. The pieces were saved and stored at the Arsenale until Bartolomeo Ferrari repaired him, altering his tail, which was previously tucked between his legs. The book upon which his front paws now stand was stolen, abandoned or lost, and had to be recast. On 13 April 1816, the lion returned to his position on top of the column. He was later removed from the column for safekeeping during World War II , and didn't return until 25 April 1991, the feast day of St Mark.

The lion's companion column holds the original patron saint of Venice, St Theodore of Amasea. We know little about St Theodore (San Todaro in Venetian), making him an odd choice for the first patron saint of Venice. Theodore of Amasea died around 306AD. He was a young soldier serving with the Roman army at Amasea (now Amasya) in Northern Turkey. When Theodore refused to celebrate Pagan worship rites with his fellow soldiers, he was arrested and later set free with a warning. He then set fire to the temple of the Anatolian mother goddess Cybele, at which point he was tortured and thrown into a furnace. Theodore's legend grew, and by the 7th century they were depicting him as a dragon slayer. Normally seen with a spear (to kill the dragon), the people of Amasea believe he saved them by wielding a cross. The first statue of Theodore (from 1372) was replaced in the 15th century, with the dragon now symbolized by a crocodile. The original 15th century marble statue is in the Doge's Palace. This one on the column is a replica.

Each column stands on an octagonal base, adorned with sculptures immortalizing the various Schools of Arts and Crafts, who helped with the monumental task of erecting them. Although they have degraded over time (nearly 1000 years), each column base shows different guilds or unions. The Column of St Mark's is now so eroded that we can identify only one –the sculpture of the greengrocers displaying their wares in a wicker basket. The trades represented at the base of St Theodore's column include a blacksmith raising a hammer to hit an anvil, and a fishmonger offering fish from a basket. The others are very faint but could be a wine seller and a butcher.

I guarantee you'll be the only travelers looking at the bases of the columns.

The Third Column

There were originally three columns. All three made it to Venice safely from Constantinople. On arrival, one column rolled off the boat into the marshy lagoon. For 20 years, a specially appointed sea master searched the lagoon for the missing column, even though raising it would have been close to impossible. In 2016, researchers tried again to find the column which had been missing for nearly 1000 years, but they too had no luck.

The Superstition

Erecting the two columns was no easy feat. Decades passed before local engineer Niccolo Barattieri accomplished the task. In return, he asked for exclusive rights to put gaming tables between the columns.

Gaming was illegal in Venice, but the engineer prevailed, and this space became an outdoor gambling den. After Barattieri's death, it became a space for market stalls, and then in the 18th century, the space between the columns became a site for public executions. The condemned were positioned, so that their last sight on earth was the clock tower directly ahead of them, announcing the time of their death.

For this reason, Venetians never walk between the columns. There is even a local saying that roughly translates to "I'll show you what time it is!" meaning, if you cross me, you too will be looking at the clock tower.

20.
The Jewish Ghetto

Did you know the word *ghetto* is Italian? Not just Italian, it's actually a *Venetian* word. *Ghèto* was Venetian dialect for 'foundry', and this was the site of the metal foundry. In 1434, the foundry became too small for the Republic's military needs, so they moved it to a bigger space. The area became a residential neighborhood known as the *Ghèto Novo*, or New Ghetto.

On 29 March 1516, Doge Leonardo Loredan gave the Jews this quarter, the *Ghèto* Nuovo. Until then, Jews could operate businesses in Venice, but they hadn't been allowed permanent residence. Even though they had been in Venice since at least the 11th century, they hadn't been permitted to have their own neighborhood. Initially, 700 Jews moved into this small area. They had their own neighborhood, could practice their faith, and were afforded protection in the event of war.

It was either a barbaric act, (by keeping Jews locked into a small area), or it was a business negotiation, (giving them the right to establish permanent homes in Venice). By putting them in the ghetto, the Venetian Republic simultaneously excluded and included them. They *excluded* Jews from parts of Venetian life. (Their highly sought-after doctors could wear black hats, while all others wore a yellow badge or hat identifying them as non-Christian.) Yet they were *included* as part of the Venetian population. They were locked in at night, the perimeters watched over by guards that the Jewish community had to pay for themselves. This became the model for all future Jewish Ghettos. To me, it seems inhumane.

The rules posed a dilemma for Jewish travelling merchants. They had to stay in the already overpopulated ghetto, but there was no room for them. So the government gave permission for Jewish merchants temporarily staying and working in Venice to stay in an adjacent area called the *Ghèto Vecchio*. The Ghetto Vecchio (Old Ghetto) is actually newer than the Ghetto Nuovo (New Ghetto).

The Jewish community were confined to the ghetto for 300 years, until 11 June 1797, when Napoleon gave them their freedom, and allowed them to become regular Venetian citizens. Affluent Jews couldn't get out of the ghetto fast enough, buying up glorious, abandoned palazzi that the aristocracy could no longer afford to maintain. The poor, working class Jews remained in the ghetto. After 1797, things went quite well for the Jewish community in Venice until the fascist racial laws of September 1938 once again deprived them of their civil rights.

In September 1943, Italy stopped being an ally of Nazi Germany, and became an occupied country. The Nazis ordered the Jews be arrested and their property seized. Some escaped to Switzerland, others to southern Italy. Over 200 were sent to Auschwitz. (There is some discrepancy with the numbers, as they sent some Venetian Jews to Trieste, but of the approximately 250 Venetian Jewish human beings sent to the camps, only 8 survived.) There is a memorial plaque to the Venetian holocaust victims in the Campo del Ghetto Nuovo, close to a memorial sculpture created in 1979 by Lithuaninan-Jewish sculptor Arbit Blatas.

Intellectuals came from all over Europe, making the community a cosmopolitan cultural hub. Although the ghetto is only a small land mass, it was full of languages. The street signs, religious services and official documents were (and still are) in Hebrew, but German, Italian, Venetian, French and Spanish were spoken in the calli. By the mid-17th century, 4000 Hebrew books were printed in Europe, and a third of them were printed right here in Venice.

The small area of the ghetto made it necessary for the community to get vertical. Look closely and you'll notice something unusual about the buildings in this sestiere –the shape and height of the windows. With no space to build more homes, the only choice was to lower the ceilings and add additional floors.

There was also nowhere to build synagogues. Many Jews lived here during the 300 years that the restrictions on the Jewish Ghetto were enforced (until Napoleon's arrival in 1797), but there was never a single "Venetian Jewish" identity. Multiple Jewish populations lived here: German, Italian, Spanish, Portuguese, so one synagogue couldn't possibly represent all the differing branches of Judaism. So, after 12 years, the community began building synagogues *inside* residential buildings. From the exterior they are completely hidden.

The five synagogues in the ghetto each represented specific ethnic sectors:

- The Scuola Grande Tedesca –German Jews
- The Scuola Italiana –Italian Jews
- The Scuola Spagnola –Spanish and Portuguese Jews
- The Scuola Levantina –Levantine Sephardi
- The Scuola Canton may have been a private synagogue, also serving the Venetian Ashkenazi community.

The synagogues are fascinating and beautiful, and they give you an entirely new understanding of the ghetto's history. They can only be visited with a Jewish guide from the community. Guided tours of the synagogues are available in three languages: Italian, French, and English.

The Jewish Ghetto is a popular tourist attraction, and a vibrant and exciting part of town. Here you'll find some tremendous eateries, including a fabulous Jewish bakery. Only Jews are permitted to live in the ghetto today, and fewer than 500 Jews still live here, but they, along with 100,000 annual visitors to the synagogues, keep the quarter feeling very much alive.

Hours: Sunday to Thursday, 10am—5.30pm (last English-speaking tour is at 3pm), Fridays from 10am—3pm (last tour at 2pm). Closed on Saturdays and all Jewish holidays.
Address: The Jewish Ghetto is in Cannaregio.

21.
Eleven Ghosts in the Floating City

Everything in Venice is just a little bit creepy, as much as it's beautiful.

–Christopher Moore

Mostly I'm in Venice in the summer when the evenings are long and languid. You stay out half the night, because you can't believe the beauty of this city, and how lucky you are to be here. Sometimes I visit in the winter, when night descends quickly, fog rolls in off the lagoon and the city suddenly turns ghostly. On winter evenings, the calli are deserted, streetlights flicker in the enveloping fog, and the city looks eerie (to someone like me with an overactive imagination).

I know my way around Venice pretty well, yet on foggy nights I can still get myself completely turned around. Even my usual haunts, like Campo Santo Stefano become unrecognizable when blanketed in gray. Apparition-like wisps of fog glide past, the flash of cold air on your neck feels like a ghostly breath, and the well in the middle of the campo, where you took selfies during the day, now fills you with an uncanny sense of foreboding. Venice is ripe for ghost stories.

You can take spooky guided ghost tours of Venice at night, which I highly recommend. You can't beat hearing a spine-chilling tale in a heavily Venetian accent while being led by someone who doesn't get lost. Especially on a foggy night.

Some of Venice's most haunted spots will absolutely give you the willies in broad daylight. So, let's go find some ghosts in the floating city.

1. Ca' Dario

Built in 1487, this beautiful marble and stone building on the Grand Canal fits in nicely with the neighboring palazzi, but it has a dark and mysterious past.

It was built by Giovanni Dario and was inherited by his daughter Marietta in 1494 after his death. After her husband went bankrupt and was stabbed to death, and her son died in a fight, Marietta killed herself. Since then, nearly every subsequent owner over the following five centuries has met with an unexpected or suspicious ending. Murders, suicides, 'accidents', violent circumstances, sudden illnesses, and bankruptcies have befallen residents of this palazzo, including a Count, a famous tenor and an American billionaire. In recent years, its ill-fated owners have included:

- Former owner British record producer and former manager of The Who, Christopher 'Kit" Lambert was pushed down a flight of stairs to his death. He reportedly told friends that he slept in a nearby gondolier kiosk to escape the ghosts that were haunting him in the palace.
- Fabrizio Ferrari, who bought the house in the 1980s and moved in with his sister Nicoletta. Shortly thereafter, he lost everything, and Nicoletta died in a car crash with no witnesses.
- Raul Gardini bought Ca' Dario from Ferrari in the late 1980s. He was involved in a corruption scandal and in 1993 committed suicide in circumstances that were never fully explained.
- In 2002, one week after vacationing at Ca' Dario, bass player John Entwhistle suffered a heart attack and died.

They call Ca' Dario "the most haunted house in the world", and "the house that kills". An inscription on the facade of the palace reads, *Urbis Genio Joannes Darius* (Giovanni Dario the Genius of the City). An anagram of this otherwise noble script reads, *Sub ruina insidiosa genero*, which translates to, "I bring treacherous ruin to those living under this roof".

Ca' Dario is easy to spot –it's gold and white. The three upper floors of the palace have four archways on the left, each with a circular window and one archway on the right. Some think beneath Ca' Dario there's an old Templar cemetery. If true, that could explain the horrendous bad luck of its owners.

Address: Campiello Barbaro 352, Dorsoduro
Vaporetto Stop: Midway between Accademia and Salute
What's Nearby: Salute Church, the Peggy Guggenheim, the Accademia.

2. Casino degli Spiriti

Lots of ghost stories take place in Cannaregio. Positioned facing the northern lagoon, where the winter mist is particularly thick and gray, Cannaregio feels extra eerie. Some say the fog is so dense because ghosts lurk in the shadows. Isolated on the edge of Cannaregio's outer coastline is a particularly haunted building, the Ghost Brothel or *Casino degli Spiriti.*

The 16th century Palazzo Contarini dal Zaffo stands proudly at the Fondamenta Gasparo Contarini in Cannaregio. Artists, philosophers and intellectuals hung out at the annex, a small ochre building below the garden, where they could gamble and frolic with prostitutes. The annex was ideal for romantic trysts and all out orgies. Tintoretto,

Veronese and Titian all hung out here. The palace and its annex were eventually abandoned.

Known to be cursed and haunted, religious cults would hold meetings here, invoking demons and spirits. There are stories of processions of torch-bearing monks in hooded robes silently walking along the path to the annex house. Some of their rituals said to have included torture and human sacrifice.

Casino degli Spiriti was then used as a hospital, where hundreds of Venetians died from the plague. Later it became a mortuary room where autopsies were performed. Plenty of tortured souls spent time here and several deaths have been associated with the Casino degli Spiriti. In 1929, they found four decapitated bodies here, each missing its right hand.

An early ghost story set here was of a nobleman's wife who was having an affair with his best friend. The nobleman found out, the best friend died, and the wife, wanting to die herself, moved into the annex with only her maid in attendance. As she watched over her lover's dead body, his ghost walked in, picked up the wife's corpse and ordered the maid to lead the way out with her lantern. At which point she fainted and remembered nothing more.

Another ghost said to haunt the annex is the painter Pietro Luzzo da Feltre. Luzzo fell in love with Cecilia, the model and lover of his fellow painter Giorgione. When she rebuffed his affections, Luzzo committed suicide. His ghost appeared in one of the windows the next night, prompting the owner to brick it up. He continued appearing in windows until they bricked them all over. Luzzo still returns on dark nights, his tormented screams echoing throughout the palace.

In 1947, Linda Civetta was murdered, dismembered, and submerged in a trunk, in front of the Casino degli Spiriti. She had come to Venice from her family's bar in Belluno to buy black market cigarettes and was carrying a large amount of money. The trunk containing her body was found a couple of weeks later. To this day, fishermen refuse to fish in front of the Casino degli Spiriti.

People have heard screams and rattling of chains here for centuries. (The sounds could also be caused by of the isolated position of the annex. The combination of the backwash and the winter winds can create a mournful howling and whistling sound.) Strange lights flicker in the dark here. The soil between the annex and the main palazzo is darker than all other soil in Venice. Cypress trees won't grow here –they all die (thought to be significant because Jesus' cross was made of cypress wood).

The annex house is perfectly positioned for smugglers, allowing them to slip in undetected under the veil of mist. Odd lights, noises, screams, and figures moving in the haze would have been the perfect way to scare away locals and law enforcement.

Address: Fondamenta Gasparo Contarini 3541, Cannaregio
What's Nearby: Madonna dell' Orto, the Jewish Ghetto, Vino Vero.

3. Poveglia Island

When an evil man dies, he wakes up in Poveglia.

Poveglia is an 18-acre, weed-ridden island near Lido. And is very, *very* haunted. So haunted, Venetians won't set foot on it. Fishermen keep a wide berth of this cursed island. It's actually illegal to go there. This island is one of the most haunted places on earth and it takes creepy to an entirely new level.

Poveglia was used as a quarantine island for the plague. The infected (and those just thought to be infected) were brought here to die a hideous death. If you showed symptoms, you were sent to Poveglia, where you were either shoved into the fires or the burial pits. People were buried and burned alive here along with the dead. Banishment to Poveglia was a death sentence. Many were dragged from their homes kicking and screaming, knowing their final days would be spent in hell on Earth. The tiny island is a giant burial ground of more than 160,000 people. Half of the soil composition is human remains.

In 1922, Poveglia was converted into an insane asylum, the perfect place to hide Venice's mentally ill. Patients reported seeing ghosts of plague victims and were kept awake at night by their tormented screaming. One of the doctors on the island did cruel experiments on patients, including performing crude labotomies with hand drills. He eventually went mad and threw himself from the bell tower, in what was either a suicide or prompted by the ghosts of the patients he had murdered. (He didn't die on impact, but later succumbed to his injuries, and I hope the ghosts were all watching and that he suffered mercilessly.) The asylum was closed in 1968 and the island once again became abandoned.

There have been ghost sightings on Poveglia for centuries. Several buildings still stand on the island –a *cavana* (boat shelter), a hospital, the asylum, housing for workers, a crematorium, a church and a 12th century bell tower. The island is uninhabited and very overgrown, and the buildings are in extreme disrepair. Squatters have left behind trash and graffiti. Drone footage shows creepy finger-like plants growing up and through the buildings. In fact, the plants alone look frightening. The bell was removed from the tower years ago, but locals say they still hear it tolling across the water. There was so much paranormal activity (or talk of it), the government declared Poveglia out of bounds.

TV shows such as *Ghost Adventurers* and *Scariest Places on Earth* have filmed here, and a quick YouTube search returns videos from people who have snuck onto the island and what they found there. One room has a metal rack where the mattresses of dead patients were hung to be cleaned before being reused. Other rooms have broken metal beds, baths, kitchen machinery and other forbidding looking mechanics. However, Police boats patrol the area and there's a heavy fine if you're caught on Poveglia.

I've never been to Poveglia, and I have zero intention of ever going anywhere near it. But I watched tons of videos while researching it for this book, several of which were pretty freaky. One in particular was made by two Brits called Finders Beepers History Seekers. I kid you not, I had only just read about the bell being removed from the tower, when I found their video on YouTube. Within minutes of them arriving on the island, you hear the bell tolling, and they're just going, "Oh listen, there's a bell," while I was shouting at my laptop, "Get out of there! Get off the island!"

Mass graves containing the remains of thousands of bodies were also discovered on two other quarantine islands nearby, Lazaretto Vecchio and Lazaretto Nuovo. The full extent of mass graves on Poveglia is not yet known.

Insider Tip: There are no public tours of Poveglia available. Visiting Poveglia is illegal. Just watch the YouTube videos instead. They're creepy enough.

4. The Ghost of Palazzo Grassi

Palazzo Grassi is a magnificent palace on the Grand Canal. The last great residence built on the Grand Canal, it is now the headquarters of the Foundation of Salma Hayek's husband, Francois Pinault, and contains a spectacular art museum. (See the **Museums** chapter.) The palazzo is also home to the ghost of a young girl, a somewhat recent resident who in the early 1900s threw herself (or was thrown) from a courtyard balcony to her death. She had reportedly been the victim of violence.

Museum employees say she is a good ghost and only shows herself to women, calling them by name. She comes up beside them and whispers their name into their ear. However, in the 1980s during renovations to the palazzo, a night watchman heard her shouting his name, urgently telling him to stop. He knew the palazzo by heart and was accustomed to walking it in the dark, but when he heard her shout, he stopped in his tracks. When he turned on his flashlight, he found that he was one step from falling through a huge hole in the floor. The ghost's warning had saved his life!

Address: Campo San Samuele 3231, Venice
Vaporetto Stop: San Samuele
What's Nearby: Opposite Ca'Rezzonico (across the canal), close to Chiesa San Samuele and Palazzo Malipiero.

5. The Bell Ringer & His Skeleton

After midnight, near the Basilica Santi Giovanni e Paolo in the Castello area you might see a giant begging for money. This is the ghost of the bellringer of the Campanile of San Marco. Fascinated by his excessive height, a Venetian scientist made this bellringer a deal –

he would give the man a large amount of money up front in exchange for the giant's skeleton upon his death.

Figuring he would outlive the scientist, the giant took the payment in advance, then went out every night, drinking himself silly. Before long, his excessive drinking brought on his premature death and the scientist collected his prize, the giant's skeleton. (The bellringer's skeleton now resides in Venice's natural History Museum. At approximately 7 feet, he was, in fact, extremely tall.) It is said that after his death, the bellringer bitterly regretted making the deal and to this day, haunts the Bressana Court next to Basilica SS Giovanni e Paolo, begging for money, hoping to get enough to buy back his skeleton.

Another version of the legend of the giant says he leaves the museum at night and walks to Piazza San Marco to go up the tower and ring the 12 bells of midnight, then walks home to Corte Bressana in Castello (next to SS Giovanni e Paolo), begging for money along the way to buy back his skeleton.

Address: Campo SS Giovanni e Paolo
Vaporetto Stop: Ospedale
What's Nearby: The hospital, Libreria Aqua Alta, Rosa Salva.

6. The Usurer's Burning Skeleton

While we are on the subject of skeletons, let's hop back over to Cannaregio to the Campo de l'Abazia. If you're there at night, look for an old man with a sack on his back. He'll beg you to help him, but don't. If you do, legend says he will turn into a burning skeleton, and you will die of fright on the spot.

This is the usurer (money lender) Bartolomeo Zenni, a miserly scrooge. On 13 May 1437, a horrific fire broke out in Campo de l'Abazia. Zenni refused to help his neighbors who were desperately trying to save their children from the flames. Instead, he escaped into the night with his sack of gold and jewels, forever condemning his soul to walk the campo and burst into flames.

Address: Campo de l'Abazia
Vaporetto Stop: Fondamente Nove
What's Nearby: Ponte Chioda, the Abbazia della Misericordia and the Casino degli Spiriti.

7. The Ghost of Campiello del Remer

Another haunting in Cannaregio, this time in the Campiello Remer near Rialto. At night, near the Mercato Rialto and along the Rio dei Gesuiti, watch for the chilling sight of Fosco Loredan emerging from the water with his wife's head in his hands.

Sixteenth century nobleman Fosco Loredan was jealous of his beautiful wife Elena, the niece of Doge Marino Grimani. One night the doge heard a woman screaming, chased by a man with his sword drawn. The doge ran after them into the Campiello del Remer but wasn't quick enough, arriving to find Loredan holding the severed head of the lovely Elena. The doge restrained himself from beheading Loredan on the spot, instead ordering him to take Elena's head to Rome and beg the pope's forgiveness. For five long months the pope refused to see Loredan, so he returned to Venice (with Elena's head), went to the Campiello and drowned himself in the Grand Canal.

Address: Campiello del Remer
Vaporetto Stop: Fondamente Nove
What's Nearby: Ponte Chioda, the Rialto Market and Ca' d'Oro.

8. The Ghost of Marco Polo's Chinese Wife

While in China, Venetian explorer Marco Polo fell in love with one of the Great Khan's daughters. She was sweet and lovely, and he married her and brought her back home. But his wife never felt comfortable in Venice and was victimized by Marco's jealous sisters. In 1298, when Marco Polo was captured by the Genoese, the evil sisters told Marco's wife he had been killed. Devastated, she set fire to her clothes and leapt from the window into the canal below. Legend says that at night, from the Milion Courtyard (where Marco Polo's houses were), you can see her ghost floating by and hear her singing a Chinese song. Although there is little documentation to corroborate this story, a few years back while renovating the Malibran Theater (built on Marco's old house) they found human remains belonging to an Asian woman, along with items of Chinese origin, a tiara and an Imperial coat.

Address: Corte Secondo del Milion
Vaporetto Stop: Rialto Bridge
What's Nearby: Chiesa Santa Maria dei Miracoli, and the Malibran Theater.

9. The Ghost of Giuseppina Gabriel Carmelo

On foggy nights, a small coffin with a candle lit on each of its four corners floats close to the island of San Michele (the cemetery island). It was a densely foggy night when a vaporetto collided with a gondola on 29 November 1904. Several people drowned, including a little girl name Giuseppina Gabriel Carmelo, whose body was never found. Her coffin appears on foggy nights so that Giuseppina can warn the boatmen, ferries, and barges, making sure they don't hit her again.

10. Tosca, the Bride of Castello

Walking across Campo San Piero in Castello late at night and watch for the ghost of a young bride. This is Tosca, looking for her ring finger (with her wedding ring attached). Tosca was a beautiful but very poor girl from Treviso, who was betrothed to a much older, very rich nobleman. She fell in love with a young hunter, and they escaped to Venice, where the nobleman tracked them down, killed the hunter, and cut off Tosca's ring finger, shouting that if he couldn't have her nobody could. On 22 September 1379, Tosca killed herself and to this day her ghost wanders the streets of Castello in her wedding dress, looking for her missing finger.

Address: Campo San Piero, Castello
Vaporetto Stop: San Pietro di Castello
What's Nearby: Arsenale, the Giardini della Biennale, Salvmeria.

11. The Ghost of Ca' Mocenigo

Giordano Bruno was a 16th century Dominican Friar. He was a philosopher, mathematician, poet, and cosmological theorist. Bruno believed the earth revolved around the sun, a theory the Catholic church opposed. In 1576 while living in Naples, Bruno angered the Catholic Church and fled north, where he lived in Geneva and then France, safely under the protection of King Henry III. In August 1591, he made the fatal mistake of accepting Giovanni Mocenigo's invitation to return to Venice. Before long, Mocenigo, unhappy with his private tutoring from Bruno and offended that Bruno planned to return to Frankfurt, denounced him to the Inquisition. The Venetian part of his trial looked favorable for Bruno but in January 1593 he was extradited to Rome, where he was labeled a heretic and burned at the stake. There is a statue commemorating Bruno in Rome's Campo dei Fiori.

Bruno gets revenge on Giovanni Mocenigo by haunting his palace. Each year on 17 February, the anniversary of his death, Bruno returns to Ca' Mocenigo to cause all manner of water-related mayhem (presumably because water was the element that could have saved him at the stake). The palace has experienced everything, from bursting water pipes, screws coming loose and valves opening inexplicably. Along with the unexplained water events, the face of Bruno, engulfed in flames, can be seen from the upper right window. He only shows himself to women.

Address: Sestiere di Santa Croce 1992
Vaporetto Stop: San Stae
What's Nearby: Ca' Pesaro, the Natural History Museum, Ponte delle Tette,

22.
Twelve Churches to Visit in Venice

Venice has always fascinated me. Every country in Europe then was run by kings and the Vatican except Venice, which was run by councils. I've always wondered why.

–Alan Furst

You might be thinking, "Meh, I don't want to see any churches …" But here's a secret about churches in Italy –the country's greatest artists painted artworks for church interiors, the greatest sculptors were hired to make statues, the greatest craftspeople created floors and ceilings and woodwork and mosaics. Churches in Italy are collections of masterpieces. The history of fashion and beauty is here on the walls. Artists painted their subjects in the styles of their day - you seldom see anyone wearing Jesus shoes. A fresco painted in 1480 will show you the clothes worn that year. A biblical story painted in 1625 shows fabrics, colors and hairstyles being worn in 1625. You can see the perception of beauty as it evolved through the centuries. From hairstyles to face shapes to body language, it's fascinating.

Regardless of your religion, your branch of religion, or your lack of religion, drop in on at least a couple of churches wherever you are in Italy. At worst, you'll turn around and walk back out. At best, you'll see incredible artwork, gain insight into the history of the town you're in and the story of its people.

Venice has 159 churches. Some are de-consecrated and repurposed; others are still calling to the faithful. If you visit a church in Venice (except for Basilica San Marco), you'll generally escape the tourists and find yourself in a cool, tranquil environment with a moment to breathe.

My goal with this chapter is to make you aware of 12 churches I wouldn't want you to miss. Maybe a couple will intrigue you enough to add them to your Venice itinerary. I'm hoping that if you get lost in Venice (it happens all the time) and you find yourself outside one of these churches, you might recognize the name from this book, and pop inside.

Most Italian churches are operational churches, which means you can't snap photos of the artwork during mass. It also means you can't enter the church wearing hotpants and a boob tube –your shoulders and thighs must be covered. (This doesn't have to be a problem. I carry a lightweight scarf with me to throw over my shoulders before I go in.)

Sometimes Venetian churches charge an entrance fee. This isn't paying for time with Jesus, it's to help offset some of the maintenance costs associated with mass tourism. If you're an art fan, those churches are where you will find the most extraordinary collections of Tintorettos, Veroneses and Titians, along with other genius Venetian painters. And you'll usually have them to yourself, or just a few others.

In this chapter, I'm not going to include Basilica San Marco, the Redentore, or any other churches that pop up in other chapters of this book. Instead, I'd like to tell you about a handful of my other favorites, starting in San Polo, working our way up through Dorsoduro, then through Castello, Cannaregio and San Marco.

1. Santa Maria Gloriosa dei Frari

The Frari is the largest church in Venice and has a tremendous wow factor.

In 1231, Doge Jacopo Tiepolo donated this little patch of marshy land to the Franciscan order of Friars (Frari) Minor to build themselves a church. Construction began in 1250 and finished in 1338. That church was too small, so work began on this current one almost immediately, taking more than a century to build. The campanile was completed in 1396, and they added the Chapel of San Marco in 1420, and the Chapel of San Pietro (next to the bell tower) between 1432 and 1434. On 17 May 1492, the church was consecrated and named Santa Maria Gloriosa.

Don't be put off by the somewhat plain facade. The Franciscans built it in 1440 and they liked simplistic exteriors. Compared to other local architecture, I always think this place looks very solid and staid, almost anchored into the marshy ground below it. There is nothing lacy or refined about this.

Inside, this church is soaring. It's huge and feels vertical. Twelve columns representing the twelve apostles divide the nave from the aisles, but while grand, they are also somehow unassuming, making it feel like one giant room. The vaulted ceilings are strengthened by huge tie-beams, keeping the church stable in a city that is technically sinking.

There's a lot to see here, so let's isolate just a few things.

A large white marble pyramid grabs your attention as you enter. This is the tomb of Venetian sculptor Canova. Like the church, this monument to the artist is enormous. Much bigger than Michelangelo's tomb in Florence, a fact which has always intrigued me.

The 124 dark wood monk's choir stalls in the center of the church are magnificent. These are the originals from 1468.

Many of the city's most celebrated are buried in the Frari, including several doges and the painter Titian. Their wall monuments are important works in Venice's history of sculpture and are well worth your time.

Don't miss Donatello's wooden sculpture of *St John the Baptist* from 1438. Donatello only created this one work for Venice.

In the sacristy Bellini's masterpiece, the triptych of the Madonna and Child with saints Nicholas of Bari, Peter, Mark and Benedict, painted in 1488, is magnificent.

Titian's *Pesaro Madonna* (1519—1526) was named for Jacopo Pesaro, the fellow in red kneeling at St Peter's feet. There's lots going on in this painting, but I'm always transfixed by the boy looking out at us. This is Pesaro's nephew Leonardo. You can't miss him –he's the only one looking directly at us and his face is bathed in beautiful light. You have to wonder what he is thinking. It's as if he just happened to glance our way and Titian caught him.

Above the high altar, Titian's *Assumption* (1516) dominates the church. This is the largest altarpiece in Venice and was possibly his first commission. It is also one of his greatest masterpieces, which is reason enough to cross Venice to see it. (Plus, the Frari is close to everything –it's not out of your way at all.)

Address: Campo dei Frari, San Polo 3072,
Vaporetto Stop: San Toma'
What's Nearby: Rialto Dridge, the Ponte delle Tette, San Pantalon.

2. Chiesa San Rocco

Just wow, wow, *wow*! Two minutes away from the Frari you'll find the elaborate white facade of the Chiesa San Rocco. Unlike the Frari, this church is resplendent with statuary and interesting shapes. Before going inside, make sure you stop to admire the exterior. Built between 1489 and 1508, it had a massive renovation in 1725, and got its fancy new frontage in 1765. Chiesa San Rocco is one of Venice's plague churches.

So who is Saint Roch?

Roch (Rocco in Italian) was born in Montpellier, France in 1348. He made a pilgrimage to plague-ravaged Rome, where he devoted himself to caring for plague victims. Rocco caught the plague in Piacenza, but survived it, adding to his celebrity. He achieved fame by performing miracles on the plague sick. Not only is he the patron saint against plagues and pestilence, but also invalids, dogs, the falsely accused, and a bunch of cities.

There are several versions of the story of his death. The most interesting has him returning to Montpellier, where his uncle was governor. The uncle didn't recognize him, thought he was a spy, and threw him in jail for five years, where he died. His true identity wasn't discovered until after his death, where it was confirmed by a birthmark in the shape of a cross.

He died on 16 August in (depending on which story you're going with) 1376 or 79, and is celebrated every year on 16 August when the doge would make a pilgrimage to this church for Roch's feast day. Saint Roch's relics have been in this church since 1485.

The Church

This church is spectacular. It has some magnificent art, but first I want to draw your attention to three massive Tintorettos, each measuring around 7.5 feet (230cm) by 21 feet (670cm). They are *Saint Roch Healing the Animals, Capture of Saint Roch at the Battle Of Montpellier* and *Saint Roch in the Wilderness.* This church is fantastic but wait until you see what comes next.

The Scuola San Rocco

This one probably should be in the **Museum** chapter, but I don't like to separate it from its next-door neighbor, the church. They're part of the same story. The Scuola Grande di San Rocco is a lay confraternity started in 1478 and still going strong today.

What are the Scuole?

In the 13th century, lots of lay confraternities popped up in northern Italy. They weren't churches, they were more like charitable organizations. By 1552 there were six in Venice, called the Scuole. Their members weren't nobles, these were middleclass working men. The rules specified they must live in Venice and work in trades and professions. Otherwise excluded from running the Republic (the nobles held all the political power), through the scuole the working class had a prestigious role in local society.

The scuole's good works included everything from organizing festivities and processions, handing out clothing, food and money to the poor, providing dowries for daughters of the poor, burying paupers, and supervising hospitals. They created a welfare system safety net to catch not only their members but eventually the entire population of Venice. They did charitable works and had a tremendous influence on the development of music. At the beginning of the 16th century, they had the first groups of musicians playing bowed instruments. The players became known as the Violoni.

Due to the almost cult-like following of Saint Roch, the Scuola San Rocco was the richest confraternity in Venice. They built a huge headquarters next to the church and hired Tintoretto to decorate it. This is where you find his most celebrated pictorial cycle. There are over 60 paintings, preserved in their original settings. They tell stories from the old and new testaments. It is breathtaking.

There is so much to see here, so I recommend getting the audio guide. The ceilings alone are beyond belief. Rather than have you break your neck looking upwards, at this scuola they give you large handheld mirrors. You'll see people walking around listening to their audio guides and looking down into their mirrors at the art on the ceiling. Put this place on your must-see list.

Of the seven scuole, San Rocco is the only one still active today. They are known for their extraordinary patronage of the arts.

Address: San Polo 3053
Vaporetto Stop: San Toma'
What's Nearby: The Frari, San Pantalon, Rialto.

3. San Pantalon

I find the lines demarking one sestiere from another as elusive as the mist floating through Venice at night. You'd think San Pantalon was in San Polo as it's so close to the Frari, but somewhere between the two we cross San Polo into the Dorsoduro.

The exterior of this church is entirely unremarkable, so much so that most tourists walk right past. But you my friend, are about to discover one of Venice's hidden gems.

San Pantalon is one of the seven saints of Venice. Born in Nicomedia in around 265AD he studied medicine and was part of the *santi anargiri* (without money), in his case practicing medicine for free. He may have been at one time the doctor to either Emperor Galerius or Maximian, until he healed a paralytic by calling on Jesus for help, and in doing so openly declared his Christian faith. At the time Christianity was illegal, so Emperor Diocletian had him put to death.

The first church was built on this site in 1161. It was rebuilt and consecrated in 1305. Originally facing Ca' Foscari, they rotated it 90 degrees to face the campo during another rebuild in 1668. Money ran out before the baroque facade was built, but you can see the holes in the front wall where the marble was going to be attached.

The interior has over 80 spectacular works of art by Veronese, Paolo Veneziano, Pietro Longhi,Antonio Vivarini and Jacopo Palma il Giovane. It also contains the largest canvas painting in the world, Giovanni Antonio Fumani's absolutely unbelievable *Martyrdom and Glorification of San Pantalon* (1680—1704). The 443 square-meter painting covers the entire ceiling. Supposedly, upon completion of the work, Fumani fell from the scaffolding and died.

Address: Dorsoduro 3703
Vaporetto Stop: San Toma'
What's Nearby: The Frari, Ca' Foscari and Campo Santa Margherita.

4. San Sebastiano

On a scorching summer day in 2018, when the cruise ships lined up like destroyers, and Venice was saturated with tourists, I happened upon this church while attempting to escape the crowds. I went inside (because why not?) and was amazed. I had accidentally stumbled upon three decades' worth of ceiling to floor masterpieces by Veronese. (It's the single best collection of his work in one place.) On top of that, I was the only one there! The church was under partial restoration at the time, and the restorers were so thrilled that I was excited, they took turns showing me their favorite pieces and telling me the stories behind them. From their facial expressions to their excited gestures, I could tell they were sharing something of great importance to them, even if I couldn't quite make out all the words. It's always thrilling when someone takes the time to passionately explain a piece of history to you.

There are also works by Titian and Tintoretto, but this is considered a monument to the work of Paolo Veronese.

Built between 1506 and 1548, San Sebastiano is one of the five votive churches of Venice, each built to celebrate the passing of a plague. Exuberant in white marble with statues and angels and gold detail everywhere, San Sebastiano is everything you would hope an Italian church would be, an absolute feast for the eyes. (But good Lord, *that art*! It's like having a secret piece of Venice all to yourself. And really, you do. Even when the city is packed with tourists, you'll have San Sebastian either to yourself, or shared with nly a few other souls.)

Address: Campazzo San Sebastiano, Dorsoduro
Vaporetto Stops: San Basilio on the Zattere side or Ca' Rezzonico from the Grand Canal side

What's Nearby: San Pantalon, the Zattere, Campo Santa Margherita.

5. Santa Maria della Salute

This is one of the most important baroque buildings in Venice. Standing guard over the Grand Canal, Salute (*sah-loo-teh*) is one of the most iconic landmarks of the city. Watching its ethereal white glow during the evening Blue Hour, you'll be convinced Salute is either a piece of magic or a creation from the hand of God. From the water it comes into view as you pass Ca' Rezzonico heading into the final bend of the canal. No matter how many times you've seen it, no matter how many times you've traveled this same route, the sight of this church will leave you thunderstruck.

In 1630, a particularly devastating outbreak of the plague killed 33% of the Venetian population. The Republic made a deal with God: end the plague and we will build you a church and dedicate it to the Virgin. The plague ended abruptly, and the doge allocated a prestigious plot of land at the narrow finger of the Dorsoduro between the Grand Canal and the Giudecca Canal. Everyone entering the city would see this monument celebrating the end of the plague in all its staggering glory. They named it Santa Maria della Salute, Our Lady of Health (or Deliverance).

Designed by Baldassare Longhena, the architect responsible for Ca Rezzonico and Ca' Pesaro, construction on Salute began in 1631 and completed in 1681, a year before Longhena's death. Instead of a normal linear style, he designed the church in the shape of a rotunda, possibly resembling Mary's crown. It also bears similarities to Palladio's work at the Redentore with its classic Roman feel, while keeping in harmony with the other domes of Venice. Check out the floors too –they are wonderful.

Most of the statues and art reference the plague. The interior is clean and bright and filled with healing white light. The church is full of Mary's symbolism. The dome represents her crown, the round interior her womb, and the eight sides of the octagon, the eight points on her star. From the octagon, eight chapels circle the church.

To the right of the main doors, three chapels each have scenes from Mary's life, painted by Luca Giordano, *The Presentation of Our Lady in the Temple, The Assumption* and *the Nativity.* The Baroque high altar designed by Longhena, has a Byzantine Madonna and Child and a group of statues called *The Queen of Heaven Expelling the Plague,* by Flemish sculptor Josse de Corte. Tintoretto's *Marriage at Cana* is in the main sacristy. Salute is full of Titians, including the *Descent of the Holy Ghost* in the third chapel on the left. From the ceilings to the tondi to other paintings, Titian is everywhere.

After all the linear churches in Venice, this one is charmingly odd. It is beautiful and feels vast and empty. I always mean to attend a service here, just to see how it works when its full of pews and people.

One last fun fact about Salute –several years ago, a statue fell from the exterior, leading Arrigo Cipriani, the owner of Harry's Bar and the Cipriani Hotel to post a sign outside: *Beware of Falling Angels,* which inspired John Berendt to name his book *The City of Falling Angels.*

Address: Dorsoduro 1
Vaporetto Stop: Salute
What's Nearby: The Punta della Dogana, the Peggy Guggenheim. The Zattere runs the length of the opposite side of the church.

6. San Zaccaria

This beautiful church is full of masterpieces from artists including Giovanni Bellini, Tintoretto, Tiepolo and van Dyck. Its harmonious facade with curved gables and arched windows is just a short walk from the Basilica San Marco.

Founded in the 7th century then rebuilt in the 9th and 12th centuries after a fire killed 100 nuns, the church holds the relics of Saint Zacharius, father of St John the Baptist. Donated by Byzantine Emperor Leo V in the early 800s, the relics are under the second altar on the right. The current church was begun in 1444 and completed in 1515, its retro Gothic style cleverly masked by architect Mauro Codussi's Istrian stone facade. Look for lunettes and seashell reliefs, disguising the original Gothic naves. Another special feature of this church is the ring of elliptical cupolas with their long, narrow windows. San Zaccaria is the only Venetian church built in this French and Northern Italian Gothic style.

The paintings in this church are spectacular. The most famous is Giovanni Bellini's luminous and magical *Pala di San Zaccaria* (*The Madonna and Four Saints.*) in the second chapel on the left. Bellini painted this masterpiece in 1505 when he was 74 years old. Originally painted on a wooden panel, it was stolen by Napoleon and moved to Paris, but returned 20 years later. The wood was warping and rotting, so they transferred the painting to canvas. (This is an extremely laborious and delicate job, where they plane off wood from the back until only the paint and a minute layer of wood remain.)

Some of the other sensational art works include the tomb and self-portrait bust of one of Venice's most celebrated sculptors, Alessandro Vittoria (1528—1608). The Cappella di Sant' Atanasio has an early Tintoretto, *The Birth of St John the Baptist.*

The nuns of San Zacaria built the chapel, using both private and public funds. These nuns were of noble birth, some were the daughters and sisters of doges. These wealthy nuns patronized the arts, in the 15th century, decorating their original church and then building a new church alongside it, supervising the work themselves.

The Tarasio Chapel was the presbytery and apse of the old nuns' church. Rebuilt in 1440, it housed the relics, including those of Saint Zacharius, before becoming a private chapel for the nuns. Look for fragments of the original 9th century tile floors under glass at the back of the chapel, and some from the 12th century are in front of the altar. The Tarasio Chapel ceilings have fabulous frescoes painted in 1442 by Andrea del Castagno. Castagno was a Florentine and painted this work half a century before the Renaisssance took hold in Venice. So, these art loving nuns were way ahead of their time. If you can, try to identify St Luke in the fresco. He is a self-portrait of the painter.

There are three well preserved gilded altarpieces by Antonio Vavarini and Giovanni d' Alemagna. The center three panels on the high altarpiece are signed and dated by Stefano di Sant' Agnese in 1385.

The left wall has a Polyptych of Saint Sabina, and the right wall a Polyptych of the Body of Christ, signed by Antonio Vivarini and Giovanni d'Alemagna in 1443. All of this art was paid for by wealthy nuns, Elena Foscari (sister of the reigning doge) Marina and Margherita Dona' and Agnesina Giustiniani.

Stairs lead down to the flooded 10th century crypt where the bodies of eight doges lie underwater. Restoration plans for the crypt include draining it and finding out what is under the concrete floor.

While you're there ...

Campo San Zaccaria is a wonderful place to escape the crowds in Piazza San Marco and outside the Doge's Palace.

In the northwest corner, a plaque from 1620 outlines activities prohibited here. Under grave penalty, you must not gamble, argue, curse or fight in Campo San Zaccaria.

The nuns at the convent stitched the distinctive *corno ducale* caps worn by the doges. On 13 September 864, the first doge to come and collect his cap, Doge Pietro Tradonico, was ambushed and stabbed to death in the campo after attending vespers at the San Zaccaria church. Another doge was murdered in Campo San Zaccaria, in May of 1172. Doge Vitale Michiel II was accused of destroying almost all the Venetian fleet and of bringing the plague back to Venice. Trying to escape the angry mob, he ran for the safety of the nunnery in the campo, but was stabbed in the Calle della Rasse, shortly before arriving.

Address: Campo San Zaccaria 4693
Vaporetto Stop: San Zaccaria
What's Nearby: The Riva degli Schiavoni, the Doge's Palace and Piazza San Marco.

7. San Francesco della Vigna

This is just around the corner from my apartment in Castello. My first time there, my landlady pointed to the leaning campanile of the church. This, she told me, is your lighthouse. When you get lost (and you will), the campanile of Francesco della Vigna will guide you home. And it has been guiding me home ever since. If not for staying around the corner, I would probably never have stumbled upon this church. It is one of Venice's least trafficked and most under-appreciated treasures.

Legend says St Mark washed ashore here during a storm. An angel told him the lagoon would be his final resting place, and a city would rise from the water with him its protector. (Take that with a grain of salt –his bones weren't hijacked and brought here until centuries later.)

It began as a small chapel in a vineyard –the *della Vigna* part of the name. In 1253 the Francescan's built a new church here, which is the San Francesco part. In 1534, 300 years later, Doge Andrea Gritti laid the first stone in a new Renaissance style church. The church was designed by Jacopo Sansovino, but his facade plans never saw completion. Doge Gritti died and was succeeded by Doge Giovanni Grimini who paid Palladio to design a beautiful facade in Istrian stone. Consequently, the exterior of this magnificent church looks more Redentore than the neighboring churches. This was Palladio's first completed ecclesiastical commission, and became a prototype for all that followed, including the Redentore.

The church is in a large campo with a Roman-looking columned portico. I always see groups of artists sitting beside the portico, painting the lovely buildings across the little rio San Francesco della Vigna. This is a secret, picturesque corner of Venice. Other than artists, residents, and me, the only people you'll run into here are nuns, on their way to wherever nuns go.

There is a crazy amount of amazing art inside this church, but it's well spaced out, so you don't feel overwhelmed. There's a beautiful Battisto Franco fresco of *Il Semolei* and an *Adoration of the Magi* by Federico Zuccari, Paolo Veronese's first Venetian commission, *The Virgin and Child Enthroned with Young John the Baptist and Saints Catherine and Anthony Abbot* (1551), and another pre 1584 Veronese, *the Resurrection.* Also noteworthy is a spectacular 1507

Madonna and Saints by Bellini and an unusual *Virgin and Child Enthroned* by Antonio da Negroponte from 1478. It's quite eccentric, with lots going on, and Jesus looks like he's about to fall off Mary's lap, but she's too busy doing prayer hands to notice. This one is also interesting because it's a rare example of an altarpiece where the Madonna and Child are not accompanied by saints. By 1300, it was normal to paint the saints with them.

Look for 15th century sculpting work by Pietro and Tullio Lombardo. Their bas reliefs depicting the life of Christ and saints are incredible. I'm fascinated with how they made it look like a breeze was blowing through the trees. In marble no less.

Save Venice has done much of the restoration work here, and if you're interested in art, it's worth checking out this church on their website, where they itemize and explain everything they've restored here to date.

The Priuli Chapel in the left transcept, has the stone upon which Sant Giustina knelt for her martydom, and a glass case with the body of Saint Cristina, martyred in 297AD at the age of 13. Her relics were transferred to San Francesco della Vigna in 1810 when the church of St Giustina was suppressed by Napoleon.

Address: Campo San Francesco 2786
Vaporetto Stop: Celestia
What's Nearby: Jonny's, one of the best kept secret restaurants in Venice, is a two-minute walk from here, Campo Santa Maria in Formosa and Campo SS Giovanni e Paolo are close too.

8. Basilica SS Giovanni e Paolo (San Zanipolo)

This was the Dominican's big church in Venice. This land was gifted to the Dominicans in around 1230. Their first church was too small, so they started building this much bigger one in the early 1300s. It wasn't finished until 1430. The marble portal was installed in 1458 but the rest of the planned marble facade was never completed, leaving it in unfinished brick. It looks quite odd next to the beautiful marble clad exterior of the adjacent Scuola San Marco (the hospital).

Rather than being named for the two apostles, the basilica is named for two random, obscure soldier-saints, also called John and Paul. Look for them in the stained-glass window with Saints George and Theodore. This church is often referred to as the Venetian Pantheon, due to the high number of doges buried here –Giovanni e Paolo has 25 dead doges, as well as Gentile Bellini (1507) and Giovanni Bellini (1516).

The doge's tombs on the front facade walls now serve as goal posts for local little boys playing soccer.

The massive, cross-vaulted interior has immense columns and wooden tie beams holding it all up. Similar to the Frari, but without the wooden choir, it seems much bigger and airier. They made the stained-glass windows on Murano and they are rare examples from that era. Of course, there's art inside too, but people mainly come here to see the spectacular tombs of the doges.

In this church, 25 doges celebrate themselves posthumously. After the 15th century, all doge funerals were held here too. Each tomb has its own statues, paintings, altars, and bas reliefs. Doges were elected from noble families, so each had centuries-long, distinguished lineage in Venice, and oodles of cash to show it off with.

The tombs of the three Mocenigo doges are huge, sculpted works of art. Sculpted by Pietro Lombardo and his sons Tullio and Antonio, Doge Pietro Mocenigo's tomb alone is worth coming to see. Pietro was a military man, so rather than saints and virgins, his tomb is carved with pagan war imagery, (other than a relief of *The Three Mary's at Sepulchre* the top).

In 1867, a huge fire here burned priceless artworks including paintings from the 15th and 16th centuries. Paintings by Bellini, Tintoretto and Titian were lost.

You must come to the Campo SS Giovanni e Paolo regardless of whether or not you want to go inside the church. The campo is gorgeous, and the hospital is ridiculously beautiful. Sitting outside at Rosa Salva with a coffee and a pastry, or a glass of wine and some tremezzini, watching life go by is one of life's simple joys.

Address: Campo SS Giovanni e Paolo
Vaporetto Stop: Opedale
What's Nearby: Rosa Salva, the hospital, the statue of Bartolomea Colleoni, Libreria Acqua Alta.

9. Chiesa dei Gesuiti

Walking past the ambulances parked diagonally along the Rio dei Mendicanti (which I do all the time because I am intrigued with the ambulance system in Venice), you end up at the Fondamente Nove. Turn left and wander a city block or so and you reach Santa Maria Assunta I Gesuiti, known as the Chiesa dei Gesuiti.

As spare as SS Giovanni e Paolo feels both inside and out, this church is a full-on explosion of over-the-top Baroque madness. Your eyes (and your brain) will not believe what they are seeing.

History

A religious order called the Crociferi (Cross Bearers) built the first Santa Maria Assunta on this site in 1155. There was a convent and a hospital caring for sick and wounded pilgrims, and crusaders. When the crusades finished in the 15th century, the hospital and convent took in elderly widows instead. There were fires and rebuilds in both the 13th and 16th centuries. Things were going quite swimmingly until 1656, when Pope Alexander VII suppressed the Crociferi.

In 1657, the complex was sold to the order of the Jesuits. The Jesuits had been kicked out of Venice in 1606 and forced to give up their church and school at Santa Maria dell'Umilita in Dorsoduro. Now Venice needed cash, so the Jesuits were allowed to return, providing they bought this complex on the outer edge of town. The noble Manin family, who have tombs here, paid for the reconstruction of the now crumbling church and for its magnificent facade. Meanwhile, the Jesuits were expelled again, this time for fighting with the pope over the right to prosecute priests who committed crimes. The old church was rebuilt in 1728, but when the Jesuits were supressed *again* in 1773, the monastery became a school. In 1804 Napoleon turned it into a barracks for his troops. In 1844 the Jesuits re-occupied the convent buildings to the north, while buildings to the south became student housing.

The Jesuits were never a popular brand in Venice. This no doubt propelled them into wanting to bamboozle the population with this completely outrageous visual banquet of a church. The wow factor here is *off the charts.*

The Church

The exterior is what you would expect for a Venetian Baroque church. The prevailing architectural theory seemed to be to put as much stuff on there as humanly possible, then add more. Consequently, this church on two levels is replete with columns and statues everywhere. They're in niches along the lower floor walls, above the columns along the second floor, and all over the roof. The exterior is crowded with statues.

Above the door, a giant Manin family coat of arms tells the world who paid for this church. (Imagine if they had known Ludovico Manin would be the Republic's last doge, who would hand over Venice to Napoleon.)

The Interior

Take a deep breath before crossing the threshold. You will not believe what you are about to see.

The Gesuiti is built to the Latin Cross style the Jesuits favored, with an aisle-less nave with three deep chapels on each side. The chapels are separated by plain pilasters –which are the only undecorated surfaces *in this entire church.* The details here are beyond breathtaking, from the ornate marble and stucco detailing to the rococco looking walls to the gold and grisaille ceilings. Look for marble inlay (intarsia) made to look like fabric, and more marble made to look like carpet in front of the high altar. And good Lord, the art! There are works here by Fontabasso and Dorigny, Titian and Tintoretto. The sacristy has twenty works by Jacopo Palma Il Giovane. The chancel is full of cherubs, angels and archangels sculpted by Giuseppe Torretti. The altar, designed by Fra Giuseppe Pozzo has ten swirling barley sugar Solomnic columns. There's a funerary monument by Jacopo Sansovino.

You'd feel like you'd stepped into some madman's fever dream if not for the fact that the inside of the Gesuiti feels light and bright and airy. It is just fantastic, and the crazy thing is, you'll find very few people here.

One last piece of information on the Gesuiti church. In 1973 it was one of the most endangered buildings in all of Venice when it looked like the back wall was about drop into the canal behind the church. Save Venice stepped in and stabilized and saved it over three years.

Visit the Gesuiti before jumping on the vaporetto to or from Murano at the Fondamente Nove C station. Fondamente Nove has wonderful little bars and restaurants along the waterfront, so you can pair visiting the Gesuiti with lunch or an aperitivo with a view.

Address: Campo dei Gesuiti, Cannaregio
Vaporetto Stop: Fondamente Nove A
What's Nearby: Midway between SS Giovanni e Paolo and our next church, Madonna dell'Orto, also close to Vino Vero.

10. Chiesa della Madonna dell' Orto

This is one of the most beautiful examples of Gothic architecture in Venice. In 1547, it became the parish church of one of Venice's most legendary painters, Tintoretto. His ashes are interred here (in the chapel to the right of the chancel), kept company by his wife and eight other family members. Madonna dell' Orto houses 11 paintings by the artist (only San Rocco has more). Also of note outside the church –look for the rare and beautiful herringbone pavement.

The History

The Umiliati built a church and monastery here in 1350, dedicated to St Christopher, the patron saint of travelers. Then, a Virgin Mary statue that had been commissioned for and rejected by the church in

Santa Maria Formosa, and which lay abandoned and languishing in a nearby orchard, supposedly started flashing lights and glowing, and (of course) performing miracles. The Scuola di San Cristoforo saw a money-making opportunity and bought the statue from the sculptor (Giovanni de Santi) for 150 ducats, which at the time was a huge amount of money. They knew having a miracle Mary *in situ* would increase donations needed for building work, so on 18 June 1377 they placed her on the high altar where she has remained ever since. The church became known as Madonna dell' Orto, or the Madonna of the Orchard.

In a hilarious turn of events in 1461, the Umiliati were run out of town by the Council of Ten for practicing depraved habits. (Can you even imagine what they must have been getting up to?!) A century later, in 1571, Pope Pius V suppressed the Umiliati order entirely.

Madonna dell' Orto then came under the stewardship of an order called The Canons of San Giorgio in Alga, also known as the Turchini because of the Turkish blue/green robes they wore. They were a religious order who didn't believe in building new churches, preferring instead to rehab old ones. They completed their restoration work in 1473. In 1669, the church was re-homed again, this time to the Cistercians, after Pope Clement IX suppressed the Canons. In 1787, only three monks remained in Madonna dell' Orto, so the Republic took over and the church became an oratory.

The church fell into disrepair, becoming a stable, a hay and wine store and even a place to store gunpowder. Under Austrian rule in 1841 terrible restorations destroyed ceiling paintings, ripped up memorial stones, destroyed the organ and even saw the facade plastered over. In 1868, it was reconsecrated and became a parish church. The ugly and ruinous restorations from the prior century were restored and fixed in 1930—31. Then the church suffered huge damage during the great floods of 1966. The church and its paintings were restored back to their former glory in the 1970s.

The Church

The interior is lovely, if simple. Rows of beautiful striped Turkish marble columns separate the aisle from the nave. The archaic capitals from the columns are from the original church. The ceiling is coffered wood, and like other churches of its size, the structure is held up with tie beams.

Four funerary chapels for four noble families line the left side: The Valier, Vendramin, Morosini and Contarini. The Renaissance Valier chapel used to have a small but priceless *Madonna and Child* by Bellini (from around 1480) which was stolen on 1 March 1993.

The Art

After the visual mayhem of the Gesuiti, Madonna dell' Orto is calmer, but it is home to some seriously incredible artwork, most famously the Tintorettos. In 1547 Tintoretto moved up the street to Fondamenta dei Mori. You can still see his house and make the same walk he did to church.

Look for the two monumental paintings flanking the altar. *The Adoration of the Golden Calf* and *The Last Judgement* were both painted around 1563, with portraits of Titian, Giorgione, Veronese and himself amongst the bearers of the golden calf. In 1565 Tintoretto also painted four of the *Five Virtues* in the vault, the fifth was painted in the 17th century by Pietro Ricchi.

There are also works here by Titian, Jacopo Palma Il Giovane and Cima da Conegliano amongst others.

The Campanile

The Campanile of the Madonna dell' Orto was built in 1332. They added the belfry in 1503. I love the eastern style onion dome and if you can zoom in close enough, you'll see a white marble "Christ the Redeemer" on top. Around the upper exterior are four statues of Evangelists from the Pietro Lombardo workshop. They restored the campanile in 1819 after a huge storm, and didn't replace the original 1424 bells until 1883.

When exploring Cannaregio, wander over here and have a look. It is a relatively short walk from the Gesuiti and is close to Vino Vero for an aperitivo, or Torrefazione for a coffee.

Address: Campo della Maddona dell'Orto, Cannaregio
Vaporetto Stop: Orto
What's Nearby: The Jewish Ghetto, Plum Plum Creations, Casino degli Spiriti.

11. Santa Maria dei Miracoli

The story of Santa Maria dei Miracoli starts with another miraculous Mary, one painted sometime around 1409. It was commissioned by a fellow named Francesco Amadi, who displayed it in a calle outside his home, and then, wouldn't you know it, miracles started happening –so many miracles that a chapel was erected to house the painting, funded with the cash people kept leaving as offerings to Miracle Mary.

Construction for a small chapel began in 1481 under the direction of Pietro Lombardo, but in 1485 Pope Sixtus IV granted permission for a larger church to be built instead. (It's still really small.) Both the exterior and the interior were clad with colorful blocks of marble interspersed with red and green prophyry. They built the exterior sides and back of the church along the canal with sturdier white Istrian stone. The exterior reminds me of Brunelleschi's love of form and balance and harmony. (If you read my Florence book, you'll know what I mean.) It is absolutely beautiful and quite, quite tiny.

With a master sculptor at the helm there are of course endless beautifully sculpted details, from the cornices to the arches around the windows, to the altar –everywhere you look you see works of art in stone, along with reliefs of prophets and saints probably created by Pietro Lombardo himself. The original Miraculous Mary painting still sits above the high altar. The church also has a coffered ceiling made of gilded and painted wood.

As lovely as the Miracoli looks today, it's hard to imagine her prior to the restoration project undertaken by Save Venice. Deterioration had set in, partly due to the proximity of the canal beside the church, partially due to air pollution and partly because of a terrible 19th century restoration. The marbles were blackened, mineral salts were leaching their way upward, and the iron supports were rusting and causing damage. During the 19th century repairs, marble panels were removed, and instead of being reattached using bronze rods as they had done in the 15th century, they were reattached with cement. Then the cement crumbled, exposing the brickwork of the church to the elements, and to salt seeping up the walls. The marble panels of the church began to swell and the future of the church looked perilous.

The rescue of the Miracoli by Save Venice took several years. Their website has lots of photos documenting the work. The research phase alone took years, as they had to use harmonic hammers to find the fissures in the building and computer technology to track the mold and salt damage. This was back in the 1990s, so computers weren't anywhere near as quick or efficient as they are now. The restoration was a multiyear project too. Each marble panel had to be removed and desalinated. Special baths were created to hold the panels, and instead of just hosing them off, each panel had to be soaked multiple times in distilled water to remove the salt.

While this was happening, the brickwork and stucco underwent extensive repair too. They replaced the rusting iron supports with steel one by one. Items that were crumbling were replaced with replicas, which had to be made from identical materials using the old techniques.

When you see the Miracoli, the magnitude of the job is staggering. Everything is made from marble panels. Once the walls were done, the ceiling had to be tackled, during which new frescoes were discovered.

Along with the restorations, the church has many intriguing elements to look at, from the Madonna and Child over the doorway to the statues and the bas reliefs around the exterior.

Tiny but mighty, Santa Maria dei Miracoli is one of my favorite churches in Venice.

Address: Campiello dei Miracoli
Vaporetto Stop: Fondamente Nove
What's Nearby: Campo SS Giovanni e Paolo, Libreria Acqua Alta, Chiesa di Santa Maria Miracoli

12 Santa Maria del Giglio

I wanted to add this sensational Baroque church partly because it is so outstanding, but also because whenever I am hanging out here a steady stream of tourists flows past, none of them seeing this absolute treasure hiding in plain sight. It is on the cruise passenger path between Rialto Bridge and Piazza San Marco, so I am steering you right into the storm, but trust me, it's worth it. Santa Maria del Giglio means Saint Mary of the Lily, the flower that Archangel Gabriel presents to Mary during the Annunciation. (It is also known as Santa Maria Zobenigo, for the Jubanico family, who founded the first church here in the 10th century.)

There were rebuilds in 966 and in 1105 after catastrophic fires, but they rebuilt the current version of this church in the last part of the 17th century. V

enetian noble Antonio Barbaro commissioned Guiseppe Sardi to create the facade of this masterpiece of Baroque theater in a grandiose tribute to himself, his accomplishments and his family. Don't expect to see Jesus & Co. on the façade — it's all Barbaro family. His four brothers take up the lower tier dressed according to the public offices they held, while Antonio had himself sculpted on the next level above the door. He surrounds himself with angels, either because it is, after all, a church, or maybe because he sees himself as exalted. The plinths under the Corinthian columns on Antonio's level depict battle scenes, while the ones on the lower-level show city plans for Antonio's military conquests, Zandar, Crete, Padua, Rome, Corfu and Split. It is completely nutty that this is on a church. But also serves as a spectacularly egotistical family album carved in Istrian stone. The facade is a masterpiece of Baroque architecture and is completely crazy.

Canaletto immortalized the church in his 1765 painting *Santa Maria Zobenigo*, but you can't get quite that angle anymore as the campo was built up sometime thereafter. In the painting you can see the original campanile of the church, which was demolished in 1774 when it began to lean too far.

The Interior

The interior is compact and has no center aisle. The artwork is dominated by 17th century artists, including the only Rubens in Venice. Kept behind bullet proof glass in the Molin Chapel the *Virgin and Child with the Young St John* is delightfully fleshy.

Tintoretto's son Domenico painted the ceiling in the Molin Chapel. There are Tintorettos in the church too, including an altarpiece of *Christ with Angels and Saints Justina and Francis of Paola*, and two pairs of Evangelists from 1577, which were inner panels from a destroyed organ case.

There is an imposing *Last Supper* by Giulio Del Moro on the inside front wall too.

Not for the squeamish, there are loads of reliquaries here with a collection of bones and such, including chunks of hair and other creepy things you probably don't want to investigate before lunch.

You'll walk past Santa Maria del Giglio when heading from Rialto or Campo Santo Stefano towards Piazza San Marco. Keep an eye out for it, and even if you don't make it inside, at least take some time to marvel at the tremendous Baroque facade, especially now that you know the crazy story behind it!

Address: Campo Santa Maria del Giglio, San Marco
Vaporetto Stop: Giglio
What's Nearby: Campo Santo Stefano, Piazza San Marco and the hidden door under the bridge.

23.
Nine Tremendous Museums in Venice

If you read a lot, nothing is as great as you've imagined. Venice is –Venice is better.

–Fran Lebowitz

Obviously, a city with so much fascinating history and an immense love of art and beauty is going to have absolutely outstanding museums, and Venice is full of them. Most are in former palaces, providing fabulous insight into the lives of centuries' worth of wealthy Venetians.

Even if you're not interested in museums, I suggest you still read this chapter –you may be surprised at what's here. Also, check online as there are many more fantastic museums in this lovely city. I've only included nine of my favorites here. You'll find four more in the **Piazza San Marco** chapter of this book (the Doge's Palace, the Clock Tower Museum, Museo Correr, and the Biblioteca Nazionale Marciana). I originally included the Peggy Guggenheim Museum in this chapter, but when you read the story of the Palazzo Venier dei Leoni, you'll see why it needed an entire chapter to itself.

The first two museums on this list are in Castello, 5 minutes' walk from Piazza San Marco. The Museo della Musica is just around the corner from Campo Santo Stefano, and all the others are along the Grand Canal.

1. Palazzo Grimani

This isn't everyone's favorite, but I love it, so it's where I'm starting. I found this museum by accident one day, wandering from Castello to Campo Santa Maria Formosa. By chance I looked along Ramo Grimani and went to investigate.

This palazzo is unique in Venice. It was the family home of Antonio Grimani, who became doge in 1521. He gave it to his grandsons Vettore and Giovanni, and the palazzo remained the property of the Santa Maria Formosa branch of the Grimani family until 1865.

The wow factor of Palazzo Grimani must have been astounding. Renovations in the 16th century added two wings, creating a central courtyard and doubling the size of the original palazzo. Vettore and Giovanni created a Roman style palace with loggias and marble colonnades. Visitors entering the inner courtyard saw ancient Roman statues displayed in the colonnades. Wanting to keep a classic Roman and Tuscan feeling throughout the palazzo, Vettore and Giovanni decorated the interior richly with stucco work and frescoes. Bypassing Venetian artists, they hired painters from Rome and Central Italy, including Francesco Salviati, Giovanni da Udine, Camillo Montovano and Federico Zuccari. This was the first Venetian home to use white stucco and mannerist frescoes.

Over the following 80 years, the building deteriorated until becoming property of the state in 1981. After a massive restoration, it reopened as a museum in 2008. Palazzo Grimani is worth visiting for the building alone. The huge rooms beaming in natural light through massive windows are incredible, the ceilings are stunning and what we can see of Giovanni's collection of ancient works may well be the city's greatest link to archaeology.

The Tribuna

The most famous room in the palazzo is the Tribuna, a room designed in the 16th century to house Giovanni's outstanding collection of ancient Roman sculptures. They display these sculptures at varying heights around the four walls of the Tribuna, a room that would have been sensational based on the sculptures alone –but there's more. The ceiling vaults upward like an ultra-tall, squared-off version of the Pantheon in Rome, meeting the Venetian sky with a huge oculus. A superb 2nd century sculpture of *the Abduction of Ganymede* is suspended from the ceiling and looks like it's whooshing up to the oculus, about to escape. It is one of the most fantastic things I have ever seen. The 1800-year-old sculpture is the Roman replica of an ancient Greek sculpture, telling a story from Greek mythology. Ganymede was one of the most handsome men on earth. Zeus, the king of the gods, wanted to kidnap Ganymede and bring him to Mount Olympus to become cup holder to the gods. So, disguising himself as an eagle, Zeus swooped down from the heavens to steal Ganymede away. Standing below and looking up, it actually feels as if the eagle is soaring up to the oculus and is about to get away. It is truly breathtaking.

Until recently, the ancient Roman sculpture collection was broken up and stored in museums around town. It has been reunited for the first time in 430 years and brought back to the Tribuna for the 2019 Biennale. They intended this to last until 2020, but the pandemic has extended the duration. Pre-Covid there was a virtual reality component, so when the collection is returned to the museums, visitors can don VR masks and see the room with all the statues in place.

The Foliage Room

After the Tribuna, the *Sala ai Fogliami* (Foliage Room) is probably the most memorable room in the museum.

The ceiling and walls were painted by Mantovano and are painted with exquisitely realistic plant life and birdlife. Mantovano even included recently discovered new world species like corn and tobacco, both of which became staples of Venetian life. (Hello, polenta!) The ceiling is amazing.

Modern Art

Entering the courtyard, pay attention to the pillars and columns with their fascinating capitals –each one is different. Look up at the ceilings as you pass through the grand, arched entryway. It is tremendous.

Some parts of the palazzo could double as 1950s office space, and feel forgotten, but then you turn a corner and find yourself in front of something fantastic. It is the most oddly laid out museum I've ever encountered, and I love it.

You'll pass the Room of the Doge on your way to the Tribuna. Giovanni and Vettore built this giant room in 1568 as part of their extension of the palace. It celebrated Antonio Grimani –grandfather, successful spice merchant and first of the family doges. They decorated the room with precious eastern Mediterranean ancient marbles like red porphyry, yellow alabaster, and green serpentine. Using 19th century photos and inventory of Giovanni's possessions, 20 sculptures were moved back to their original 16th century locations in this room, including an Imperial Roman Dionysus and a huge bust of my favorite emperor (the gay one, Hadrian).

The main room, which is huge, has a permanent exhibition of 12 really large modern art works by Georg Baselitz, created specifically for this space. Personally, I don't really understand this part of the exhibition and wouldn't make the trip specifically to see it, (I come here for everything else). Even so, it's pretty cool.

Tickets

Palazzo Grimani is on the same ticket as Ca'd'Oro, so you can combine visiting the two. It is also free on the first Sunday of the month.

Address: Ramo Grimani 4858, Castello
Vaporetto Stop: Midway between San Zaccaria and Ospedale
What's Nearby: Libreria Acqua Alta, Campo Santa Maria Formosa, Campo SS Giovanni e Paolo.

2. Fondazione Querini Stampaglia

The Fondazione Querini Stampaglia is one of Europe's best preserved, most meticulously maintained and most important house museums.

The Querini Stampaglia were a very affluent Venetian family, and this magnificent palace was their home until the last of them, Conte Giovanni, died. This place gives you a glorious window into the daily lives of the very wealthy in Venice.

Conte Giovanni said it should be a place for the exchange of knowledge, not just a museum. He also bequeathed the family library of over 350,000 books, but with a caveat: The library must be open to everyone and must open when the other Venetian libraries were closed. As such, this library, considered one of the most beautiful in all of Venice, is even open on Sundays.

The museum is on the *piano nobile*, the living quarters and reception rooms of a Venetian palace. From the lavish interiors to the frescoes, the collections of rare and precious furniture, porcelains, fabrics, sculptures, and paintings by everyone from Tiepolo to Bellini to Longhi, the palace reflects the culture and traditions of Venice across the centuries, and the heritage of this noble family.

The museum opened in 1869. It combines some modern art and architecture (the Carlo Scarpa designed garden) with the old. It is also an event space and has a series of modern/contemporary art exhibitions each year. A must-see in Venice, check the calendar online to see what exhibitions are happening while you're in Venice.

Address: Campo Santa Maria Formosa 5252
What's Nearby: Libreria Aqua Alta, Campo SS Giovanni e Paolo, 5 minutes from Piazza San Marco.

The Piano Nobile

In historical Venetian houses/palaces, the *piano nobile* was the 'noble floor'. *Piano* (*pea-ah-noh*) means floor, and *nobile* (*noh-bee-leh*) refers to the noble folk living in the palace. The ground floor at water level is where merchant boats pulled in to warehouse their goods. The next floor up is the main floor or piano nobile, where the family lived. Some palaces have two main floors and the piano nobile would be on both. The servants would live on the attic floor, above the luxurious floors used by the noble family.

3. Museo Di Palazzo Mocenigo

If you love the Venetian history of beautiful clothing and costuming, be prepared to die a little.

This was the family palace of the San Stae branch of one of the most important families in Venice's illustrious history, the Mocenigo family. *Seven* members of this family became doges. This Gothic-style palace was rebuilt at the beginning of the 17th century.

In 1945, the last member of the family, Alvise Nicolo' Mocenigo, bequeathed the palazzo to the city, designating it to be a "Gallery of Art to supplement the Museo Correr".

In 1985 it became the Museum of the History of Fabrics and Costumes. Textiles and costumes from Palazzo Grassi, and the Cini, Correr and Guggenheim collections were all moved here under the one roof. It also has a library of the history of fabrics, costumes, and fashion across the centuries, particularly from the 18th century. Five rooms are dedicated to the history of perfume in Venice, replete with art and an interactive multimedia display. It's quite fantastic.

Here again, you'll experience centuries in the lives of wealthy, important Venetian families. Walking the *piano nobile* just for this reason would be worth the visit. But Good Lord, the costumes! They are magnificent. And they're not just hanging against walls either. Mannequins wear the costumes, while actively *doing something.* Groups of mannequins are arranged in social context, not just sitting or standing, but leaning into one another, acting out their lives. This brings the costumes to life. You can better imagine the clothes as they were intended, functioning in their elaborate Venetian lives. I absolutely loved this.

Address: Santa Croce 1992
Vaporetto Stop: San Stae
What's Nearby: Ca' Pesaro, the Church of San Stae.

4. Ca' Pesaro

If you enjoy modern art, put this on your must-see list. Ca' Pesaro is home to works by Kandinsky, Klee, Klimt and Chagall, along with modern Italian artists such as De Chirico, Boccioni and Sironi. The collection is just remarkable.The 19th and 20th-century paintings and sculptures are on the first floor, while the second floor houses the Oriental Art Museum, Europe's most renowned collections of Chinese and Japanese art.

This is one of the most important palaces in Venice. It was built for the uber wealthy Pesaro family in the second half of the 17th century by the superstar architect Baldassare Longhena. (Longhena also created Ca' Rezzonico and the beautiful church of Santa Maria della Salute.) The three-story Pesaro palace has frescoes by Pittoni, Bambini, Trevisani, Brusaferro and Crosato. Its most famous fresco *The Triumph of Zephyr and Flora* by Tiepolo was transferred to Ca' Rezzonico in 1935.

Duchess Felicita Bevilacqua La Masa donated the palazzo to the city, to become a Modern Art Museum. The original Modern Art Museum was in Ca' Foscari but moved to the larger (and brighter) Ca' Pesaro in 1899.

One fascinating aspect of this museum is the use of light. From the canal, you don't quite realize just how bathed in natural light the interior is. The windows seem larger from the inside, flooding the gallery with light. Another stunning feature of the palace is its huge foyer, which is built around a Venetian well.

Address: Santa Croce 2076
Vaporetto Stop: San Stae
What's Nearby: Ca' Mocenigo, Ca' d'Oro, the Rialto Bridge and Santa Maria Gloriosa dei Friari are all within about 500 meters of Ca' Pesaro.

5. Ca' d'Oro (Galleria Giorgio Franchetti)

The Grand Canal is lined with amazing palaces. One of the most remarkable is Ca' d'Oro, The House of Gold.

The design was influenced by the Doge's Palace. Wealthy merchant Marino Contarini built this Venetian Gothic palace in 1420, intending it to be the most lavish palace in Venice. The Contarini were one of the founding families of Venice and one of the oldest families of Italian nobility. (On top of that, they produced eight doges.)

Known as the house of gold, the facade of Ca' d'Oro was flamboyantly covered in gold leaf, tempered with expensive pigments of vermilion and ultramarine. It must have been an incredible sight, glistening in the morning light and glowing as the sun went down. It would have screamed money, which, of course, was the goal! You would automatically assume the glistening golden house on the Grand Canal must belong to the wealthiest man in town.

Look for the delicate pinnacles and intricate loggia shapes, that almost look like sculpture. From the water, each level of the facade gets more ornate, lifting the eye upwards, creating the illusion that the palace is taller than it actually is. At the same time, a solid horizontal emphasis makes it seem wider than it is. The style is uniquely Venetian, a blend of Byzantine, Islamic, and Gothic architecture. You'd think each design element of the exterior would be chaotic when thrown together, but the styles interweave beautifully, looking symmetrical and harmonious. It is beautiful.

The palace changed hands multiple times over time and decline set in. At one point, the palace was semi-derelict. The worst moment in its history came in 1847 when a Russian, Prince Troubetskoy, bought the palace for his mistress, a ballerina named Maria Taglioni. The prince stripped the palace facade of its marble, tore out the open staircase and even sold the original well head. All of Venice was horrified. Art critic John Ruskin frantically tried to sketch the palace before it was too late.

Ca' d'Oro was rescued in the late 19th century by art enthusiast and collector Baron Giorgio Franchetti. He restored the palace, the staircase and the well, then moved in his collections of paintings and sculptures and coins. He donated the palace to the city in 1916.

This palace has always fascinated me. Walking past, you can look into the lower floor, the courtyard, staircase and well.

The art museum is on the first and second floors (second and third floors to Americans) and is surprisingly light and airy. The most famous painting here is *Saint Sebastian* by Andrea Mantegna, (1431—1506) painted near the end of the artist's life. Also look for a sculpture by Tullio Lombardo (1455—1532) called *Young Couple*, Titian's *Venus at the Mirror*, 16th century Flemish tapestries, and Renaissance pieces looted from churches in the Veneto by Napoleon.

Step out onto both loggias and take in the view over the Grand Canal. Each view needs to be seen from both inside and out. To my untrained eye, the arches give the optical illusion of being bigger from the inside.

I absolutely love Ca' d'Oro and hope you will make time to see it. Entrance for Ca' d'Oro is on the same ticket as Gallerie dell' Accademia and Palazzo Grimani. Get there first thing in the morning and watch the Grand Canal from the loggia. Watch the boats and barges delivering goods and taking away the trash before the tourist action is in full swing.

Address: Calle Ca' d'Oro 3934, Cannaregio
Vaporetto Stop: Ca' d'Oro
What's Nearby: Ca' d'Oro is just across the canal from Ca' Pesaro and Ca' Mocenigo, and the Rialto Market.

6. Gallerie dell'Accademia

There are masterpieces by Venetian artists all over the city, but nowhere has such a majestic collection all in one place as the Accademia. This museum has works by the greatest names in Venetian art. This is one of Europe's most magnificent, specialized collections and covers 500 years of art created in and around Venice.

This smallish museum has only 24 rooms, but the rooms themselves are sumptuous. The collection is mostly in chronological order, making it fascinating to follow as the centuries roll out. I won't list all the artists represented, but the big names are here, including Bellini, Canaletto, Andrea Mantegna, Tiepolo, Tintoretto, Titian and Paolo Veronese. Giorgio Vasari is here too. The most famous work is Leonardo da Vinci's *Vitruvian Man*. This drawing on paper is very sensitive to light and is displayed only on rare occasions.

Entering the first room of the Galleria, look up at the gold and blue ceiling. It's decorated with masses of individually carved wooden angels. Each angel has eight golden wings and looks down at you with its own individual facial expression. No two are the same. They are fantastic! This is the work of Marco Cozzi, a 15th century woodcarver and artist. He created this spectacular ceiling between 1461 and 1484.

Address: Campo della Carita' 1050, Dorsoduro
Vaporetto Stop: Accademia
What's Nearby: The Peggy Guggenheim, Santa Maria della Salute, Bar Foscarini.

7. The Pinault Collection (split between two locations)

Did you know, Venice is one of the world's premier destinations for exceptional collections of modern art? Francois Pinault, French billionaire and husband of Selma Hayek, has amassed one of the world's most important collections of contemporary art –more than 3000 works from the 20th and 21st centuries. He keeps much of it here in Venice split between two locations –Palazzo Grassi and the Dogane, displayed in a rotation of absolutely blockbuster exhibitions.

Palazzo Grassi

First, let's talk about the palace (it is also in the **Ghosts** chapter). This was the last palace built on the Grand Canal prior to the fall of Venice and is in a completely different architectural style to the others. Unlike the neighboring Venetian Gothic palaces of the 14th and 15th centuries, this palace was built in the Neoclassical style. It's huge and symmetrical and has no lower mercantile openings. (The openings where boats bring merchandise for storage.) The palace was built by Giorgio Massari between 1740 and 1772, after he finished Ca' Rezzonico, across the canal.

The Grassi family lost their fortune and sold the palace in 1840. It then had a succession of owners until the Fiat group bought it in 1983. Gianni Agnelli made it an exhibition space, and from 1983 until 2005 it was internationally renowned for its exhibitions. After Agnelli's death in 2005, the Fiat group terminated its tenure at the palace and Francois Pinault stepped in.

Pinault hired Japanese architect Tadao Ando to redesign the interior. Tadao created magic with natural light, making it feel airy and bright and a perfect place to show modern art. The art museum opened in 2006. The museum doesn't have a permanent collection, instead works are rotated, changed and updated constantly. There are spaces within the museum where artists create their installations, and it is always changing. You can come here over and over and always find something new.

Even if you're not into modern art, the palace is worth seeing!

Hours: Closed Saturday and Sunday
Address: Palazzo Grassi, Campo San Samuele 3231
Vaporetto Stop: San Samuele
What's Nearby: La Fenice, Campo Santo Stefano, 10-minute walk to Piazza San Marco.

The Punta della Dogana

The Punta della Dogana is the triangle-shaped building next to Santa Maria della Salute at the tip of Dorsoduro, straddled by the Grand Canal on one side and the Giudecca Canal on the other. Built in the 15th century, this was the customs house of Venice. It was renovated in 1677, then again in the 18th and 19th centuries.

In April 2007, Pinault and Tadao Ando transformed the 5000 square foot building into a center for contemporary art, to host curated exhibitions from the Francois Pinault Foundation collection. When planning your trip to Venice, check the exhibition schedule online as it is constantly changing.

Punta della Dogana has the best view across the Grand Canal to San Marco and the Doge's Palace. I love walking the length the Zattere from the Dogana to the very end. The views across the Giudecca Canal are beautiful and peaceful and the Zattere is lined with fabulous bars. This is a glorious spot to escape the tourist crowds and sit on the waterfront with a Prosecco and a snack. Combine your visit here with a visit to the Salute church.

Hours: Closed Saturday and Sunday.
Address: Punta della Dogana, Dorsoduro 2
Vaporetto Stop: Salute
What's Nearby: Santa Maria della Salute, The Peggy Guggenheim, the Zattere.

8.Museo della Musica

If I try another word for music, I always come back to the only one, Venice. – Nietzsche

As a former cellist I love this tiny museum. Did you know that Venice has been an important music center since the Middle Ages? Not only was music played everywhere, Venice was famous for making magnificent musical instruments, highly sought after by professional musicians throughout the centuries.

In 1501, Ottaviano Petrucci printed the first book of music in the world, after which Venice became the world capital of music publishing. Venice also had the most opera houses of any city in the world. The glorious stage sets and innovative stage machinery used in the Venice opera houses not only defined style across the centuries, they were imitated all over Europe. Back then, opera performers were the movie stars and rockstars of the time. Opera was madly chic.

Antonio Vivaldi, virtuoso violinist and one of the greatest baroque composers, was born in Venice. He composed many of his violin concertos here. Vivaldi wrote several operas in Venice, some of which were considered avantgarde at the time. Some old-school musicians thought he was too modern, which of course just makes him more interesting. What you may not know about Vivaldi is that he was also a catholic priest and as part of his duties he was assigned to the Ospedale della Pieta', an orphanage for abandoned girls. At that time, orphan boys were taught a trade while orphan girls learned music. Vivaldi worked there from 1703 to 1715 and then again from 1723 to 1740. He wrote many of his works to be performed by the girls at the Pieta' and their all-girl ensemble. Vivaldi moved to Vienna after meeting Emperor Charles VI. The emperor died shortly after Vivaldi arrived, before he could get royal patronage. Vivaldi died in Vienna in poverty within a year and was buried in a mass grave with no tombstone. In his lifetime, Vivaldi composed many concertos for a variety of instruments, sacred choral works and over 40 operas. He is perhaps best known for his violin concertos, the *Four Seasons*. For two centuries, Vivaldi's name all but disappeared, then in the 20th century, his music experienced a revival of sorts and once again became widely played all over the world.

The Museo della Musica is a niche collection exploring 300 years of music in Venice, with a collection of around 150 musical instruments from the 17th to 19th centuries. Throughout the history of manufacturing of musical instruments, Italian violin making has always been considered the very best in the world. This museum has examples of violins from the different regional luthier schools of Italy. Along with violins, violas and cellos dating back to the 1600s you can also see harps, mandolins, even historical flutes.

There is a section of the museum dedicated to famous composers, including our friend Vivaldi.

This is a small museum, just one large room in the Church of San Maurizio. It is one of the few free museums in Venice.

Address: Chiesa San Maurizio, Campo San Maurizio, San Marco
Hours: Open 10am—7pm daily
Vaporetto Stop: Giglio
What's Nearby: Campo Santo Stefano, Accademia Bridge, Teatro La Fenice, Piazza San Marco (10 minutes' walk).

9. Ca' Rezzonico

Ca' Rezzonico is a house museum, so is more about showing you how the excessively wealthy lived, than lining up lots of paintings to walk past. To understand Venice, you need to understand the level of opulence, decadence and staggering displays of wealth in its history. For several hundred years Venice was the merchant capital of the world, and therefore the center of wealth –and what's the point of having all that cash if you don't flaunt it? Ca' Rezzonico flaunts it, and by God, it's fabulous. This is a magnificent example of the grandiosity of 17th and 18th century Venice. Ca' Rezzonico is one of the most luxurious palaces on the Grand Canal.

Our story starts with (of course) one of the noble families of Venice, this time the Bon family. In 1667 they began building a monument to themselves, hiring the biggest name in architecture, Baldassare Longhena. He designed Ca' Pesaro and Santa Maria della Salute, so came with huge bragging rights. Two major problems impeded this palazzo being completed: Longhena died in 1682, and the Bon family realized the project far exceeded their finances. Construction halted, and the palace sat unfinished for nearly 70 years.

In 1750 Giambattista Rezzonico, a freshly minted new noble (the family bought their title), bought the building and hired Giorgio Massari, the most fashionable architect of the day to finish the project. The Rezzonicos were a newly rich banking dynasty, so not only had the cash to build the palace, but they also needed to show they had crazy amounts of money. Their home reno was an astounding display of wealth, from the Tiepolo frescoes to the Flemish tapestries. Ca' Rezzonico became famous for its unbelievable interiors.

The ground floor feels airy and huge, with clean stone lines from the canal entrance to the back garden entrance. A dramatic, sweeping staircase transports you up to the *piano nobile*, where the fun begins. Before we go further, remember Venice was a party city, with endless glamorous masked and unmasked parties, taking everything to excess at a level not seen elsewhere. The best way to impress people with your wealth was to have a lavish party room, and this one doesn't disappoint. The ballroom at Ca' Rezzonico stops you in your tracks. It is enormous and over-the-top lavish. The gigantic golden chandeliers alone are worth the visit, but the rest of the room, with its frescoes and gold accents, is just astounding. It's like walking into a fairytale.

Tiepolo was in Germany at the time, working for the Prince of Wurzburg, so the frescoes commission was given to Giambattista

Crosato, a highly original painter, fresh from working for the court of Savoy in Turin. Crosato worked alongside one of Tiepolo's trompe l'oeil painters, Giralamo Mengozzi Colonna, who used genius illusionary techniques to make the room look even bigger. He ringed the room with pale pilaster strips topped with gilded capitals, interspersed with fake statues and reliefs, and gray marble columns. The opulent use of gold squeals money, while the pale, vertical pilasters and columns shoot your eye heavenward to the beyond glorious ceiling. Giorgio Massari removed the original ceiling, exposing the entire height of two floors of the palazzo. Not only was the effect spectacular, but it was also unrivaled in Venice, both in size and in decoration. At the center of the ceiling is a giant Crosato fresco of Apollo the sun god vaulting upward with his horse and chariot, radiating his light across the four corners of the world, represented by girls of different races. This Apollo symbolism showed up often in patrician houses. It was their way of alluding to their own radiant future, and their ridiculous wealth. Just in case you didn't catch who all this money belonged to, the Rezzonicos installed a giant coat of arms opposite the entrance.

The Rezzonicos lightning fast rise up the social ranks peaked in 1758. Not only did they buy their way into nobility (which wasn't rare at the time), they also got themselves a family pope! In 1758, in a move of Medici-level strategy and genius, Giambattista's son Carlo was elected Pope Clement XIII. The family's tenure at Ca' Rezzonico ended shortly thereafter when they moved to Rome. The family glory didn't last long though, as the family died out in 1810 when the last male heir died.

During the 19th century, the palazzo changed hands several times and had a series of interesting tenants. The poet Robert Browning lived here with his son Pen from 1887 until he died here in 1889. Cole Porter rented the palace from 1926 to 1927. Eventually the original furnishings were stripped away, and it was an empty shell in 1935 when the city purchased it to become a museum of 18th century art. Frescoes and paintings were stripped from other palaces in the city and installed at Ca' Rezzonico, making this a truly remarkable museum where you can experience art in a home similar to that for which it was created. There is an enormous amount of art, including Tiepolos and Canaletto. On the third floor, look for the replica 18th century Venetian pharmacy built with original materials.

If you've been to Naples, you may have seen *The Veiled Christ.* One of the most fascinating sculptures I've ever seen, Christ lies there covered by a diaphanous veil, made of marble. You can't get close to him though, and you can't take photos. Here, in the Antonio Guardi room, *The Veiled Woman* by one of the 18th century's most renowned sculptors, Antonio Corradini, uses the same concept. And here, you can get up close and take all the photos you want. I'm always intrigued by this piece. The style became fashionable at that time, so it's not exactly rare, but even so I challenge you to figure out how on earth he did it! The woman, thought to be an allegory of Purity, tilts her fully formed, beautiful face, which is covered by a flimsy transparent veil –and it is made from a single piece of marble. If anything, the marble veil makes the piece even more sensual. Honestly, it is astounding. Google the bust first to see why it needs to be on your must-see list. (Just by coincidence, Corradini took his own life in Naples while working at Capella Sansevero, where *The Veiled Christ* is.)

As you walk through Ca' Rezzonico, remind yourself that this wasn't a royal palace, just a private home.

Address: Dorsoduro 3136,
Vaporetto Stop: Ca' Rezzonico
What's Nearby: Barca san Barnaba, the Ponte dei Pugni and Ca' Foscari.

24.
Peggy Guggenheim and the Ladies of the Palazzo Venier Dei Leoni

Well behaved women seldom make history...

Palazzo Venier dei Leoni has a fascinating recent history, involving three iconic women who, across the best part of a century, lived wild and irrepressible lives here. They revitalized a rundown palace, infusing it with excitement, glamor, art and an enormous amount of sex.

Along the way, they shook up the old guard of Venice, leaving their mark on the city and the world. One of these women is one of the most influential patrons of 20th century art.

The Unfinished Palace

Our story starts in 1749 with the Venier family, one of Venice's oldest noble families, and most powerful dynasties. Their ancestry included three doge's, 18 procurators of St Mark's, bishops, consuls and admirals, and a family tree tracing back to Roman Emperors Valerian and Gallienus. This was a family with the bragging rights and the wealth to build themselves the casa to end all casas, and they decided to celebrate themselves with a massive palace on the Grand Canal.

The Venier wanted the largest palazzo in the toniest of neighborhoods, just along from the Doge's Palace. Theirs would be the biggest, most glorified McMansion on the block. A 5-story palace with a gleaming white neoclassical facade, a ground floor, a mezzanine, *two* piani nobile and an attic. There would be columns and pilasters and a triple arch sequence on each floor. (The neighbors were not happy.) It would be the most modern building around.

The project plans and a wooden model can be found today in the Museo Correr. The palace would have been stunning. However, a confluence of events halted everything, leaving only the first floor completed. Some say the Venier ran out of cash, others say they ran out of heirs. Noble Venetians farmed their daughters out to convents, preventing them from marrying and diluting the family fortune, so it makes sense a lack of boy babies could halt construction on what was to be a seriously enormous palace. Either that or Napoleon came to town and ruined everything. Whatever the reason, the palace was never built higher than the ground floor.

Some speculate that a lion lived temporarily in the palazzo's garden, but Palazzo Venier dei Leoni was more likely named for the eight Istrian stone lions' heads at the water level on the facade. (Look for them –they're wonderful.

You can't miss this palace. Your eye will be drawn to it immediately, because it is the only single-story palazzo on the Grand Canal. It looks decidedly odd. It's bright white, and at first glance you think it is a modern building. But look a little closer and you'll see it is beautiful and very old.

After the fall of the Republic, the palace stood empty. Decay set in, and at one point the basement was used as a cheap boarding house. Then, in the 20th century, three eccentric and fascinating women turned the palazzo around, and today it is one of the most celebrated and important art museums in the world.

Luisa Casati

In 1910, one of Italy's wealthiest and most eccentric heiresses, Marchesa Luisa Casati Amman, moved in. Bored with aristocratic life in Milan and suffering from crushing introversion, Luisa saw the unfinished palace as a mythical stage upon which to reinvent herself. Luisa was an introvert but was also completely wild. She created a theatrical persona –an extreme 1910 version of Lady Gaga.

She turned the derelict interior of Palazzo Venier dei Leoni into a festival of gold, glass and marble, but left the exterior crumbling, dirty and overgrown. Accompanied everywhere by her African manservant and a cheetah, she collected a menagerie of exotic animals, including monkeys, peacocks and a flock of albino birds that she dyed different colors to suit her mood. Luisa walked Venice at night with her pet cheetah, completely naked under a fur coat. She also had a wax dummy made of herself, its wig made from her own hair. The likeness was so acute that it is told that she sat motionless next to it at candlelit dinner parties and guests couldn't tell which was which.

She was a muse and a model for big artists of the day, including Boldini, Troubetzkoy and Augustus John. She modeled for Man Ray and was hostess to the avantgarde Ballets Russes. Their costume designer, Leon Bakst, designed outrageous costumes for her, which she wore to major events and her lavish parties. Her outfits included a peacock head dress dripping with the blood of a freshly killed chicken, and an outfit covered in light bulbs, powered by a generator. One of these costumes had her dressed as St Sebastian, wearing armor pierced with illuminated arrows. This outfit wasn't quite the raging success intended –faulty wiring gave her an electric shock so severe they say it flipped her over backwards. She was six-feet-tall, but rather than minimizing her height or hiding from it, she wore elaborate headpieces to make herself even taller.

Luisa Casati saw herself as a living work of art. Along with extreme outfits and wild hair (which was sometimes dark, sometimes red), she dilated her pupils with belladonna, and rimmed her eyes with kohl to make them more dramatic. She added multiple layers of false lashes, sometimes making them from strips of fabric.

Her parties at Palazzo Venier dei Leoni were legendary and, like herself, a piece of extreme theater. The internet has pages of photos of her crazy outfits and wild parties. She didn't socialize at these events, instead veering between not speaking to her guests and standing like a statue –a piece of human art. At one party she drugged a giant snake, had it painted gold, and wore it around her neck.

Luisa's Venetian life ended at the onset of World War I. She resumed the mad theater of her life in Paris; the stories getting crazier as the years unfolded. In the end, she became an opium addict, blew her fortune and ran up $25 million in debt. They sold off her palaces and all her belongings. She lived the last years of her life in poverty, in a one-room flat in London, where she was seen rummaging through trash cans looking for feathers to put in her hair. (They now think Luisa was probably on the autism spectrum.)

She has lived posthumously as a muse to artists and fashion designers including John Galliano, Dries Van Noten and Karl Largerfeld, and was the namesake of Georgina Chapman and Keren Craig's fashion house, Marchesa.

Palazzo Venier dei Leoni is more exciting to visit when you know about Luisa. I think of her as a blend of Lady Gaga and Daphne Guinness –brilliant, theatric, extreme, and in a league of her own. The more you read about her, the more fascinating she becomes.

Viscountess Doris Castlerosse

Twelve years after Luisa left Venice, another intriguing woman took up residence at Palazzo Venier dei Leoni: The Viscountess Doris Castlerosse.

Born Doris Delevingne, she is the great aunt of models Poppy and Cara Delevingne. Doris grew up working class but gained access to London society by becoming a courtesan. Her list of lovers was long and distinguished and included Winston Churchill *and* his son. Churchill famously painted "*Viscountess Castlerosse on the Terrace at the Chateau de l'Horizon 1933*". It's Doris, reclining on a green sofa, perfect bare legs stretching to eternity, looking all come-hither-y.

Doris had a wild reputation. Prince George bragged about getting in trouble with King George V for going to her parties. Doris got her title by marrying Valentine Browne, the Viscount Castlerosse. (As a result, his mother, Lady Kenmare, irate that he married a call girl, cut him off financially.) No end of shenanigans ensued. She divorced the Viscount and resumed being supported by her lovers. (I'm leaving out a lot here, so look her up. Her story is fascinating and *completely crazy*.)

In the mid-1930s, she met and became involved with New York socialite and multi millionairess Margot Hoffman. Margot was completely besotted with Doris and bought her the empty Palazzo Venier dei Leoni, where Doris reinvented herself as a Venice *salonniere*. She renovated the palace with stucco walls, antique sconces and frames, and glossy black marble bathrooms. Like Luisa before her, she threw legendary parties here, this time attended by such luminaries as the young Prince Philip and actor Douglas Fairbanks. The painter Derek Hill described Doris as "one of the chicest and most attractive people that ever existed".

The fun ended with World War II. Doris and Margot relocated to New York, where the millionairess grew tired of Doris, and left her. Doris was left stranded in war-time America with no way to get home, until eventually, Winston Churchill secured her safe passage back to London.

In 1942, intentionally or by accident, Doris died of an overdose of sleeping pills.

PEGGY GUGGENHEIM

It is always assumed that Venice is the ideal place for a honeymoon. This is a grave error. To live in Venice or even to visit it means that you fall in love with the city itself. There is nothing left over in your heart for anyone else. –Peggy Guggenheim.

The third iconic woman to take possession of the Palazzo Venier dei Leoni was the American heiress and art collector Peggy Guggenheim.

Stifled by the misogynistic New York art scene, Peggy escaped to Venice to start a new life. In 1949 she paid approximately US$60,000 for the Palazzo Venier dei Leoni, moving in with her superlative collection of 20th century art. She lived at Palazzo Venier dei Leoni for 30 years, until her death at age 81.

During World War II, soldiers had occupied the palace. They'd destroyed the luxurious salon created by Luisa and Doris. The palace was once again crumbling, its interior walls now covered in graffiti. Breaking with convention, Peggy stripped the palazzo to a bright, white, simple interior. This was a stroke of genius, as the white walls were perfect for displaying her magnificent collection of modern art –the 326-piece collection of paintings and sculptures now known as the Peggy Guggenheim Collection. The collection includes works by Pablo Picasso, Jackson Pollack, Joan Miro', Salvador Dali', Willem de Kooning, Mark Rothko and Wassily Kandinsky. Biographer Mary Dearborn maintains that Peggy's art choices affected the course of 20th century art history. Hers is considered one of the world's most outstanding collections of modern art.

Like the two women before her, Peggy threw wild parties that shocked and delighted Venetians and her guests alike. One of my favorite stories is the party where Peggy paid homage to her father's death on the Titanic. (She was 21 when he died.) She re-enacted the sinking of the Titanic, walking from her terrace out into the Grand Canal, naked as a jaybird. Not only that, but she also took the entire orchestra with her, having paid them to do it. As if *that* wasn't crazy enough, her gondoliers had to row out to rescue her! (You couldn't pay me to put a naked *toe* into the Grand Canal. I'd be convinced rot would set in and make it fall off. The thought of someone willingly walking their naked nether regions into the canal has me equal parts horrified and dying laughing. At the time, it must have seemed completely outrageous and totally insane. Which of course, makes me love Peggy even more.)

Her party guestlist over the years included everyone from Marlon Brando to Tennessee Williams, Igor Stravinsky to Somerset Maugham. She is said to have had more than 400 lovers, so she was busy with more than just art and parties.

In Venice she became known as l'ultima dogaressa, or the last female doge, floating around in her private gondola in her trademark jazzy sunglasses, her dogs snuggled in her lap.

–Judith Mackrell

Peggy's Lhasa Apsos dogs were all buried in the garden. She joined them when she died from a stroke in 1979. In the garden a plaque commemorating Peggy is right next to the plaque commemorating each of her 14 dogs. They're interred next to her so they could enjoy the afterlife together.

On her death, she bequeathed her palazzo and art collection to her uncle Solomon's Guggenheim Foundation. Four decades later, it is still embroiled in an endless legal battle as her descendants fight over it.

The Peggy Guggenheim Collection opened to the public here in 1980. With 400,000 visitors annually, it is one of the most visited and most popular museums in Italy.

INTRIGUE

There are many fascinating, quirky, stories about Peggy. I recommend Googling her before coming to Venice, because the more you know about her, the more you'll want to see the world she created here.

In John Berendt's fabulously gossipy book, *The City of Falling Angels*, his stories about Peggy Guggenheim, her legendary parties and absolute eccentricity are fascinating, funny and also quite sad. He adds a layer of intrigue with his stories about Jane and Philip Rylands, a couple who emerged from nowhere, and infused themselves into the life of elderly American violinist, Olga Rudge. If Berendt is correct, the Rylands conned Olga into signing over the extremely valuable rights to the papers of her long-time lover, poet Ezra Pound. They then smuggled them out of Olga's house. It's an intriguing story that ends with the papers squirreled away in the archives at Yale.

(The Olga Rudge home is close to Peggy's in the Dorsoduro.) Once the Rylands were done fleecing Olga, they moved onto their next wealthy elderly lady, Peggy Guggenheim. They insinuated themselves into her life, and he became the director of her museum. (In Rylands' defense, under his direction for 35 years, the Peggy Guggenheim Collection became one of the most visited art collections in the world.)

I haven't researched it further, so can't verify the accuracy of Berendt's story, but the book does make a visit to the Guggenheim more exciting.

There is something delicious about the fact that this palace, built to celebrate the male Venier egos, fell to ruin, only to be rescued and rehabilitated by three defiant, single women, who railed against conventional morality, and lived their lives on their own outrageous terms.

I hope that even if you're not a fan of modern art, the stories of Luisa, Doris and Peggy will still intrigue you enough to come visit the Palazzo Venier dei Leoni.

If you enjoy contemporary art, the Peggy Guggenheim Museum is *not to be missed.*

Recommended Reading

If you're interested in learning more about the Venetian lives of Luisa, Doris, and Peggy and the craziness they brought to the Palazzo Venier dei Leoni, I highly recommend Judith Mackrell's book *The Unfinished Palazzo: Life, Love and Art in Venice.*

Also recommended: John Berendt's *The City of Falling Angels.* His look into Peggy, the Rylands and Olga Rudge, along with the fire at the Fenice Opera House, will add another layer of interest to your trip.

Address: Dorsoduro 701—704
Vaporetto Stop: Accademia or Salute
What's Nearby: Santa Maria della Salute, the Accademia, the Zattere.

25.
Isola San Giorgio

Venice, its temples, and palaces did seem like fabrics of enchantment piled to heaven.

–Percy Bysshe Shelley

One of the most iconic views of Venice looks from the San Marco *piazzetta* across the water to the island of San Giorgio with its beautiful, Palladian style Basilica. For centuries, this has been a favorite view of artists. More recently of photographers too. For a truly iconic photo, crouch in front of the gondolas at San Marco and photograph the island with them bobbing in the foreground. If you can swing it during either of the blue hours, or when the mist is rolling in, you will have a postcard-worthy image.

In the winter, cold air from the mountains meets the warmer (but still cold) water of the lagoon, creating a mist thick enough to slice with a bread knife. When this happens, the view from the campanile on San Giorgio shows only the tops of the buildings of Venice, as if they're rising out of a fairytale cloud. It is simply magical. So, rather than just looking at the island from San Marco, I recommend taking a trip over there. From the San Zaccaria vaporetto stop, just beyond the Doge's Palace, the #2 vaporetto takes approximately 3 minutes to reach San Giorgio.

There is a lot to see from the island. San Giorgio has the very best views of the Doge's Palace and San Marco, especially from the campanile, and most tourists coming to Venice know nothing about it.

Island History

Isola San Giorgio used to be called the Island of the Cypresses. In 790, they built the first church here, and almost 200 years later, in 982, Doge Tribuno Memmo gave the island to a Benedictine monk named Giovanni Morosini to start a monastery on. This was fine until 1223, when an earthquake destroyed all the buildings and the Benedictines had to start over. The island stayed with the Benedictines until Napoleon got his hands on it in 1806, when he expelled the monks and used the island for military warehousing. The monastery was left in ruins after 150 years of military occupation. In 1951, Count Vittorio Cini bought the island and restored it to its original beauty. He established an international cultural center here called the Fondazione Giorgio Cini. The island also has beautiful gardens and woods, and a glass museum.

The Church

The island is best known for the Palladio-designed church of San Giorgio Maggiore (1566—1610). This was Palladio's first complete church project and was drastically different to the lavish Venetian Renaissance architectural style of the time. Palladio loved the clean lines, balance, and harmony of ancient Roman and Greek architecture. The front facade of Palladio's church here resembles an ancient temple. Looking at the front of San Giorgio Maggiore, you can identify two triangular pediments above four majestic columns surging upward, supporting the top pediment while providing perfect visual balance. It's absolutely beautiful. You'll see these same shapes across the water in another Palladio church, the Redentore on Giudecca.

The interior of the church is sparse but luminous. White walls in a Latin cross are illuminated by high windows, offset by pilasters and soaring white Corinthian columns. After all the busy churches *full* of artwork, this one feels calm and open, allowing you to breathe and quiet your mind. Being Venice, it does of course house masterpieces, including Tintoretto's *Last Supper* and *Jews in the Desert.* In the Capella dei Morti you will find Tintoretto's *Entombment of Christ* and two paintings by Jacopo and Domenico Tintoretto, *The Risen Christ with St Andrew* and *The Coronation of the Virgin with Saints.*

THE CAMPANILE

This bell tower is where you get the very best views of Venice. The tower is 63 meters tall (206 feet) and offers a 360-degree panorama, encompassing all of Venice, the lagoon, and the islands. In the campanile, the nine church bells play in C# Major, harmonizing with church bells on Lido.

Across the centuries, the tower has kept falling over. The original bell tower collapsed during a storm in 1442. Its replacement fell down in 1726. The next one was built in 1729, and fell over in 1774, this time killing a monk and wounding two others. You can see the 1729 tower in a painting in the Accademia, called *St Mark's Basin with San Giorgio and the Giudecca.* Look a little closer at the painting and you'll see that it had an onion-shaped dome. They rebuilt the current campanile in 1791. The current campanile hasn't been immune from trouble. In 1993, lightning struck the wooden angel on top, which now resides in front of the ticket office.

San Giorgio doesn't get a fraction of the crowds waiting to go up the campanile in San Marco, but I still recommend going up the campanile when you first get to the island, in case a large group arrives. My only caveat is if it's foggy and the sun is coming out later. This is the view to die for, so you want to get your timing right. You can take an elevator right to the top.

The Monastery

In 1433 Cosimo de' Medici took refuge at the monastery here when he was exiled from Florence, and Cosimo brought his architect Michelozzo with him to Venice. Few people owned books in 1433, so Cosimo had Michelozzo build a public library. Ostensibly this was to show his gratitude to the people of Venice for letting him live there, but really it was a calculated and brilliant political move. (You'll find a more comprehensive version of this story in *Glam Italia! 101 Fabulous Things to Do in Florence.*)

That library burned down in 1614 and was rebuilt in 1640 by Baldassare Longhena, another architect who pops up all over Venice. Longhena also designed the wonderful grand staircase, the *novitiate*, guest quarters, infirmary, and the monastery facade.

The monastery was an important cultural and artistic center in Europe. The monks built relationships with both Florence and Padua, making it a favorite spot not only for Cosimo but also for foreign dignitaries visiting Venice. In fact, the monastery was so highly esteemed that when the French occupied Rome in 1799, the Papal Enclave convened here to elect Pope Pius VII. The cardinals met in the *chorum nocturnis* (night choir) where you can see Carpaccio's *Saint George Slaying the Dragon.*

In 1560 Palladio built a new refectory and Paolo Veronese painted his massive *Wedding Feast at Cana*, which remained here until Napoleon stole it. The original is now in the Louvre in Paris, but a reproduction hangs here where the original was. Napoleon also stole the most valuable books from the Longhena library.

The monastery has two sets of cloisters. The Cloister of the Bay Trees was built 1516—1540 and then Palladio's Cloister of the Cypresses, which was begun in 1579, the year before he died, but not finished until the mid-1600s.

THE FONDAZIONE GIORGIO CINI

In 1951, Count Vittorio rescued San Giorgio in memory of his son, Giorgio, who had died in an air-crash in 1949. The monastery is now the Fondazione Giorgio Cini, an extremely prestigious international cultural institution.

The foundation dedicated their residential research program and institute, The Branca Center, to the scientific, cultural, and artistic legacy of Venice. It offers postgraduate scholarships in art history, music (the Vivaldi Institute), literature, and drama. The Fondazione Giorgio Cini also maintains archives of Venetian history and is constantly adding new programs and projects. In 2016, a new concert venue opened on the island, in a 19th century *squero* (gondola repair shop). Check their schedule when planning your Venetian sojourn.

The Foundation has meticulously restored the island's monastery buildings, which are primarily used for workshops and conferences pertaining to The Branca Center interests. They have also hosted G7 and UNESCO conferences here. You can only see inside this extraordinary complex with a guided tour (which I highly recommend).

THE LABYRINTH

Recently, the Foundation opened the Borges Labyrinth to the public. Inspired by the stories of Jorges Luis Borges, this kilometer-long maze made of 3200 boxwood plants is spectacular. The audio guide for the maze has a soundtrack written by Antonio Fresa and recorded by the Orchestra of the Teatro La Fenice. Reservations are required to visit the labyrinth –check the website first.

You'll find information about the guided tours on the CINI website, www.cini.it/en/guided-tours

When you've seen enough of Isola San Giorgio, take the #2 vaporetto to the next stop on the list: Giudecca.

26.
Giudecca

Venice, the most touristy place in the world,
is still just completely magic to me.

–Frances Mayes

Giudecca is eight interconnected islands stitched together to make one long, thin island in the Venice Lagoon, opposite Dorsoduro. This is an artsy community populated by working class Venetians, artists and expats spending big money on gentrifying old palaces.

There is some speculation about how it got its name. One thought is that it came from a 14th century Jewish settlement. Another thought is that 9th century nobles sentenced to *giudicato* (exile) were sent here.

Giudecca is known for large palazzi with gardens. In the early 20th century, a film studio moved in, factories were built, and for a time it was the industrial port of Venice. Old granaries and warehouses on the east side of the island have now been converted into the luxurious Belmond Hotel Cipriani, and the port activities have since moved to Marghera.

Giudecca alone is reason enough to devote more than just a day or two to Venice. This is a fantastic place to escape the tourists. Here, you can walk the entire length of the fondamenta, stopping at cafes, restaurants and art galleries lining the Giudecca Canal, and get an absolutely glorious view of Venice. There is a romance to Giudecca, its old squares, churches and views of the San Marco basin have long called to artists. Honestly, it is just lovely.

For 500 years, the strikingly beautiful white church of Il Redentore has dominated the Giudecca skyline. Except, of course, when a gigantic cruise ship passes though the Giudecca Canal, blocking the view of everything. Supposedly these big ships have now been banned from the Giudecca Canal, but I've hears this story go back and forth so many times I'm hesitant to get my hopes up.

The best way to explore Giudecca is just to wander the island with no particular agenda. You'll stumble across fabulous and fascinating sites, enjoy artisanal gelato, have lunch with a view, and if you're lucky, catch the totally breathtaking sunset. So, the following are ten sites just to keep an eye out for while you wander, listed from the east end of the island heading west.

1. THE BELMOND HOTEL CIPRIANI

My favorite place for an upscale aperitivo, I tell you all about this one in the earlier chapter about **Madly Chic Places for an Aperitivo**.

2. THE CHURCH OF SANTA MARIA DELLA PRESENTAZIONE (LE ZITELLE)

This church has an intriguing history. It is the third Venetian church designed by Palladio, after San Giorgio and Il Redetore. Santa Maria della Presentazione began construction in 1581, the year following Palladio's death, and was completed in 1588. The church has a temple-like facade with a large dome and two small bell towers, and an almshouse extends to a cloister behind the church. The church interior is interesting, particularly the polygonal floors and the paintings by Francesco Bassano, Antonio Vassillacchi (a student of Veronese), and Palma the Younger.

The Jesuit Benedetto Palmo created the refuge known as Le Zitelle (The Spinsters) in 1558. It was a place to safely stash girls from poor families whose beauty put them at risk of forced prostitution, and the first 40 girls arrived here in 1561. The girls, as young as 12, were protected here, and learned trades like playing music and lacemaking. When they turned 18, they could choose between a life in the nunnery or marriage. If they chose marriage, the church would provide them with a dowry and find them a suitable husband. When the project needed more space in 1581, the almshouse was built.

The church and associated buildings have been deconsecrated and now operate as a luxury hotel (Palladio Hotel and Spa), so you can go and see some of it, but it requires booking in advance.

The Zuecca Project Space occupies the ground floor of the former convent. (Zuecca is dialect for Giudecca.) Exhibitions revolve around the concept of displacement, which has been part of the historical fabric of Venice since the beginning. Check their upcoming exhibition schedule online.

Address: Fondamenta Zitelle 33
Vaporetto Stop: Zitelle

3. Casa dei Tre Oci

A gorgeous example of late 19th century/early 20th century Venetian architecture, this is a must-see on Giudecca. In 1913, the artist Mario de Maria (also known as Marius Pictor) built this extravagant private residence. It was called Casa dei Tre Oci (The House of Three Eyes) because of its three beautiful ogival windows. Mario designed it to be a home-studio. After his death, his son Astolfo (a painter) lived there with his wife Adele. Until the late 1980s, it was a vibrant, active place where artists worked, and visiting intellectuals hung out. When Astolfo died, Adele stayed on and welcomed internationally renowned figures in the arts with her next husband, Giulio Macchi.

The Fondazione di Venezia purchased the building in 2000. It underwent a substantial restoration before reopening in 2012. Casa dei Tre Oci is one of the best examples of neo-Gothic architecture in Venice. It now operates as a venue for spectacular photography exhibitions from major international names, including Newton, LaChapelle, Bischof, Roiter, de Biasi and Scianna. The Fondazione di Venezia also keeps their photographic archives here, including over 100,000 images taken by the de Maria/Pictor family and the Italo Zannier archive comprising over 2000 photos from the 19th century to today.

If you love photography (and fashion photography), check online to see which exhibitions will run while you are in Venice. This is one of those goldmine finds that most tourists haven't heard of.

Address: Giudecca 43
Hours: 11am—7pm every day except Tuesday
Vaporetto Stop: Zitelle.

4. Villa Heriot

This Venetian palazzo now operating as a university for art restoration, originates with fascinating French woman, Anne-Marie Heriot (later known as Cyprienne Heriot).

Anne-Marie was the daughter of a French wool spinner, and worked as a sales assistant at the Grands Magasins du Louvre department store in Paris, where she met and married the owner, Zacharie Olympe Heriot. She was the inspiration for *Au Bonheur des Dames*, Emile Zola's novel about everyday life in a Paris department store. The two made an interesting couple. They owned several magnificent properties, were philanthropists and great patrons of the arts.

Heriot had a military background and converted one of his properties in the south of France into a school for military orphans aged 5—9 years. The Ecole Militaire Enfantine Heriot opened in 1887 and, over the next 80 years, became home to over 4500 military orphans. When Olympe died in 1889, Anne Marie stayed involved with the orphanage, expanding the grounds and opening her chateau in the Cote d'Armor to the children for holidays. She spent much of her inheritance on charity, educating children, and her passion for buying, creating, and restoring villas.

Anne-Marie had architect Edouard Arnaud design the magnificent Villa Cypris in Cap Martin on France's Azure Coast. Italian painter Raffaele Mainella designed the villa's interiors and gardens. Around this time, she started calling herself Cyprienne Heriot. In 1911 she again hired Mainella, who was living in Venice, to transform the cloister of the Abbey of San Gregorio (in Dorsoduro) into a residence. They collaborated again in 1926 when she bought an empty piece of land on Giudecca. She had Mainella create this picturesque, neo-Byzantine home with a sprawling garden and gorgeous views over the Venice lagoon. The home had been originally named Villa Michelangelo for the artist who had hidden on Giudecca 400 years prior, and was renamed Villa Heriot. The property comprised a main house for the family, a second house for guests, a servants' quarters and a covered boat dock, along with a large garden.

Villa Heriot starred in the aristocratic social scene from 1929 until the outbreak of World War II, when the parties stopped and the Heriots returned to France. The Germans requisitioned the villa during the war, after which the allies took it.

Cyprienne Heriot died on 5 December 1945, aged 88. Her son Auguste II either sold or donated the property to the city of Venice in 1947, stipulating it was to be used as a school, in the family tradition of supporting and providing education for young children. The main house became the Carlo Goldini Elementary School, and the guest house became a refuge for children with tuberculosis.

In the 1970s, Villa Heriot became the headquarters for the International University of Art Restoration in Venice, and is now the International Institute of Art. You can visit the house, garden, archives and library during open hours, or take a guided tour. One feature to keep an eye out for is the fabulous bifurcated staircase in the main house.

Address: Calle Michelangelo 54
Vaporetto Stop: Zitelle.

5. The Redentore

One of the most famous buildings in all of Venice is the beautiful Palladio-designed church of Il Redentore (The Redeemer). It was built to thank God for delivering the people of Venice from the plague of 1575—76, when 46,000 Venetians (30% of the population) died.

The church was consecrated in 1592 and handed over to the care of the Order of Friars Minor Capuchin, who still care for it now. Notice the lack of tombs. The Capuchins never allowed families to inter their dead inside the church, so this is the only building in Venice that is exactly as the architect built it. Of course, there is some pretty remarkable art here too, with works from Tintoretto, Veronese, and Bassano.

This church is considered to be one of Palladio's greatest works. He designed it as a respite from the decadence and debauchery of Venice, giving it a pure, cleansing, classical style. Inspired by the Pantheon in Rome (look for the similarities), the 15 steps up to the entrance symbolize the 15 steps of the temple of Jerusalem. Palladio used a gentle gradient to meet his requirement that "the ascent of the faithful will be gradual, so the climbing will bring more devotion".

The smooth white lines of Il Redentore instantly calm the optical busyness of Venice. Inside, the church is remarkable. It is the divine color –all bright white and full of light, and feels very vertical, as though all the pure white energy is soaring upwards. I think it's fantastic, almost built like a Roman temple. The view from the balcony, looking down, is symmetrical and stunning.

Every year on the third Sunday in July, Venice celebrates one of its favorite festivals, *Il Redentore*. For centuries, shortly before the third

Sunday in July they would erect a pontoon bridge connecting the church to the Zattere on Dorsoduro. On that third Sunday, the doge and the senators would walk across it to take mass at Il Redentore. A major celebration followed.

Today, they celebrate Il Redentore with one of the most spectacular fireworks displays you will ever see. The lagoon fills with boats, everyone picnics and drinks Prosecco, those without boats line the Zattere and the waterfront of Giudecca. The following day there is a procession across the pontoon bridge. It is a spectacular event.

Address: Redentore, Giudecca.
Vaporetto Stop: Redentore.

6. Convento Santa Cosma e Damiano

Founded in 1481 by Marina Celsi, this was one of the most prestigious convents/female monasteries in all of Venice. Several of the most influential noble families parked their daughters here, including the Contarini, the Falier and the Giustini. (Remember, daughters marrying into other families diluted family fortunes, so unless there was an advantageous match to be made, it was thought better to offload spare daughters into convents.) This convent followed strict Benedictine rules of encloisterment, confining the girls as if they were imprisoned. Although starting with only 15 nuns, by 1508 the convent had 100.

In 1806, Napoleon turned the convent into a warehouse, then a barracks, and the remaining 32 nuns moved to San Zaccaria. In 1887 it became a hospice for cholera victims. In 1897, the Herion brothers converted it into a textile factory, destroying the interior. In the 1990s, the church became office space for small businesses, while the convent became housing. At one time, it was full of incredible artwork by the likes of Tiepolo, Tintoretto and Molinari. They moved some of the art into museums, but much was lost. Look for Girolamo Pellegrini's fresco *Virgin With Female Saints* in the chancel's dome.

In the 1980s, the convent became part of a council re-qualification initiative, revisiting the Venetian history of *Casa e Bottega*, where an artisan lived above his workshop. The project created 10 workshop studios in the cloisters, each with an apartment above it on the first floor. This little art commune is called the **Artisti Artiginani del Choistro**. These are local artists creating traditional Venetian products, including masks, glass, paintings and all kinds of cool stuff. You will find tremendous souvenirs here. For lovers of Murano glass, the workshop of **Stefano Morasso** offers all kinds of interesting pieces, from jewelry to bowls and glasses. Stefano is from Murano.

Another workshop to visit is the paper shop **Carta Venezia**. Fernando, the artisan here, makes incredible handmade papers and handmade paper things –lampshades, jewelry, notepaper and notebooks, bookmarks –all kinds of wonderful items that make unique souvenirs and gifts. Before moving to Venice, Fernando's background was in graphic design and teaching graphic design, and his work is magnificent. He creates and uses cotton paper because of its strength and durability, so you're not buying something flimsy. I consider his workshop to be amongst the best-kept secrets in Venice.

Address: Calle Cosmo, Giudecca 620
Vaporetto Stop: S. Eufemia.

7. Chiesa Sant' Eufemia

Another fascinating little church well worth visiting. Founded in 865 and dedicated to four saints, Euphemia, Dorothy, Tecla and Erasma, the name got shortened to the first saint, Euphemia and before long, the locals referred to it as *Famia.* All these centuries later, most still do. It was renovated in 952 and then had some more work done and was reconsecrated in 1371. The church received two more facelifts, one in the 16th century and another in the mid-18th century.

The portico is from 1596, from the church of SS Biago e Cataldo, which was demolished to make space for the Stucky Flour Mill, which is now the Molino Stucky Hotel. Giovanni Stucky donated the portico to San Eufemia in 1883, along with the crucifix above the main door. Inside, although it maintains its original Veneto-Byzantine form, you can really see the centuries of reconstruction. There are columns and capitals from the 11th century. The plaster on the lower walls is chipped away, revealing old brickwork, so you can see and feel the old shell of the building. Meanwhile, above it the flouncy rococo decor it is all white, pale green and gilt. There is tremendous art here too, including works by Veronese, Giambattista Canal, and Bartolomeo Vivarini.

There is also a very interesting sculpture of the Pieta. Instead of lying in Mary's lap, Jesus is draped over a rock. Mary holds out his left arm and has her right arm raised above him, probably doing something important, but at first glance, it looks like she is going to hit him over the head with a rock! Have a look and let me know what your first thought is when you see her! (I think she actually has cloth in her hand but it makes me laugh every time I see it.) Also, Mary looks about 12 years old. I'm intrigued by this piece.

The views from the inside the church looking outward are wonderful –your eye is drawn to the Zattere across the water.

There is also a lovely little hidden, walled in vegetable garden in the back of the church.

Address: Giudecca 680
Hours: The Church of Sant'Eufemia is open to the public Monday to Saturday, 8am—noon, then again from 3pm—5pm. On Sundays it's open 3pm—7pm.
Vaporetto Stop: Palanca.

8. Le Convertite

This was an Augustinian convent and a hospice for reformed prostitutes and other sexually besmirched women. (Does this imply that these women made a conscious choice *not* to become a countess or an aristocrat's wife?) Santa Mary Magdalena became known as *Le Convertite* because of its mission to convert fallen women.

Le Convertite gained notoriety when Fra Giovanni Pietro Leon made the 400 nuns into his personal harem. He would test a nun by fondling her during confession. If she refused his attentions, he would congratulate her on her chastity and then imprison and punish her until she eventually gave in. The Council of Ten found out about it and in 1561 beheaded the randy rector in Piazza San Marco. It took 13 tries with an axe before they gave up and just chopped his head off with a knife. (Taken as a sign from God that mere execution wasn't punishment enough for him, his remains were then burned.)

In 1806 under French rule, the convent became a hospital, then in 1857 under Austrian rule, it became a jail. Now it is the women's prison of Venice. Rather than punishing the women imprisoned here, the prison works on teaching the women skills and trades to rehabilitate and integrate them back into society. They grow some of the best organic produce in the city, create artisan goods and clothing, some of which are sold at the Biennale shops, and produce a range of toiletries (soaps, shampoos, lotions and gels) for the Bauer Hotel group. Some of these are also sold through a co-op.**

You can't visit the prison itself, but on Thursday mornings you can shop at the market the prison sets up on the fondamenta outside. Shopping at the Thursday morning market is a great way to support this effort *and* score yourself some top quality fruit and veges.

** There is also a retail clothing arm of the project. See Banco #10 in the **Shopping** chapter.

Address: Fondamenta delle Convertite
Vaporetto Stop: Palanca.

9. Fortuny

In 1919, Spanish fashion designer Mariano Fortuny purchased this former convent and turned it into his production area and factory. He had been living in Venice since he was 18, and worked out of the family palazzo (Palazzo Fortuny) until moving the business to Giudecca. He opened for business in Giudecca in 1921.

Fortuny developed his own brushes and dyes, as well as his fabric and textile patterns, drawing inspiration from Catalan motifs, Morris prints, and Greek clothing. He created a revolutionary system to make the designs look carved into the fabrics. They are exquisite.

The world famous Fortuny fabrics are still produced here, using the original machines and maintaining Mariano's secret processes to treat the cotton, developed over 100 years ago.

The property has beautiful gardens where they host wildly chic events.

Address: Giudecca 805
Hours: You can visit the showroom and gardens by appointment only, Monday to Friday, 10am—1pm then again from 2pm—6pm
Vaporetto Stop: Palanca.

10. The Molino Stucky Building

Next to Fortuny on the far west edge of Giudecca, this neo-Gothic building began its auspicious life in 1884. Giovanni Stucky's father, a mill owner from Switzerland, married into the Italian Forti family. Giovanni built a flour mill on this site, which later became a pasta factory.

Giovanni was the city's largest employer, employing 1500 workers each day. The success of Stucky Pasta made him the richest man in Venice. He was popular too, so everyone was devastated when he was murdered in the railway station by a mentally unstable former employee. Stucky had just celebrated 25 years in business. The factory declined from 1910, despite the valiant efforts of the workers to keep it going. By 1955 it closed down entirely.

In the 2000s, the Hilton group converted this building into a 5-star hotel with 379 rooms, a 2000 seat conference facility, a rooftop swimming pool, one of the best health clubs in Venice, and one of Venice's famous night spots, the Skyline Bar. The views from the Skyline alone make the bar's €14 spritzes worth every time.

The building also offers surprisingly affordable and really beautiful Airbnb apartments. They share the Hilton facilities, including the complimentary boat shuttle service to Zattere and San Marco. This can be a brilliant spot to enjoy luxury, right on the water, while avoiding the crowds –even in the middle of summer.

Address: Giudecca 810
Vaporetto Stop: Palanca.

Getting to Guidecca

You can reach Giudecca quickly and easily on the #2 vaporetto from San Zaccaria (just up from St Mark's Square). Make sure you get on the correct #2 –both go to Ple. Roma, one via the Giudecca Canal (this is the one you want) and the other via the Grand Canal. The #2 goes from San Zaccaria to San Giorgio (3 minutes) then 3 more minutes to Zitelle, followed by the Redentore and Palanca stops. You can also take a vaporetto from Zattere to Palanca (Molino Stucky).

Giudecca is so small it doesn't matter which vaporetto stop you use. The one-way ride is €5 instead of the normal €7,50.

When you get there, take a pleasant stroll along the fondamenta, stop for a drink along the way and enjoy the gorgeous views and the calm atmosphere.

27.
Lido

It seemed like a magical city, floating on the lagoon
as if conjured by an enchanter's wand.

–Kate Forsyth

Lido is an 11km/7-mile-long barrier island separating the Venice Lagoon from the Adriatic Sea. It looks completely different to the rest of Venice, and visitors come here for a completely different experience. This island has cars and buses, which even after all these years still give me a jolt when I see them. Lido is home to 20,000 people, spread across the island, from the main town at one end to a village at the other. It is also home to the Venice Film Festival and has staged runway shows for design houses such as Chanel. With its luxurious hotels and villas built in the Liberty style of the 19th century, and wide boulevards, there's a chic glamour to the island.

I consider Lido a guilty pleasure when I'm in Venice, and I always block out an extra day just to come here (or at least an afternoon). Here's why: Lido has absolutely gorgeous beaches stretching the full length of the island that would satisfy every Italian beach dream you've ever had. Don't worry –I'm not sending you for a dip in the cruise ship polluted waters of the lagoon. Instead, you and I are going to head to the other side of the island, only a 10-minute walk from the vaporetto. A few steps from the vaporetto stop, turn left onto a wide sweeping boulevard that will escort you from the lagoon across to the Adriatic. This is Granviale Santa Maria Elisabetta, and it literally drops you off at the beach.

The Adriatic coast of Lido is full of award-winning, pristine beaches. There are public beaches, hotel-owned stretches of beach and (my favorite) Italian beach clubs or *stabilimenti*, where you can rent sunchairs and a beach umbrella, perfectly lined up in rows. Most beach clubs have a bar serving light food. You get a locker with a key in which to stash your valuables, and the changing rooms are clean and private. The beaches here are lovely, and they are super clean. The swimming conditions are idyllic. Even better, the tourist crowds don't seem to know about it. Welcome to Italian summer life!

I love people-watching here. People in neighboring sunchairs invariably end up chatting with me and inviting me to swim with them. So even when I go to Lido by myself, I'm never alone.

There is more to this island than lounging on a gorgeous beach and swimming in the most perfect water, though. If you can bear to tear yourself away, here are some other things you can do while you're here.

1. Walk with Marlena di Blasi

This is where Marlena di Blasi first lived when she moved to Venice to marry Fernando. I highly recommend reading all of her books, starting with the first, the gorgeous *A Thousand Days in Venice: An Unexpected Romance*. Wander Lido and discover the places she talks about. The way she writes will open a portal in your brain that washes everything with beauty.

2. Rent a bike

There are bike rental places all along Granviale Santa Maria Elisabetta, each with excellent bike rentals. It is lovely riding a bike the length of the Adriatic coastline, taking in the fabulous hotels and villas, enjoying the shade of the trees, and admiring the beauty of the beaches. If you do this in the morning, you can spend the afternoon at the beach.

3. Stroll the Gran Viale

Granviale Santa Maria Elisbetta (commonly known just as Gran Viale) is full of shops and eateries. After the hustle and bustle of the tourists in Venice proper, it feels low key and glorious.

4. Visit the Tempio Votivo

Just along from the vaporetto stop, this landmark is one of the first buildings you'll notice as you arrive on Lido. Its huge green dome and cylindrical white building are hard to miss. This is a church and war memorial, built between 1925 and 1935 to celebrate Venice emerging from World War I somewhat unscathed, and in particular for its deliverance from the bombing raid of 27 February 1918. The Tempio Votivo is one of the most recent major religious buildings constructed in the lagoon (constructed 100 years ago).

5. Visit the church and monastery of San Niccolo'

Turn left when you exit the vaporetto stop and wander up to the church and monastery of San Nicolo' (the patron saint of sailors). Strategically placed at the main access to the Adriatic Sea, this was the final stop for ships departing on expeditions. In 1071 with the Basilica San Marco still under construction, Doge Domenico Selvo was elected and crowned here. In 1099, the first crusade departed from here. In 1100, the relics of St Nicholas were interred here after being stolen from Lycia in Turkey, and spending some time in Bari. There are paintings here too, by Palma il Vecchio and Palma il Giovane.

This is an 11th century single nave church, with a 16th century renaissance cloister. The baroque campanile was built between 1626 and 1629. The three church bells have been in place since the 16th century, ringing in the key of G Major. (Nearby the bells of San Giorgio Maggiore ring in C# Major.) Initially San Niccolo' was a Benedictine monastery, but in 1770, the Franciscan monks took over.

This church is where Venice would celebrate its traditional thanksgiving mass for the Sposalizio del Mare (Marriage of the Sea) ceremony. Every year, the doge came here on his special boat as part of the celebration.

You may recognize San Niccolo' from film and television. The James Bond franchise has used San Niccolo' in two movies –*Casino Royale* in 2006, and in 1979's *Moonraker* it was used as the MI6 headquarters. In 1971, the film *Death in Venice* was shot here.

San Niccolo' is adjacent to the next place on the list, the Old Jewish Cemetery.

6. Wander the Old Jewish Cemetery

Venice had one of the largest Jewish communities in all of Europe. In 1386, they were permitted to have their own cemetery, providing it was away from the city. The Republic allocated them land on (mostly uninhabited) Lido Island.

This cemetery is at the north end of Lido, built on property belonging to the monastery of San Nicolo'. It used to be larger, but in the 16th century Venice reclaimed some of the land and the northern end of the cemetery was lost, along with its tombstones. A few hundred grave markers from the lost area were moved into the remaining cemetery and piled on top of what was already there, creating a second level of tombstones. In 1774, the Jewish community abandoned this cemetery and moved to a larger one nearby with its entrance on Via Cipro.

This old cemetery had fallen into ruins, then in 1929, the section closest to the lagoon was reappropriated to extend the lagoon road. Now only one sixth of its original size, the Old Jewish Cemetery holds roughly 1200 burial monuments, tombstones, sarcophagi and grave markers. These range from the traditional simple form to very ornate, including some with family crests. In 1999, Save Venice began draining the swampy land, excavating and restoring sunken grave markers and tombstones dating from around 1550 to the early 17th century.

The tree-filled cemetery with its trove of medieval stone artwork is oddly beautiful and really quite fascinating. You can visit it by appointment, Sunday through Friday. It is closed on Saturdays and all Jewish holidays. If you are interested in Venice's Jewish history, I recommend hiring a local guide and combining a visit here with a visit to the Jewish Ghetto in Cannaregio.

7. Visit the Armenian Monastery

Since 1717, the small island of San Lazzaro degli Armeni, just off the coast of Lido, has been home to the Armenian Catholic Monastery of San Lazzaro. The poet Byron stayed here for a while to study Armenian. The monastery even has a permanent exhibition devoted to him and his stay on the island. Also of note is the island's publishing house, established in 1789. This is the oldest continuously working Armenian publishing house in the world. Every day, the monks here offer a tour of the island.

8. Go to Malamocco

At the southern end of Lido, a series of bridges take you to a picturesque little village on its own miniature island. This is Malamocco. Wander the island and take photos –it's a lovely place. Look for the Piazza Maggiore, where you will find the Church of Santa Maria Assunta and the Gothic style Palazzo del Podesta'. The palazzo was home to mayors of Malamocco until 1339. It is now the village museum. Also, check out the Ponte Borgo, the oldest bridge in Malamocco. This place is full of character and beauty and completely off the main tourist radar.

9. Eat in Pellestrina

Pellestrina is another long, thin barrier island. At its southernmost tip, it is just across from the port town of Choggia. This is an island of fishermen and lacemakers. While it's not as pretty as the other islands, Pellestrina is known for its phenomenal seafood.

From Lido, either take the #11 bus or ride your rental bike to the ferry at Porto Santa Maria del Mare. It's very close. You can't get lost on Pellestrina –the island is only a couple of streets wide and is ideal for walking or biking.

Fans of Donna Leon's Commissario Brunetti series will know this island from the book *A Sea of Troubles*. I adore visiting the places from books and movies I've loved, so the Brunetti connection makes this a fun spot for lunch in one of its two restaurants. Don't expect fancy but do expect exceptional seafood.

10. Spend an Afternoon at the Beach

I'm repeating myself here, but if you're a beach lover and want to escape the crowds, reward yourself with a swim in the Adriatic Sea and get an Italian tan. Wander along the promenade and choose the prettiest beach club or relax on a public beach. It's an experience not to be missed!

28.
Murano

Anyone who knew the recipe of the alchemists could make gold, but only the artisans of Murano could make glass so fine, one could nearly touch one's fingers together on either side; cristallo without an imperfection or blemish, clear as the sky, with a sparkle to rival that of diamonds.

–Ruth Nestvold

Murano is an absolute joy. I love taking the vaporetto to the Colonna stop, then just walking everywhere. The vaporetto goes through the canals, but Murano is so small that unless it's raining, I recommend just wandering.

In my experience, the crowds hang out along the Rio dei Vetrai –the main "road" from Colonna and through the heart of the glass shopping district. True, it is a beautiful stretch of waterway with shops and eateries but move on beyond there and you'll find fewer tourists and more local life, serene campi with trees and benches, historic buildings and gorgeous views. Here is the Murano you will fall in love with, at a leisurely pace.

Murano is a collection of seven small islands connected by bridges. Approximately one mile northeast of Venice, it is small, requiring only about 30 minutes to walk from one end to the other. Murano has thousands of years of history. The Romans were here, then in the 5th century it became the home to refugees from Altino. In the old, *old* days, Murano made its money as a fishing port and through salt production.

In 1291, Doge Pietro Gradenigo ordered that all Venetian glassmaking furnaces move to Murano. The reason was twofold: furnaces posed a huge fire risk to Venice, and Venetian glass was not only unique, but it was also the most coveted glass in the world. By keeping all the glassmakers on an island, the doge secured Venetian glassmaking secrets and techniques from the prying eyes of international merchants (and spies) walking the streets of the port city. There was a catch though – Murano's glassmakers were forbidden to leave the Republic.

In the early 1300s, Murano became famous for making mirrors and glass beads, after which it became Europe's main glass producer for everything from glass goblets to chandeliers. The glass masters of Murano invented new methods and technologies including enameled glass (*smalto*), crystalline glass, glass with gold threads (*aventurine*), milk glass (*lattimo*) multicolored glass (*millefiori*), and imitation gemstones. They also made miniature glass beads, which were threaded by the impiraressa and used around the world as trade beads. The industry became so highly esteemed that by the late 14th century, daughters of glass masters could marry into Venice's noble families.

In the 15th century, Murano became a popular location for summer palazzi and resorts for the wealthy. In the 19th century, orchards and vegetable gardens in the countryside of Murano were torn out to make room for more housing. The island population peaked in the 15th and 16th centuries when it reached as high as 30,000. Now around 5500 people live on Murano. Throughout the April to October tourist season it gets a daily influx of people coming enjoy wandering and exploring, and to see demonstrations of glass blowing.

THE GLASS FACTORIES

Glassmaking has a 1000-year-old history on Murano. Not visiting a glassmaker while you're here would be practically a crime.

When in Italy, I am always looking for Christmas presents, birthday presents and business gifts. I love giving something different and special, and the recipients always love them. And, of course, I find amazing gifts on Murano.

Recently, while wandering in and out of glass shops along the Rio dei Vetrai I found these unique, square glass paperweights with designs inside them. While the wife of the glassmaker was explaining how they make them, I spotted a design that reminded me of the logo for a Kenzo perfume my mother and I both used to wear. (Hilariously, when I actually looked at a bottle of Kenzo Flower, the two designs were nothing alike.) I was so excited about it, and the saleswoman was excited that I was excited. She found another almost identical one so that I could buy one each for my mother and myself. The two paperweights were small enough to carry around in my handbag all day, and I have to tell you, sitting here at my desk writing this book, every time I glance over at my not-Kenzo paperweight, it brings me so much joy.

I was back and forth through Murano several times in 2021 with my tour travelers, some of whom shipped back substantial pieces, and others who, like me, picked up small items for souvenirs or gifts. When walking past the shop with the paperweights a few months later, this same woman popped her head out, smiling from ear to ear, and asked me if my mother enjoyed her gift.

That's one thing I love about experiences like this –interacting with lovely human beings, buying items that are a part of the local culture, putting money into the immediate local economy (even if it's not a huge amount of money) and coming away from it all with something unique that has an emotional value to me.

If you read my book about Florence, you'll already know about me going crazy buying up everything in the Catherine de' Medici fragrance at the Farmacia in Santa Maria Novella. All of which brings me so much pleasure every single time I use any of them. I think that's the key to buying souvenirs when we travel –picking up locally made items which have some meaning for you.

(In case you're wondering, my mother absolutely loves her paperweight. Funnily enough, she immediately saw the similarity to the Kenzo design too!)

Covid and the Furnaces

The Covid pandemic had a horrible impact on the glass industry. In March 2020, for the first time in who knows how long, Murano's furnaces, which burn 24 hours per day, 7 days per week, were forced to shut down and go cold. When Italy closed down all nonessential work for three months, that included the glass furnaces on Murano. I don't know how many of the roughly 100 historic furnaces have been rekindled at the time of writing this book. While on the island in 2021, I was told many were still not burning, and some may be shuttered for good.

Turning off the kilns is a challenging and expensive process. At Schiavon, they showed me a ceramic basin inside the kiln, which cracks whenever the furnace is cooled, even if cooled slowly. The basins cost thousands of euros to replace. Also, when you reignite the furnace, it takes 10 days to heat it to adequate glass-working temperatures, and it costs up to €10,000 per kiln. With such excessive costs, not all furnaces will reopen. Many that have are still suffering from the excruciating costs. Your support of these businesses, even by only buying something small, is very important.

And Then There are the Fakes

As if loss of income and horrendous cost of re-starting weren't enough, Murano glassmakers have to compete with counterfeit sellers in Venice. Many Murano furnaces have showrooms or shops in Venice, but so do the Made In China knockoff merchants. (I've talked about this extensively in the **Shopping** chapter and suggested specific tools to avoid being ripped off.) One way to avoid being hoodwinked by cheap Chinese knockoffs (at Murano glass prices no less) is to come directly to Murano. Along with buying the real deal, you can see the furnaces and watch the masters at work. Having observed the furnaces in action, I have a whole different appreciation for Murano glass, its history, the dedication of the glass-workers, the astounding complexity of what they do, and what makes it incredibly special.

There are many furnaces on Murano, so instead of listing all of them, I'm going to include only two on my list of things to do on Murano. I hope that you will check out several others while you're here, because each has its own story and its own specialty.

10 Things to Do on Murano

These are my favorite things to do here, including a lunch spot I would happily dine at a hundred times. I've included the vaporetto stops to give you an idea of where on Murano each place is, but I suggest you just walk –everything is within a very small area.

1. Museo del Vetro

This museum is dedicated to the history of Murano's glass industry. Housed in a 17th century palace, it became a museum in 1861.

During the peak of the Murano glass trade in the 19th century, local glassmakers donated massive amounts of their work to the Vetro Museum, so it has an expansive collection that really takes you through the craft across generations of families.

The space is light, bright and well thought out. I suggest checking out the website (below) and booking tickets if this interests you.

Address: Fondamenta Giustinian 8
Website: museovetro.visitmuve.it
Vaporetto Stop: Museo.

2. Seguso

When John Berendt's book *The City of Falling Angels* came out in 2005, I gained an entirely new appreciation for Murano glass. I've mentioned Berendt several times in this book, because *The City of Fallen Angels* introduced me to many new characters in Venice and set me off on some entirely different explorations and experiences in the floating city. I'm one of those people who seldom remembers facts and figures but tell me a good story about a building or its inhabitants and I remember it forever. Without Berendt I never would have gone snooping around Dorsoduro looking for Ezra Pound's house, nor become fascinated with Save Venice and their restoration of Santa Maria dei Miracoli. In fact, since reading it I'm interested in everything they do. The book marked the beginning of my obsession with Peggy Guggenheim, and my fascination with Seguso.

Seguso has been making Murano glass for over 600 years, and is mentioned in documents in the Venice archives, dated 3 May 1397! The family was so highly esteemed they were added to the Libro d'Oro of Murano in 1605, affording them noble titles and privileges.

Their business was successful during the 16th and 17th centuries, their products sought worldwide, from as far away as the brand new country of America. Seguso glass is displayed in over 75 museums around the world, including the V&A in London and MOMA in New York. The family has made pieces for popes and princes. It is not only one of the largest furnaces in Murano but is also one of the most highly esteemed. Archimede Seguso died in 1999 but his sons have continued the business.

Seguso's showrooms are a must-see. They also have an absolutely fantastic guided event called Seguso Experience that shows you the furnaces and glass blowing and takes you through the family history and the history of glassmaking on Murano. I recommend checking out the videos and reviews on their website. This is no ordinary tour and you will want to do it. It was awarded Attraction of the Year for Italy in 2016 — it's that good! A booking is required (see website below) and although you hear about people lucking out and getting last-minute reservations, it sells out fast.

Address –Furnace: Campiello San Maffio 1, Murano
Address –Murano Showroom: Fondamenta Venier 29
Address –Venice Showroom: Dorsoduro 723 (near the Peggy Guggenheim)
Website: www.seguso.com

3. Schiavon Art Team

I love bringing my Glam Italia Tour groups to see this place. Schiavon Art Team is one of the most famous glass factories in Murano. You can watch a glass blowing demonstration here and wander their factory showrooms. There are two other showrooms/shops –in Murano and in Dorsoduro.

The showrooms at the furnace on Fondamenta Serenella are huge and give you a fantastic insight into what makes this glassworks so incredible and sought after worldwide. It really is spectacular. To watch a glass blowing demonstration, you need to book ahead on the website below.

Max (Massimiliano) is a 6th generation glass blower. He left his father's firm more than a decade ago to reopen his grandfather's old furnace at the current location. His work is vibrant and exciting, combining old techniques with his modern vision. This is one of my favorite places to watch a glass blowing demonstration.

Address –Furnace and Showroom: Fondamenta Serenella 18 (turn left when you exit the vaporetto at Colonna and follow the walkway along the sea for about 3 minutes)
Address –Rainbow Art and Beads: Fondamenta Vetrai 63—64, Murano
Address –Max's Studio in Murano: Fondamenta Manin 32, Murano
Address –Max's Studio in Venice: San Vio, Dorsoduro 869.

4. Basilica Santa Maria e San Donato

This basilica is a must-see, if not for the spectacular mosaic floors, then for the dragon slaying accomplishments of one of its patron saints. This is one of the oldest churches in Venice.

In the 7th century, the Muriani and Muraneschi families founded this church, dedicating it to Saint Mary. It had a Veneto-Byzantine rebuild between 1125 and 1140, at which time it received the incredible mosaic floor, and became the recipient of the relics of the dragon slaying bishop, Saint Donato of Arezzo. Donato was a performer of miracles, bringing a woman named Euphrosina back from the dead, returning sight to a blind woman named Syriana, exorcising a demon that was tormenting the son of the Roman prefect of Arezzo, and (my personal favorite) fighting and slaying a dragon who had poisoned the local well in Arezzo. A set of rib bones from the dragon are behind the altar at Basilica Santa Maria e Donato. (They're probably mammoth bones or some other extinct creature.)

The floor is made from precious Mediterranean stone, serpentine and porphyry, and measures 500 square meters (5382 square feet). Along with geometric patterns, it also features figurative animals including a peacock, an eagle, two roosters carrying a fox, and some griffins. It is quite remarkable and definitely worth coming to see. The floor was damaged in the great flood of 1966 and was the beneficiary of a large rescue effort by Save Venice.

Horrific flooding in November 2019 submerged the floor again in corrosive water, causing massive damage and again Save Venice came to the rescue. A team of restorers along with master mosaicist Giovanni Cucco have been repairing damaged and missing tesserae (the individual pieces used to make mosaics). Interestingly, parts of the church that Save Venice restored in 2012—2015 withstood damage from the recent flooding. This shows the benefit to be gained from constant maintenance of some of Venice's really old buildings. Unfortunately, it is excruciatingly expensive. During the repair work, they removed a rotting wooden door and wooden staircase, revealing more mosaic floor that had been hidden for who knows how long?

Even just the exterior of the Basilica is fascinating and well worth visiting while you're in Murano.

Address: Calle San Donato 11
Vaporetto Stop: Museo.

5. Alessia Fuga

Alessia makes incredible jewelry and pieces from Murano glass. Her collection is fabulous, and her shop is a great place to pick up something special to bring home. She has items at a variety of price points. Have a quick look at her website so you are familiar with her style and then add her to your must-see list for Murano. She also offers workshops for all ages. (I talk about Alessia in the shopping section but wanted to bring her up again here, so remember to pop into her store, which is close to the Basilica of SS Maria e Donato.)

Address: Rio Tera San Salvador 12
Website: www.AlessiaFuga.com
Vaporetto Stop: Museo.

6. Chiesa di San Pietro Martire

Although somewhat unassuming from the outside, there are staggering works of art inside this church. There is a Tintoretto, two Bellinis, works by Palma il Giovane, Veronese, da Lodi and Guiseppe Porta. There is also an Ecce Homo from 1495.

This naked brick building is one of two parish churches in Murano. The original church and convent on this site burned to the ground in 1474, and they built the current church in 1511. From the outside you can see Renaissance arcades and columns, possibly the remains of the original 16th century cloister, a 16th century portal and above it a vast rose window. The free-standing bell tower dates back to 1498. The interior is high and spacious and airy, with an interesting combination of arches and columns and white Murano glass chandeliers hanging below a wooden ceiling. During restoration work in 1922—28, the original frescos above the pillars were discovered. Restorations in 1981 included roof repairs and rotten brickwork being replaced, and Save Venice financed repairs to the stonework of the bifora window above the side door.

Address: Fondamenta dei Vetrai, Campiello Marco Michieli 3
Vaporetto: Murano da Mula.

7. Santa Maria dei Angeli

This church has a fascinating history that involves our friend Casanova.

Ginevra Gradenigo, a noblewoman forced to become a nun by her father, donated the land for the monastery, and the original church was built here in 1188. The original building was demolished and rebuilt in around 1529 and it remained one of the favorite convents to stash the daughters of Venice's prestigious families. The nuns were known to sneak out at night and have affairs. King Henry III of France, son of Catherine de' Medici, even popped by in 1574.

The church exterior is unassuming, but of course, there are treasures inside, including fabulous frescoes, Carrara marble carvings, and a ceiling with 40 round paintings depicting Apostles, Evangelists, Prophets, and angels surrounding a crowned virgin. The altarpiece, *The Annunciation* by Pordenone, is from 1537 and is considered the artist's greatest work. Thanks to Napoleon, the convent was closed and stripped of much of the artwork in 1810. It was restored in 1861 and reopened in 1863.

Casanova often came here for mass on Sunday, not because he was devout, but because (according to his memoir) the woman he loved, 22-year-old MM (Marina Morosini), was a nun here. The daughter of a nobleman, she was not happy being forced into convent life. Apparently, she instigated the affair, dropping Casanova a note after a church service. Casanova acquired a secret apartment near San Moisè in San Marco for their trysts –a five room apartment with white marble fireplaces and an octagonal bedroom with a mirrored ceiling. The apartment came with the services of a private chef who delivered luxurious meals via a dumbwaiter so the guests' identities would remain secret. The wealthy nuns were accustomed to sneaking out by night and apparently MM did so dressed as an elegant boy, her long golden hair braided down her back. Her previous lover, French Ambassador Joachim de Bernis, escorted her in the gondola and, according to Casanova, the affair went on for months.

The convent building where MM lived was demolished in 1810. The church was divided into two parts, with the nuns' ancient chorus made into a military hospital, and the rest of the church was kept intact. When you enter, you walk along a corridor with several doorways before you reach the church proper.

Address: Fondamenta Cristoforo Parmense 48 C
Vaporetto Stop: Murano Venier.

8. Campo Santo Stefano

This wide-open city square (campo) is one of the most visited spots on Murano. The two biggest draws are the 19th century clock tower which can be seen from far away, and the abstract blue glass sculpture in the middle of the campo, the *Comet Glass Star* by Simone Cenedese.

The campo is at the end of the Rio dei Vetrai (on the Faro side of the waterway) where it meets the Grand Canal of Murano. It only takes a couple of minutes to walk up here.

Address: Campo Santa Stefano
Vaporetto Stop: Faro.

9. Palazzo da Mula

This wonderful old palazzo was an important building historically (although now it's a municipal building).

This was the luxurious summer home of the da Mula family and later used as a summer residence by other families from Venice's Golden Book (the book of nobility). One of the coveted features of the palazzo was the garden and inner courtyard. With land in short supply and therefore super expensive, the courtyard was unique. Some of the summer guests enjoying this courtyard over the centuries included the Queen of Cyprus, the Mocenigo, Contarini, Pesaro, Giustinian and the Trevisan families.

The Palazzo da Mula is a fabulous example of Venetian Gothic architecture. Built in the late 12th or early 13th century, it went through multiple restorations over the centuries, but the façade remains unaltered. The three-story palazzo has tremendous Venetian-Byzantine arches and windows, white balustraded balconies, tiles, bas reliefs and *patere* embedded in the wall. It is gorgeous and packed with history.

You get your best view from Ponte Longo and across the Grand Canal along the Fondamenta Venier. At the end of Rio dei Vetrai hang a left on Murano's Grand Canal and the Ponte Longo and the Palazzo da Mula are just ahead of you.

Address: Fondamenta da Mula 152
Vaporetto Stop: Murano da Mula.

10. Lunch at Della Mora

I ate here recently with one of my Glam Italia Tour groups and it was fantastic. I can't even take credit for choosing the restaurant –my group went to find a place to eat while I helped a client in a glass shop. When choosing a restaurant, I'd told them …

- choose a place full of Italians,
- find an outdoor table (it was a gorgeous day),
- don't get a table on a major thoroughfare.

They chose Della Mura and grabbed a table in the outdoor area around the corner from the Rio dei Vetrai. The place was packed –I can't believe we got a table.

Apart from the German couple behind us, the tables were full of Italians. This is always the best sign –way more accurate than a Trip Advisor review or anything a magazine or book will tell you. Italians only eat where the food is fantastic and won't waste time or money on tourist fare.

Our waitress had a mass of curly black hair, a huge smile and was totally engaging and fun. The service took a while (every table was full), but the wine was wonderful and *oh good lord* –the food! I would wait forever for a lunch like that. We each ordered something different, and everything was amazing. Now that I know about it, I keep coming back here!

Della Mora is a great place for traditional Murano-Venetian food, so think incredible seafood, seafood-based pastas, and tremendous mixed fried foods Venetian style.

Address: Fondamenta Manin 75
Vaporetto Stop: Faro.

INSIDER TIPS

1. Don't take a "free" boat ride to Murano. The free boats are arranged by specific glass factories and you'll be under substantial pressure to buy from them. You can get there easily by vaporetto.

2. Have a look at the glass consortium's website www.Promovetro.com before you go. It will give you an idea of who's who. I like having a rough idea of which glass factories and shops I want to visit before heading to the island.

3. Avoid the touts outside the shops trying to call you inside. It helps to have a plan of where you want to go ahead of time.

4. Visit everywhere else on your list before going to the glass shops, unless you have a demonstration booked. You don't want to be carrying glass all over the island. Also, once you've been exploring, you'll be more relaxed, you will have found some glass factories away from the crowds, and you'll be less likely to feel overwhelmed by all the action at the beginning of the Rio dei Vetrai.

Getting to Murano

To get to Murano by vaporetto you have three options:

Vaporetto #3 departs from Piazzale (Ple.)Roma, goes to Ferrovia (train station) and from there straight to Murano. It circles inside Murano, stopping at Colonna, Faro, Navagero, Museo, da Mula, Venier and then back to the train station and Ple Roma. The ride out takes about 20 minutes.

Vaporetto #4.1 circles Venice counter-clockwise. From Fondamente Nove B, it stops at San Michele (the cemetery island), then at Murano Colonna, taking only about 10 minutes. The #4.1 also stops at Murano Faro, Navagero and Museo before coming back.

The #4.1 from Ple. Roma takes over an hour to get to Murano, so from there you are better taking the #3.

Vaporetto #4.2 is a good choice to come back from Murano. It goes clockwise and takes about 20 minutes to get to Fondamente Nove.

Vaporetto #12 goes from Fondamente Nove A to Murano Faro, Mazzorbo, Torcello and Burano (sometimes to Treporti and Punta Sabbioni too).

Murano has two main vaporetto stops: Colonna, at the bottom of the island, and Faro, which is 3 minutes further on. If you want to visit more than one island, catch the connecting vaporetto at Faro.

29.
Torcello

Venice is a complicated place, physically and spiritually, and it is extraordinarily difficult to establish Venetian facts. Nothing is ever quite certain.

–Jan Morris

Compared to Murano and Burano, few people come to Torcello. It's not sparkling and full of brightly colored houses and it doesn't have a roaring glass trade or lace business. It does however, have a 7th century cathedral with spectacular Byzantine mosaics, and is well worth a visit.

Fewer than a dozen people live on Torcello, one of whom is the parish priest. I can never decide if the island looks abandoned or like a superbly kept secret. When I leave (or if it's a cloud/ misty/ moody day), it feels like Torcello is a desolate and lonely place, and I always think it would be the perfect setting for a murder mystery or a ghost story. I love it.

The History of the Island

Torcello is the first important part of the story of Venice. When the Roman Empire fell (around 450AD), Torcello was the first island where the Veneti refugees settled as they escaped the barbarians and Attila the Hun. Over the next 200 years, repeated invasions of northern Italy sent more and more people to the relative safety of the island. The Bishop of Altino found safety here, and in 638 Torcello became the official seat of the bishopric for more than 1000 years. The people of Altino brought with them the relics of St Heliodorus, who became the island's patron saint.

Around the 5th century, the buildup of silt and sand made the ancient port of Altinum unusable, so a new port was built on Torcello. (A complex system of piers and warehouses has since been discovered, built on reclaimed, raised land. There must have been housing for workers too.) Shipping was a more viable way of moving goods than by land. With the fall of the Empire, the roads were no longer in great condition, and with marauding savages coming down from the north, the roads were no longer safe either. It made sense to focus on shipping, and Torcello was a brilliant spot to base it from. Torcello quickly became an important trade center. By the 10th century, it had an estimated population between 20,000 and 35,000. For a long time, it was the primary port in the lagoon, and a more powerful trading center than Venice.

By the 14th century, traders opted for the more amenable Venice instead. Silt from the rivers had increased swampiness around the island, making navigation treacherous for ships. Torcello's expanding swamps created massive numbers of mosquitos, and major outbreaks of malaria. The people of Torcello were forced to move to Burano, Murano and Venice. As they migrated, they took the stones that had built their houses with them, intending to use them to build new homes and businesses elsewhere. Just a handful of buildings were left behind.

In 1689, the bishop's seat moved to Murano, and by the time Napoleon arrived in 1797, the population of Torcello was down to 300.

Archaeologists have uncovered ancient history in Torcello too, predating the fall of the Roman Empire. They found wooden infrastructure with bricks and amphorae, along with signs the lagoon was used for fishing and salt harvesting during the Roman Empire. With infrastructure already in place, it makes sense the Veneti chose Torcello as their base.

1. The Legend of the Devil's Bridge

Shortly after disembarking the vaporetto, we stumble on a ghost story. Walking along the Strada della Rosina, you pass two eateries, the Taverna Tipica Veneziana and Al Trona di Attila, then come upon an unusual bridge –the Devil's Bridge. Like the Chioda Bridge in Cannaregio, this bridge has no balustrades, and has low, wide and deep steps that you could gallop across on a horse.

According to legend, during the Austrian occupation of Venice, a Venetian girl fell in love with an Austrian soldier. Her family was opposed to the traitorous relationship, so they killed him. Heartsick, the girl asked a witch to help her, and the witch agreed to meet her on the island of Torcello, which at the time was a remote place ideally suited for magic rituals. The witch called on the devil, and they made a deal. The Austrian boy was brought back to life, but in exchange, the witch promised to bring the soul of a recently deceased child to the island every Christmas Eve for the next 7 years. The witch died in a fire shortly after and couldn't honor their pact. To this day every Christmas Eve the devil comes to his bridge in Torcello disguised as a black cat, seeking the souls he was promised …

2. Locanda Cipriani

Another reason to come to Torcello is to eat or stay at Locanda Cipriani. Owned by the Cipriani family for 80+ years, this is a reception site, an exquisite restaurant (Cipriani restaurants are revered worldwide) and an upscale hotel, albeit with only five rooms. Locanda Cipriani is the perfect place to hole up and write a book. Hemingway did exactly that for an entire season, writing his masterpiece *Across the River and into the Trees.* Daphne du Maurier wrote her short story 'Don't Look Now' on Torcello. Be sure to look at the Locanda Cipriani guest book. Everyone who is anyone has been here, from royalty to presidents and prime ministers, fashion designers like Armani and Versace, artists, writers, and numerous actors, from Charlie Chaplin to George Clooney, 80 years' worth of celebrities have left their gratitude in the guest book and reading through it is a treat.

Address: Piazza Santa Fosca 29
Website: www.LocandaCipriani.com

3. The Church of Santa Maria Assunta

This fascinating little basilica is Torcello's biggest draw. One of the most ancient churches in all the Veneto, it contains the oldest mosaics in all of Venice and the surrounding area, dating from the 9th (some say the 7th) through to the 12th centuries. Not only the oldest church in the Veneto, this is also the oldest surviving structure in the lagoon. Santa Maria Assunta was built in 639 and renovated in 864. Not much of the original stonework survived the renovations, other than part of the central apse wall, and the old baptistery, which is now part of the current church's facade. The current church was built to the same plan as the original. The final renovation was in

1008, with a couple of additions in the 13th and 14th centuries –this church is *old.*

I especially love the mosaics. The main apse has a breathtaking 11th century mosaic of the Virgin Hodgetria. She stands against a gold background, above a semi-circular register of standing saints. If you enjoy Byzantine mosaics, as I do, this staggeringly brilliant work is not to be missed. The ring of saints is from the original 11th century Byzantine mosaicists, but the standing Virgin was reworked after suffering earthquake damage a century later.

There are other important works here too: *The Apostles, Christ Pantocrator, The Annunciation, The Ascension, Doctors of the Church, The Agnus Dei, The Crucifixion, The Anastasis* and the incredible *Last Judgment.* In total these works are overwhelming, when broken down into sections they are beyond spectacular.

Take time to look at the *Last Judgment*, as no doubt the parishioners from the Middle Ages did every Sunday when exiting the church. They couldn't read or write, so the way to brutally enforce the church's doctrine and make the parishioners obey the rules was through terrifying pictorials like this one. Look at what happens to those who Jesus passes judgment against.

A couple of years ago I had the good fortune to be the only person in the church. A fellow who worked there took the time to walk me through the various sections of mosaics and explain everything moment by moment. Even so, I could still come back a hundred times and notice something new every time. My advice is that if it feels like too much to take in, just focus on small details. If the small details feel overwhelming, step back and look at the total image. (This zoom in/zoom out theory applies to all of Venice.)

4. The Bell Tower

The freestanding bell tower was built during Torcello's financial peak in the 11th century, and stands tall like a navigational beacon. For a small fee, you can climb the bell tower and enjoy views stretching to the snow-capped mountains on one side and across Venice on the other. You can imagine how the island must have felt by the time Napoleon arrived. The population had dwindled into the hundreds, and the palazzi, churches and monasteries that had been here for centuries were all gone. There's a sadness about its beauty, but it is tremendous.

5. Santa Fosca

Adjacent to Santa Maria Assunta is the 11th century church of Santa Fosca. This lovely Venetian-Byzantine church is built to a Greek cross plan, has a shaded portico in front and around five sides. The columns of the porticoes are topped with Byzantine capitals. The church is a circular shape. All the once glorious palazzi, churches and signs of a thriving city had been plundered for building materials and completely removed, so the architecture jumps out at you and holds your attention. It demands it.

Santa Fosca is majestic. This was once a flourishing town, yet when you stand in this emptied campo and look around at these old buildings, the pieces of ancient columns, statues, wells, and the bas reliefs on the walls, it has an abandoned, desolate feel to it.

6. The Torcello Museum

Across from the cathedral, in a 14th century palazzo, you'll find the Torcello Museum. This was once the seat of government. The museum has medieval artifacts mostly from Torcello, along with archaeological finds from the Veneto, from the paleolithic time through the Roman period. These treasures spill out into the campo, down the side of the house, and onto the old walls around it. I love ruins and old treasures, so I love spending time in Torcello. If you're pressed for time, you may want to skip the museum and just wander around outside.

The museum is closed on Mondays.

7. Attila's Throne

In front of the museum, facing the two old churches, is a large stone chair known as the Throne of Attila. The most feared barbarians were the Huns, led by a fellow named Attila. Attila was so brutal and ferocious he was called the Scourge of God. In 452AD the Huns destroyed the city of Altinum, just 15 km southeast of Treviso. This event propelled the people of Altino to flee to the relative safety of Torcello. In a way, it is fitting that there be some kind of recognition of the barbaric Attila in the heart of town. Except this chair actually has nothing to do with the leader of the Huns and possibly wasn't even built until a century after his death. In all likelihood, it was the seat of the bishop or the magister militum –the governor of the island –who probably sat here when chairing council meetings or administering justice.

The chair is 1500 years old and you are free to sit in it. Just as rubbing the nose of the wild boar in Florence guarantees you will come back, legend says sitting in the Throne of Attila means you will come back to Torcello. I sit in it every time.

8. Casa Museo Andrich

Remember how I said fewer than 12 people live on Torcello today? Since 2003, one of these people is Paolo Andrich, nephew of the artist Lucio Andrich, who cares for his legacy.

Lucio Andrich and his artist wife Clementina de Luca lived in the sacristy of the Borgognoni church in the 1960s, and spent the next four decades creating more than 1000 pieces of art which are now on display in the Casa Museo Andrich.

This house afforded the artists a sensational view of the Palude della Rosa marshlands and the lagoon. The landscape here is drastically different from the rest of Torcello. From the shoreline, you can look out at the salt marshes and land formations and get an idea of how the entire lagoon was formed, and how fragile the ecosystem is. It is quiet and peaceful and serene.

I always think Venice has the most beautiful light in the world. When you pair that with the scenery here, you can understand why artists would move in and never leave. Its beauty also draws in flocks of flamingos from March through September.

Casa Museo Andrich is a house museum full of Lucio and Clementina's work. It also has an educational farm and meticulous private gardens. Tours of the property and the museum are led by Paolo and his dog Wagner.

Address: Fondamenta dei Borgognoni 4
Website: www.museoandrich.com

Where to Eat?

Along with Locanda Cipriani, there are several places to enjoy a quiet lunch far from the madding crowds of Burano, Murano, and Venice. All are event spaces frequently booked for weddings and parties, as well as great casual spots to enjoy authentic Venetian cuisine.

1. Osteria al Ponte Del Diavolo

Here you'll find an outstanding menu based on fresh, seasonal ingredients. The cuisine is Venetian with a strong emphasis on seafood and fresh pastas. Check out their website for has mouthwatering photos of their food.

Address: Fondamenta dei Borgognoni 10
Hours: Closed Mondays
Website: OsteriaAlPonteDelDiavolo.com

2. Ristorante Villa 600

This is a 17th century farmhouse once used by fishermen, now refurbished and quite beautiful, with lovely grounds. Villa 600 serves modern Venetian cuisine. It is part of the slow food movement and the zero-kilometer movement, which means that all ingredients are sourced locally and travel zero kilometers to get from farm to table.

Address: Fondamenta dei Borgognoni 12 (about 200 meters from the vaporetto stop)
Hours: Closed Wednesdays
Website: Villa600.it

3. Ristorante Al Trono di Attila

This property also has lovely grounds and outdoor spaces, along with an exceptional menu predominantly featuring local seafood.

Address: Fondamenta Borgognoni 7
Hours: Closed Mondays except during summer
Website: AlTronoDiAttila.com

Getting to Torcello

From Burano and Murano Faro, take the vaporetto #12.

From Burano, the vaporetto #9 runs between the two islands every 30 minutes.

30. Mazzorbo and San Francesco del Deserto

Mazzorbo

This is one of the least visited islands, even though it is connected by a bridge to the most touristed one (Burano) Fewer than 300 people live in Mazzorbo. Known for artichoke fields and wonderful wine, the island has a tremendous history and a Michelin Star restaurant.

The History of Mazzorbo

Originally called Maiurbian (*magna urbis,* which means "major town"), Mazzorbo was an important commercial center for centuries because of its proximity to Torcello. This lasted until the 11th century, when Venice became the economic and social capital of the lagoon. Over the following centuries, the island's financial glory slipped away, but it remained a vacation island for wealthy and noble Venetians. Few signs of the golden age remain today, but it does have a tremendous old church.

1. Santa Caterina Monastery

Between the 7th century and the 17th century there were four monasteries and five churches on Mazzorbo. Only one remains, the lovely Santa Caterina Monastery. The original church on this site was built in 783 as part of a Benedictine nunnery, then in the 14th century it was replaced with the current Romanesque-Gothic one. No traces of the first church remain. Santa Caterina was restored in the 16th century, then unfortunately again (badly) in 1922—25. In 1806, during Napoleon's rampage, the nunnery was demolished, and the church became a parish church.

This really is a pretty church and well worth visiting. Look for the 1368 marble relief of *The Marriage of Saint Catherine* over the door, and Salviati's *Baptism of St Catherine and St Mary Magdalene* over the high altar. There is also a *barco* (nun's gallery) and a *carena di nave* (ship's hull ceiling). Veronese's *Santa Caterina di Mazzorbo* used to hang here too, but now lives in the Pitti Palace in Florence.

The walkways around the church are lovely, with lots of interesting pieces of history to look at. The campanile is special too. Its age is unknown but was part of the old convent building. It underwent restoration in1762 and is famous for having one of the oldest bells in Venice, cast in 1318.

2. Tenuta Venissa

Wine making is a really important tradition in Mazzorbo, and this winery is an insider secret. The masses of tourists spilling off every vaporetto docking across the bridge in Burano are completely oblivious to it. But you, my friend, are now in the know.

Tenuta Venissa is a 2-hectare agro-tourism venture with a Michelin Star restaurant, an *osteria*, a boutique hotel, gardens, and a vineyard, ensconced within the walls of an ancient monastery. The nine gardens on the property supply the two eateries and are tended by many of the older folks living on the island.

The gardens grow local artichokes known as Violetti di San Erasmo, prized for their *castraure* (very tender tips). The young artichokes are so tender they are normally served stripped of the outermost leaves, then finely sliced and served raw in a salad tossed with extra virgin olive oil, lemon, black pepper and Grana Pandano cheese. If they're on the menu (they're seasonal), these are a must-try.

And Then There's the Wine ...

The winery is special because it is the **only place in the world** that farms the Dorona di Venezia grape. This varietal, documented in the 15th century and exclusive to the Venice area, was considered extinct until recently. The *oro* part of the grape's name comes from the Italian word for gold, in this case the golden green color of the ripening grape and the color of the wine. Dorona is also known as Uva d'Oro, the golden grape.

Gianluca Bisol, of Bisol Prosecco fame, owns the winery. There are a few versions of this story, but basically a monk on the nearby agricultural island of San Erasmo found three specimens of the grape in an unused and forgotten corner of his churchyard. The specimens were DNA tested and found not only to be the real thing but also the only known plants in existence. Bisol, who has exclusive rights to the grape, used cuttings from these three plants to build the Mazzorbo winery. The Venetian grape thrives in watery environs, and both the vines and the grapes have a resistance to mildew diseases that would befall other varietals. Tenuta Venissa has been producing Dorona wine since 2010. This alone is unbelievably special, but Bisol levels it up further. Dorona produces a very small volume of wine, all of which comes in *handcrafted bottles of Murano glass*. Each bottle is numbered, signed, and hand pressed with a label made of gold leaf. The label design changes each year to reflect the vintage.

Restaurants on the property are part of the zero-kilometer slow food movement. Fish is sourced from the lagoon, vegetables grown on the property, and the Prosecco comes from nearby Piave, with apologies for how far it has traveled to get to your table. (It's 30km, but no Prosecco grows on Mazzorbo.)

If this is your first trip to Venice, I recommend staying in Venice, but if you're making a repeat trip and you want something super special, check out staying within the monastery wall at the wine resort. There are only a few rooms. You can find out more on the Venissa.it website.

Insider Tip: Instead of disembarking the vaporetto at Burano, get off at Mazzorbo. The 5-minute to walk from here to Burano takes you across the vineyard and is really pretty. When you reach Burano, the tourists from your vaporetto will still be milling around trying to decide where to go.

San Francesco del Deserto

This 4-hectare island lying between Burano and Sant Erasmo is another insider secret that 99.9% of people who've visited Venice have never heard of.

During the Roman era, the island was known as Isola delle Due Vigne –the island of the two vineyards. It is now the home of a very old monastery.

Apparently in 1220, St Francis of Assisi stayed here on the island, getting a little R&R after returning from the East and the 5th Crusade, where he met with the Sultan of Egypt. There was a small Byzantine church on the island where St Francis and his travel buddy

Friar Illuminato da Rieti did their praying. At the time, the Isola delle Due Vigne belonged to a fellow by the name of Jacopo Michiel. According to legend, St Francis planted his stick into the ground, and it grew into a pine tree, and birds flocked there to sing to him. They don't specify how long it took this pine tree to grow, but it's fun to think of it as being like Jack and the Beanstalk. In 1233, Jacopo donated the island to the Franciscan Order of monks, and it became known as Isola di San Francesco.

The monks built a beautiful monastery here with two cloisters, the first from the 1200s, the other from the 1400s. (The first cloister suffered considerable damage from Napoleon's goons but was rebuilt during the second half of the 19th century.) In the early 1400s, the current church of San Francesco was built over the original Byzantine church. The 1400s also brought outbreaks of malaria, rampant in these marshy, swampy islands, so for a while the monks had to abandon Isola San Francesco, and it became known as San Francesco del Deserto (deserted). The monks returned when the malaria outbreak subsided but left again when Napoleon's troops turned the island into a warehouse and stashed gunpowder there. It remained abandoned during the Austrian rule, but a convent/monastery was re-established in 1858.

Today you can visit the island and take a guided walk with the monks. (Book a guided half-day tour through IsoladiBurano.it) The monks only speak Italian, so it's helpful to go with a bilingual guide.

The island is private, so vaporetti don't stop here. You can arrive by private boat, either a taxi from Burano or a local *bragozzo* boat. When you disembark, you'll see a large wooden cross and a cobblestoned path leading to the monastery and adjacent church. A monk will answer the doorbell and accompany you around the island. The friars raise a few animals here and have lovely gardens full of trees and flowers. There are two notable terraces offering stunning views of both the lagoon and of Burano.

San Francesco del Deserto is not an island to stay on –it doesn't have services or souvenir stands for visitors and only has accommodation for the monks. It's perhaps not ideal for your first visit to Venice, unless you are staying a couple of weeks or have come specifically to look at churches and monasteries. However, if you have been to Venice before and are looking for some more obscure places to visit, this is a cool one to add to your list.

31.
Burano –Isola dei Pescatori (Fishermen's Island)

How can any place on earth be so astonishingly, ludicrously pretty? And so ridiculously photogenic?

I bring every single Glam Italia Tour group here, and as I typically end one tour in Venice and start the next one here immediately after, I often only have a few days between visits. Yet every time it is just magical. Even after seeing a million photos and videos of Burano, and knowing exactly what to expect, nothing really prepares you for the kaleidoscopic explosion of color and absolute loveliness of this picturesque little island. The beauty never wears off.

About Burano

Burano is 4 miles/7km from Venice, beyond the much larger Murano, just below Torcello, and linked to Mazzorbo by a bridge. It has a year-round population of around 2000.

Made up of five tiny island neighborhoods (sestieri), Burano was originally divided by four canals. They joined two of the neighborhoods (San Martino Destra and San Martino Sinistra) by filling in a canal to make the main street and piazza on the island (Via and Piazza Baldassare Galuppi). The other three island neighborhoods are San Mauro, Giudecca and Terranova. (The 6th sestiere was Mazzorbo –sestieri = 6ths.)

Like neighboring Torcello, the Romans settled in Burano before the Veneti fled here. There are three stories telling how the island got its name:

1) They named it for one of the city gates of Altino from where the first refugee settlers came,

2) They named it for the Buriana family,

3) The original settlers may have come from Buranello, 5 miles south of Burano.

Take your pick, which (if any) is true.

Burano became a thriving community, governed by Torcello, but with none of the importance or privilege of Torcello and Murano.

In the 16th century, the local women rose to international fame with their unique handmade lace. (I went into this at length in the **Shopping** chapter.) Burano lace was coveted worldwide and became the lace of European royalty and aristocrats until the handmade lace trade was ruined by the industrial age. Burano experienced a lacemaking revival in 1872 when the lacemaking school opened. Now most of the lace sold on the island is machine made, with some finishing done by hand. You can still find a circle of Buranelli women sitting outside stitching lace, but because of the time required to make even a small piece, it is no longer cost effective.

Burano is most famous for its brightly painted houses. Some say they painted the houses a vibrantly colored rainbow of pastel hues, so the fishermen could tell which was theirs when they returned home on dreary, foggy days. Others say it was to signify the demarcation of one house from the next, as most share common walls. Whatever the reason, there is actually a system behind the colors of the houses. You can't just paint your house any old color –you have to apply to the local government, who gives you a list of colors approved for your specific house.

Burano's fishermen still depart in the earliest hours of the morning, returning in time to sell their catch to local restaurants.

1. The Leaning Tower of Burano

From every point on the island, you can see the leaning bell tower of San Martino. The tower (*campanile*) was built in the 16th century. At first it had a bronze angel on top, but in 1867 she was damaged in a tremendous storm, after which they replaced her with a cross.

The campanile is part of the church of San Martino, in the Piazza Baldassare Galuppi. A church stood here in 959, but the current structure is from the 16th century. You'll notice it has no facade, and the back end abuts into houses. It's worth popping inside to see Tiepolo's *Crucifixion* (on the right-hand side) which dates back to 1719.

2. The Lace Museum

While you're in the piazza, pop into the Museo del Merletto (Burano Lace Museum). Discover how local women supported their fishermen husbands and fought poverty by making this remarkable lace. You also learn what makes Burano lace so special, so special Leonardo da Vinci chose Burano lace cloth for the altar in Milan's Duomo.

Address: Piazza Baldassare Galuppi 387.

3. Shopping

From the piazza, you look straight along the main street, Via Baldassare Galuppi. It is full to bursting with wonderful eateries and really fantastic shopping, especially for those who enjoy lace and/or linen. (Be sure to read the **Shopping** chapter of this book before coming to Burano.)

4. Bepi's House/Casa Bepi Sua

You may have seen Bepi's house on postcards –it's probably the most famous house on the island. It is also, without a doubt, the most colorful house on the island. I adore stories like this one.

Bepi, whose real name was Giuseppe Toselli, loved color and loved to paint. Every day you would find him painting geometric designs on the wall of his house. Once he completed the job, he would start over, layers and layers of circles, triangles and squares in oranges, reds and blues, yellows and greens –the colors of the rainbow. Apparently, he painted something extra every day until he died. (The interior has since been restored, but the exterior remains the same.) But there is more to Bepi's story. He was also a movie buff who, as a young man, worked as a maintenance man and janitor at the island's movie theater, the Cinema Flavin. When the cinema closed down, Bepi started staging outdoor summer movie nights for the local children. By hanging a white sheet on the wall of the storehouse opposite his own colorful house, he used a huge old movie projector to show movies. From old Laurel and Hardy films to cartoons and crazy performances of Ridolini the clown, for years the children of Burano enjoyed Bepi's cinema under the stars. This tradition continued until he died in the 1980s.

To find Bepi's House from via Baldassari Galuppi, turn right onto Calle del Pistor until you reach the little square of Corte del Pistor. It takes all of 2 minutes, assuming you stop and take loads of photos along the way.

Mangia!

Personally, I would happily ride a vaporetto for 45 minutes just to eat on Burano. And I frequently do. There are plenty of fantastic places and it really is a tremendous place to dine alfresco with all the ridiculously beautiful views. Burano is known for glorious Venetian seafood, risottos, and Bussolà cookies.

GÒ Risotto

Goby (or sand goby) is an almost translucent, bony little fish, that gets caught in fishermen's nets. They have little flesh and aren't much use for anything. Not wanting to waste anything, somewhere way, *way* back in history, Burano fishermen began boiling goby to make a fish stock/broth from them, and then adding that stock to risotto. (The goby bones are strained from the stock before it is added to the risotto.) This stock recipe has never changed. The recipe for GÒ Risotto has been a closely kept secret for generations. The most famous place to eat this delicately flavored dish is da Romano on the via Baldassare Galuppi. But you'll find it on many menus.

This is a slightly soupy risotto that stays bright white like the local lace, it gets sprinkled with finely cut parsley, and it tastes like the history of the prettiest island you've ever seen. This risotto dish is specific to Burano.

Buranelli/Bussolài

This cookie is available everywhere in Venice, but make sure you eat some on the tiny patch of land from which they came. They are fabulous with an after-lunch macchiato.

They're made from all natural ingredients with no bad oils or chemicals you find in industrially made cookies. Bussola were durable, healthy foods that wives could send out with their fisherman husbands, ensuring their men had some nutrition and energy while working at sea. They also became the festival cookie of the island, especially popular at Easter. One of my Venice guides told me the local women on Burano traditionally rent out their bakery ovens on the island for a few hours a few days before Easter to cook massive amounts of bussola.

Moeche

If you're in Venice during *moeche* season, you must try this lagoon delicacy. Every restaurant will have them on the menu, and they are fantastic everywhere. I come here for them any time I can.

For centuries, every spring and fall, moeche (softshell crabs) are harvested from the lagoon. There is only a 5—6 hour window between the crabs shedding their hard shells and the new shells hardening, so the Venetian moeche fishermen (*molecanti)* monitor the crabs who are due to molt, store them in tanks, and harvest them as soon as the shell sheds. Both male and female crabs shed in the spring, but only the males also shed in the fall.

Moeche are soaked in seasoned, beaten egg before they're dredged through coarse flour and deep fried Venetian style (light and crispy) until golden brown. The flavor is intense yet also delicate. They are served with sea salt and lemon and are best paired with a crisp Prosecco. (To be fair, I think everything is better with a glass of Prosecco.)

Where to Eat on Burano

I have never had a less-than-wonderful meal on Burano. Considering I've been coming here for more than half my life, it's fair to say I've had plenty of meals in plenty of restaurants over the years. Here I've had mostly lunches, because coming here for lunch is one of life's great joys. We've chatted about risotto at da Romano, but I want to tell you about two other eateries here.

1. Al Gatto Nero (The Black Cat)

You cannot talk about eating in Burano and not talk about Trattoria Al Gatto Nero. Without a doubt, this is the most famous eatery in Burano. With good reason –the food is incredible. Incredible enough to be a favorite of presidents and prime ministers, royalty and Hollywood A-listers. You seriously never know who you'll see here, but the star of the show is the unbelievably fantastic food.

The entire Bovo family works at the restaurant, every day. In Italy, your community is family too, so the trattoria always keeps a table open for local Burano folks. Several years ago, I heard about a Hollywood super A-lister, who, after raving about his amazing fish, was walked to another table to be introduced to the man who caught it.

Everything here, including the pasta, is made by hand. The fish is caught locally, probably by someone sitting across the room from you.

This once was a rugged, rustic fishermen's haunt until in 1965 Ruggero Bovo, who had dreamed of studying music, ended up taking over the trattoria and along the way became a brilliant chef. For decades, Al Gatto Nero has been written about all over the world. It is also a Michelin restaurant. This place is legendary.

Ruggero's son Massimiliano, who looks like a cross between Alan van Sprang (King Henry on *Reign*) and Jason Statham, runs the front of house. Massimiliano learned English while at college in Scotland, so he has a Scottish accent. When he speaks, you'll think you're in a Guy Ritchie movie. It's beyond fantastic.

Like his father, Massimiliano is passionate about the food here at Al Gatto Nero. He is also a sommelier and runs the wine list. He will choose the perfect wine for you, partly because he knows his stuff, and partly because this morning he met the fishing boats and chose what you'll be eating.

Insider Tip: Book your table at Al Gatto Nero as many months in advance as possible. A killer concierge might be able to get you in at the last minute, but otherwise this trattoria is booked out every day, and with good reason.

Address: Via Giudecca 88.

2. Trattoria da Primo

I eat here all the time. Everything that comes to your table is from this immediate area. This is another family story, and once again the family is just wonderful. If you tend to be chatty (and I always am), you'll meet the entire family –Paolo, his wife and all four daughters.

Back in the 70s da Primo was a cicchetti bar, run by Paolo and Primo, who married two sisters from the island. Ten years later (give or take) they became a full restaurant, specializing in the foods of the lagoon. Over a plate of *moeche*, the famous Venetian softshell crab, I learned the family story. Unfortunately there was also wine, and I had the great idea of having this chat in Italian instead of the English they all speak fluently, so now I'm not sure if Paolo used to *catch* the fish or if he spent his mornings *choosing* the fish ... either way, his mornings were busy.

The four sisters grew up in Burano and will tell you about living on the island, their castle home, growing up with the restaurant. You don't just leave here with a full belly; you also feel like you've made new friends. They have a regular clientele of famous football players, fashion designers and actors, who keep coming back and who they also treat like friends.

Everything here tastes amazing, comes with a story, and is tied up with the history of Burano. The menu depends entirely on the catch that came in this morning. Along with the softshell crab (which is seasonal, so not available year-round), the risottos and pastas here are incredible. My favorite is the seafood pasta, which changes daily with the catch, is light enough to not weigh you down on a hot summer day, yet leaves you completely satiated.

You must find room somehow for their homemade bussolai cookies, which are not to be missed. Although recommended with sweet dessert wine, they are also fantastic with a macchiato after lunch.

Address: Piazza Baldessare Galuppi 285.

Wander Around Burano

There is much more to Burano than just shopping and eating. Anywhere this pretty needs to be explored. Walk up and down every street, turn corners just because they're there, do your best to see every part of the island. It's tiny, so exploring doesn't take long and it's impossible to get lost. Away from the principal thoroughfares you'll find brightly colored streets with few if any tourists. Enjoy everything your eyes land on and take yourself some really remarkable photos. Burano is absolutely gorgeous.

Insider Tips

- Burano gets packed with tourists, so either come early in the morning or plan on being here later in the day. If cruise ships are in Venice, assume Burano will be full of tourists between 11am and 3pm. By arriving in the early morning, it's easier to get all the photos you want without a bunch of fanny-packed folks getting in the way.
- Whether planning a morning trip or an afternoon trip, make sure lunch in Burano is involved!
- Burano gets tons of sunshine –probably no more than the rest of the islands, but it seems like more, so be sure to pack sunscreen because you will need it.
- Buy Burano cookies to bring home. S shaped or round, they are a must!

Getting to Burano

By vaporetto, there are a few ways to get to Burano.

From San Zaccaria, take the #14 vaporetto. It takes 45 minutes, stopping at Lido, Punta Sabbioni and Burano. Some stop at Punta Sabbioni and don't continue to Burano, so check before boarding.

From Fondamenta Nove, the #12 vaporetto stops at Murano, then Mazzorbo, Torcello and Burano. You can also take the #4.1 to Murano and from the Murano Faro stop connect with the #12. I do this all the time.

Whichever vaporetto you take, expect a 45-minute trip one-way.

32.
Acqua Alta and MOSE

It's so easy for me to get caught up in the feeling of a city like Venice, where everything is just beautiful color and gorgeous buildings that are so peaceful. You can roam around and get lost in the labyrinth.

–Nanette Lepore

Acqua Alta

Venice, the city built on the water, periodically suffers from high tide flooding called a*cqua alta*. Different to regular high tides, acqua alta is *mostly* a seasonal phenomenon and *mostly* takes place from October to January (there are always anomalies –global warming is affecting the frequency and even the seasonal times it happens).

The flooding is temporary. After a few hours, the water drains back out to sea. It can be as minor as a high tide creating puddles in Piazza San Marco, or as major as a 6-foot deep (187cm) flood. Two extreme floods have happened in recent history –the worst in November 1966, the second worst in 2019.

WHAT IS ACQUA ALTA?

To understand acqua alta, first you need to understand the lagoon. The Venetian lagoon is separated from the Adriatic by two long, narrow barrier islands, Lido and Pellestrina, and two barrier peninsulas, at Jesolo, and Chioggia. Three inlets run through these natural barriers and are used for shipping channels and access for smaller boats.

Along with the regular high tides, there is a seasonal phenomenon of extra high water. These very high acqua alta floods are caused when a high tide *plus* a full or new moon occurs with low atmospheric pressure, allowing sea levels to rise higher than normal. Add in the warm strong Sirocco winds coming up from the south/southeast and the cool, strong Bora winds blowing down from the north/northwest, and it can be problematic.

The geography of the Adriatic complicates the situation even more. This long, narrow sea has more extreme tidal events than the rest of Mediterranean. The shape of the Adriatic causes an oscillating water motion called a *seiche*. The first seiche can raise the sea level by as much as half a meter and lasts a period of 21 hours. A secondary seiche also occurs with the period of about 12 hours. They coincide with the tides, but are more significant when there's a full moon, new moon or an equinox.

When you combine high tide with the full moon, the Adriatic seiches *and* the Sirocco wind blowing northward, pushing excess water into the lagoon and making the outflow of water difficult, Venice experiences extra high acqua alta. The Bora wind prevents water from draining back out of the lagoon, making two high tides overlap. This spells disaster for Venice.

What's Normal?

Venice is used to a certain level of these high tides. For 16 centuries, they've developed ways of dealing with them, like ground floor businesses erecting *paratoie* (small private flood barriers that block most of the high water). They work most of the time.

One of my friends lives in a ground-floor apartment. If he's not home to raise everything up himself, a friend will pop in and do it for him. It is just part of ground-floor life. I've been in Venice when there has been low-level acqua alta, and ground-floor shops in low-lying areas use pumps to drain water into the calli outside, while shopkeepers use rubber brooms to push out the remaining inch or two of water. Venetians are incredibly resilient. When the water starts to subside, they get right back to normal life. Shops and bars still open with a foot of water on the floor, and rubber booted waiters and customers carry on as though nothing happened. It blows my mind. Thankfully, I have never been in town when a big flood hit.

Flood Sirens

A siren system alerts residents when an extra high tide is coming.

1. A single protracted blast of the siren in a long, drawn-out tone means that water is expected to peak at 110cm. Piazza San Marco is 90cm above sea level, so a single siren means the piazza is going to be under 20cm/10 inches of water. Other parts of the city may notice nothing much at all. City workers will erect ramps to walk across, shopkeepers will put merchandise up high, everyone will pull out their galoshes, and life will go on largely as normal.

2. A siren with a second note in a higher pitch warns of an expected water level of 120cm. Piazza San Marco will be under 30cm/12 inches of water and 29% of the city will experience flooding.

3. A siren with a third ascending note warns of an expected 130cm water level.

4. The fourth and final siren, with four tones each higher than the one before, warns of an expected 140cm water level, roughly 2 feet above the level of Piazza San Marco. At this point 54% of Venice will be flooded.

There are no more sirens. Beyond four, there is no knowing how severe an emergency is looming. This is what happened in November 2019. No one saw what was coming.

How Man Made It Worse

The first way man has exacerbated the flooding of Venice is Global Warming. (I refuse to use the cleverly repackaged, less scary term Climate Change. I call it what it is –Global Warming.)

The next way man has made the situation worse is by digging deep channels in the lagoon for huge ships to pass through, and by creating Porto Marghera. Marghera is an industrial port just behind Venice on the mainland. To build this industrial nightmare, parts of the lagoon full of low-lying islands called *barene* were filled in to make solid ground. The barene worked like natural sponges, absorbing significant amounts of excess water caused by acqua altas. With them filled in, there was nowhere for the excess water to go. Then, a deep channel was cut through the lagoon so oil tankers could reach the port. The tanker channel crosses the lagoon to the Adriatic through the Malamocco inlet. These deep channels for freighters and cruise ships have meant more water flooding into the lagoon. As a result, the city has been subjected to even higher tides.

Even more frightening, if they move the big cruise ships to Marghera (as has been proposed), deeper channels will need to be dug to accommodate them and flooding will get disastrously worse.

How Frequent are Bad Floods?

The first documented flooding of the lagoon was 17 October 589AD, when Paolo Diacono recorded in the *Historia Langobardorum* that all the rivers with mouths into the Adriatic had overflowed at the same time –no doubt after heavy storms.

The city archive has maintained records of flooding in the calli and campi since the Middle Ages. Although these events were significant enough to be documented, the floodwater high mark was **25% lower** than it is now. Floods are now more frequent than ever before, have vastly greater intensity and are harder to contain.

In the last 50 years, floods above 110cm sea level are twice as frequent. Floods above 140cm are called "exceptional floods". From 1870—2000, there were only nine of these exceptional floods (and only one between 1872 and 1936). In the 19 years from 2000 to 2019, there were 11.

The worst flood in the history of Venice occurred on 4 November 1966. Water reached 194cm/6'4" above sea level. A plaque on the north exterior wall of the campanile in Piazza San Marco marks the height. Standing next to it you can imagine how horrifying it must have been, especially with the hurricane-force winds blowing, waves crashing into buildings and all the electricity down.

The next biggest flood happened on 12 November 2019, reaching 1.84cm/6 feet above sea level. This flood was compounded by high tides, the moon, and winds of over 75 miles per hour coming in two different directions, causing massive waves to slam up against the buildings. Anticyclones over the Azores and eastern Europe blocked the winds. Meanwhile, a small cyclone roared up the Adriatic. Global warming is mostly responsible for the size of this catastrophic flood, but environmental experts point out that digging the massive channels to allow enormous ships into the lagoon has made the situation incrementally worse. This digging started in the 1960s, and the biggest flood in Venice's history happened shortly thereafter.

The more you dig, the more water you get.

The MOSE Flood Barrier

In 2003, the government began work on mobile flood barriers at the three inlets where the Adriatic meets the lagoon. The $8 billion project known as MOSE (*Modulo Sperimentale Elettromeccanico*/Experimental Electromechanical Module) uses 78 steel box-gates, flooded with water, laid flat on the seabed. When they forecast high tides at a given level, air is forced through the barrier gates, pushing them up. The gates can hold back tides as high as 10 feet.

After years of delays and corruption, MOSE was first put to use on 3 October 2020. An acqua alta was forecasted to reach 135cm (4'5") occurred, but the gates went up and flooding was avoided.

Since then, MOSE has been deployed successfully, but there have also been incidents where it wasn't activated in time and the city experienced flooding. In one of these, the forecast had been for tides to reach 125cm, which was 5cm below the level MOSE is activated. The water reached 135cm, by which time it was too late to activate the gates.

33.
Sustainability in Venice

Responsible tourism is the future of travel.

–Simon Reeve

Sustainable Travel

Travelers (as opposed to tourists) travel to experience something different, something we don't have at home. And there is no place more unique, more different, than Venice.

I've always been one of those people multi-level marketers can spot across a crowded Target store. They chase me up and down the aisles, promising untold wealth if I just listen to their sales pitch. Religious recruiters in the US spot me a mile off, too. They're always trying to lure me into their wacky brand of religiosity. So when the sustainable travel folks were vying for my attention, I assumed they wanted me to eat vegan food, drive an electric car, avoid deodorant, and sleep in a hammock. All of which are fine –they're just not my preferred style of travel.

At some point I saw a TED Talk about sustainable travel and realized it wasn't so scary –I was doing most of it anyway (even though I'm not a vegan, love deodorant and sleeping in beds, and rent petrol cars when I travel). I just didn't realize it. I wasn't doing things specifically to be a sustainable traveler –these things just made sense to me and enhanced everything I love about world travel.

There are two types of travel: unsustainable tourism (also called mass tourism), and sustainable travel. If your mode of travel is unsustainable, then without even realizing it, you are contributing to the destruction of the place you're visiting. This is especially important when you're visiting somewhere as fragile as Venice. Unwittingly, you become part of the massive, catastrophic problem.

Conversely, even if you're completely oblivious to the cause, if you exercise sustainable travel practices, you become part of the solution. In all honesty, if you've made it this far through this book, there's a good chance you're already a mostly sustainable traveler, or at least a traveler who wouldn't knowingly be part of the destruction of the most unique city on earth.

What is Sustainable Travel, and Why is it Crucial to the Survival of Venice?

Sustainable travel is a way of traveling and exploring a destination, while considering both the current and future environmental, cultural and economic impact of your visit. It is meeting your needs as a traveler, without damaging the host community. In its simplest form, it's treating Venice with respect in order to keep this magical destination alive for future generations. Sustainable travel is a way of enjoying everything a place has to offer, really experiencing the destination, and leaving it in condition to be enjoyed by both the local community and other travelers for generations to come. Traveling this way, you not only protect the place you're in, but you also have an incredibly fulfilling, wonderful travel experience. Everybody wins.

There are three pillars to sustainable travel: Economic, Cultural, and Environmental sustainability.

Were this a talk given by UNESCO or any of the important

organizations desperately trying to save endangered destinations, they would now go into some weighty discussion on a global impact scale. But this is you and me talking about a trip to Venice, so I'll be specific.

Economic Sustainability

Economic sustainability ensures every euro you spend will hit the ground and stay right here in Venice. Mass tourism creates a massive income for international corporations, but these corporations keep their billions offshore. Although they send millions of bodies through Venice every year, it doesn't necessarily benefit the local economy. In fact, to a large degree, they paralyze it. Mass tourism pushes so many people through a destination, it's impossible for local businesses to keep up. So, in order to keep their businesses financially viable, they import cheap labor to do everything from selling Made in China souvenirs to cleaning hotel rooms, and they do it well below minimum wage. The people who live here can't compete and are forced to go elsewhere to find jobs. This happens everywhere invaded by mass tourism.

It also forces local businesses out of business. Supply and demand pushes rents to an unsustainable level and before long, local restaurants get replaced by McDonald's and Subways. (I am not kidding.) Mass tourists grab something cheap and quick to eat that resembles food at home –they didn't travel to try local cuisine. The bulk of the money spent at international food franchises doesn't stay in Venice. The food is not locally sourced, so it doesn't benefit local farmers. It comes prefabricated, so it doesn't involve local chefs and restaurant workers. The bulk of the profits go to the franchisor, a gigantic multinational corporation.

When we travel, every dollar we spend can and will bring change –either positive or negative. Make a responsible choice.

Cultural Sustainability

Cultural sustainability is preserving the culture that made Venice so special in the first place. It encompasses everything from local cuisine to craftspeople and artisans, customs, traditions, and its unique history –things that separate it from a soulless destination like Las Vegas. Cultural sustainability also involves practicing a way of travel that allows the local people to keep living here.** Once they're gone, it's all gone.

**In 1971, just under 109,000 people lived in Venice. Mass tourism and the powerful negatives associated with it have forced the exodus of a thousand local people each year –people with family histories running centuries-deep in this city. At the time of writing this book, fewer than 51,000 actual Venetians live here.

Environmental Sustainability

Environmental sustainability means not destroying the local environment. This includes things like trash, sewerage, damage to the bridges and *calli*, damage to the buildings (the prime source of which may surprise you), and damage to the lagoon.

Want to know more?

For an in-depth, really fascinating look at mass tourism and sustainable travel, watch destination expert Doug Lanksy's TED Talks. He makes the concept easy to understand, backs it up with data, and shows you the tiny adjustments you can make when traveling anywhere in the world, which will have a massive positive impact AND improve your trip.

The Solution

You'll find that by taking a simple action (that is often the more enjoyable choice anyway), you'll hit multiple sustainability pillars at once, without even thinking about it. And you'll have more fun.

Below, you'll see how a single simple choice can make a world of impact.

SPEND WISELY

Make sure the money you spend hits the ground here in Venice. Not every type of tourist has the same cost–benefit ratio. Day trippers (including cruise ship passengers) account for 73—80% of the tourists in Venice, *yet they only make up 18% of the tourism economy.* Meanwhile, 14% of visitors to Venice spend at least one night in a hotel, but they make up 48% of the tourist economy. A June 2021 article in Bloomberg quoted global management consulting firm The Boston Consulting Group that in 2019 Venice had 25 million tourists. Of those 25 million, 76% (that's a staggering 19 million people) were day trippers and only spent between €5 and €20 each.

Think about that for a moment. Cruise passengers and day trippers don't pay daily tourist tax and barely spend anything while they're here. They're just taking up space!

There are many easy ways to make your trip to Venice economically sustainable:

- Stay overnight, ideally several nights. (With so much to see and do here, one night is never enough, anyway.)

- Be selective about where you stay and how you book it. Only stay in locally owned hotels, B&Bs and vacation rentals, and book directly when you can.

Accommodation

Let me give you an example. For simplicity, let's say you spend $100 per night on accommodation.

If you stay with a multi-national hotel group, approximately 16% of your nightly fee goes to the corporation, bypassing Venice entirely. Third-party booking sites take another 25% that also never arrives in Venice, so your $100 per night spend only brings $59 to Venice. Instead, find the best price on a third-party site, then contact the business directly to ask them to match it and book directly with them. It hasn't cost you a penny more, and you just redirected all the money to Venice.

Shop Local

Shop with local artisans. (To clarify, I don't mean the long-haired hippie dude smoking weed and selling homemade honey at a farmer's market. Not that there's anything wrong with that, but when I talk about artisans, I'm referring to local people making local products and providing local services, keeping the culture alive.) This might be a shoe designer or a mask maker, a chef, or a glassblower.

The Made in China souvenir stands now occupy multiple storefronts, pushing out local businesses. Do you really need a $10 knock off mask or the other junk they sell? Heads up: the junk factories in Asia making this trash don't usually operate to environmentally sustainable standards –or often even to humane standards. Factory conditions are horrific, workers including children work excessive hours for terrible pay. Is that $10 mask really worth it?

Choose instead to purchase a quality, artisan-made souvenir from any of the businesses listed in the **Shopping** chapter of this book (or any of the multitude of other artisan businesses I didn't have room to include). You don't have to spend a fortune; most places invariably have plenty of inexpensive handmade items for sale too.

When you buy from local craftspeople, the dollars you spend stay in Venice, paying their rent, buying local groceries from local vendors, keeping these Venetians living in Venice. You are helping to stop Venice from turning into a giant Walmart. This is decision is also culturally sustainable.

GET A LOCAL GUIDE

Hire a local licensed guide, even for just a few hours. Don't hire one through a booking site –they take a fee from the guide. Instead, use my list of local licensed guides in Venice (I keep it updated on my website, so you know that my PDF list is as current as possible). These are the guides I've worked with before and vetted. They're all great. And if they're already booked, they'll refer you to another local licensed guide. You can download the PDF here: www.glamitaliabooks.com/Venice-Private-Guides

Local licensed guides are the gatekeepers to all the great stories and details about this city. They are the frontline, keeping the culture alive for people like you and me. Often in a heavily touristed city like Venice, the time you spend walking around with a tour guide (whether alone or in a small group) is your most extended time to socialize with a local Venetian. Most other interactions are brief, but this is a solid three or four hours (or longer). Your guide can give you a fabulous window into Venetian life, what it was like growing up here, how the place works. It adds so much dimension to your experience.

On one of my recent tours my guide Emanuele pointed out where he went to high school and where they went for PE. My group asked him a million questions about it, about going to school here, about how you get to school when it's pouring rain (there's no cars), about everything you can imagine regarding growing up in Venice. They were enthralled, and it delighted him that they found it so interesting. They still talk about how fantastic it was to just chat with him, and how much they loved learning about life in Venice.

It was a simple example of cultural sustainability and economic sustainability not just having a positive impact on Venice, but on the traveler experience, too. Our greatest travel experiences involve human connection. The hours spent walking with Emanuele and also with our cicchetti tour guide Monica, had my travelers feeling really connected to Venice. To them Venice will always be a living, breathing thing, a home to real people. This human connection made them absolutely love Venice.

In addition to increasing your Venetian experience, hiring a local guide is a brilliant way to inject money directly into the local economy. It pays their rent, buys their food, pays for their life right here in Venice. This is also culturally sustainable, as licensed guides are the ones keeping the stories and the history alive.

Eat Local

Eat in Venetian-owned and run eateries and bars. (Remember, in Italy you get coffee in a bar.) Don't buy American fast food in Venice. Avoid eating in foreign-owned pseudo-Italian restaurants. These venues may look like Italian eateries at first, but a quick look at the menu will reveal all. (I go into this in more depth in my first book, *Glam Italia! How to Travel Italy.*) A Venetian-owned and run eatery will make fresh food daily. If it's a foreign-owned tourist joint, the sauce on your pasta probably came out of an industrial-sized can.

If you're unsure, ask local shop owners, artisans, your local guide, your hotel/accommodation host, your gondolier –any local Venetians you are interacting with, where you should eat. Food is hugely important to all Italians, and Venetian food is really important to Venetians.

It doesn't have to be expensive to be good in Italy! Food in Piazza San Marco is always expensive, and the same rule applies anywhere targeting tourists. But places where the locals eat, are not particularly pricey. They cook with fresh, locally sourced, seasonal ingredients, so you're not only supporting the local business and staff, but by extension you're supporting local farmers and fishermen too. This choice is culturally sustainable by supporting the local style of cuisine, and environmentally sustainable.

Respect the Residents

Venice is already a challenging place to live but imagine trying to get your kids to school, go to work, go to the dentist, bring home groceries –the normal stuff of life, with thousands of extra people blocking the bridges and the narrow *calli*, refusing to let you pass.

How frustrated and irritated do you feel at home when you're stuck in a traffic jam after a long day at work? Multiply that by a few thousand, every day for months.

The key to any travel experience, anywhere, is to be a good guest. Any place suffering from mass tourism also suffers from the rudeness and entitlement of mass tourists who think just being here should award them something. So, treat the place and the people with respect. Simple things like letting someone pass, making eye contact and smiling (even if they don't smile back) can make a difference.

Don't ride the vaporetto during rush hour, especially not the #1. Let locals get to and from work without having to climb around you. Venice is an amazing city to walk through, anyway. If it's raining, sit in a bar and have an aperitivo or a coffee until rush hour passes.

Explore

Get away from the main tourist areas. Of course, you need to visit Piazza San Marco –it would be madness not to –but explore other parts of the city too. This is where you'll find the Venice you fall in love with, the cool under-the-radar shops and restaurants, the stretches of old fondamente with views unspoiled by fanny-packed, sweaty tourists. Away from the masses, you'll find empty churches full of staggering art, random *calli* and *campielli* full of architectural treasures, and quiet benches where you can sit in the shade and enjoy a gelato.

Consider Your Footprint

Be mindful of the trash you create. In the US we have a very trash-excessive society, so most of us, when traveling, don't consider how damaging it can be. For most of us (like me) the goal to create *zero* trash is far too extreme to achieve at home, let alone on vacation. But being mindful of the volume of trash you create nudges you into different choices, which then impact your level of environmental sustainability.

Only consume food while sitting in an eatery/bar/restaurant (other than gelato). This hits all three principles of sustainability – environmental, cultural (supporting the local food culture) and economic (supporting local business) It also enriches your Venetian experience.

Use reusable bottles. The worst trash you can create is the single-use plastic bottle. Rather than buying bottle after bottle of water, just buy one and refill it. Where possible, do your drinking sitting at a bar (cafe). You seldom see me without a bottle of water, but I refill the same bottle over and over, and that bottle comes home with me at the end of the day. If you have to dispose of your trash where you're staying, be aware of exactly how much non-biodegradable trash you are creating.

Tourist congestion. Part of the environmental damage to Venice is damage to the bridges and walkways of Venice. Watch where the cruise ship people go, then go somewhere else. Every time you break away from the masses, you take a measure of stress off the bridges and calli. This also heightens your experience and diverts you into new places that will make you fall in love with Venice.

Don't take a cruise. The single most damaging thing you can do to Venice as a tourist is to arrive or depart by cruise ship.

The Single-use Plastic Bottle Curse

I like to illustrate the impact of single use plastics this way:

If 4000 people disembark one cruise ship for a few hours and each buys, drinks, and disposes of one bottle of water, Venice has 4000 extra plastic bottles to deal with (believe me, cruise ship tourists are not bringing their trash back to the boat with them). What if it's a hot day and each person buys 2 bottles of water? Or 3? There is seldom just one ship in port –frequently 5 ships are docked at once. That's 20,000 people buying bottles of water, and (best-case scenario) Venice has to dispose of 20,000 single-use plastic bottles in one day. (Of course, in reality, it is vastly more than that.) Are you as horrified by this as I am?

It is pretty safe to assume that mass tourism created at least 25 million plastic bottles for Venice to dispose of in 2019 alone. Paid for how? By whom? 19 million of these visitors were day trippers and didn't even pay a tourist tax.

The Cruise Industry and Venice

The experts are right, he thought. Venice is sinking. The whole city is slowly dying. One day the tourists will travel here by boat to peer down into the waters, and they will see pillars and columns and marble far, far beneath them, slime and mud uncovering for brief moments a lost underworld of stone.

–Daphne du Maurier

Cruise ships bring thousands of passengers to Venice all at once, dumping them in the city's historic center. These tourists hang around for a couple of hours, maybe buy bottled water and a slice of pizza, create trash and sewage, and cause environmental damage without offsetting it with an economic balance. This type of tourist is economically *un*-sustainable. Don't be one of these.

Cruise passengers eat breakfast on the boat and are back on board later in the day to hit the all-you-can-eat buffet. At best, they might have lunch in Venice. (I say "at best" because some cruises sell passengers boxed lunches.) They invest almost nothing in the local economy. Mass tourism doesn't care about the impact it has on the destination or its local community –it keeps forcing more and more people through until something breaks. Then it finds a fresh new destination. However, that's not all. In addition to damaging the culture of the city of Venice, the cruise industry is damaging the landscape.

The cruise industry damages two major environmental aspects of Venice that I want to address here. The first is the lagoon; the second is the buildings.

THE LAGOON

The Venice lagoon is a shallow body of water. At around 550 square kilometers, it is the largest wetland in the Mediterranean basin. Much of the lagoon is only inches/centimeters deep.

The engineering marvel that has kept Venice standing for over 1000 years is a combination of human genius and the very specific ecosystem of the lagoon. Remember how we talked about Venice being built on top of millions of wooden pilings driven down into the lagoon bed, and how when the wood interacts with the silt and the water and no oxygen, it petrifies? This delicate balance of silt runoff from the rivers and the twice daily flushing and washing from the tides of the Adriatic Sea creates a perfect environment.

Mudflats, salt marshes and tidal shallows make up 80% of the lagoon. These naturally absorb some of the excess water during the high tides, and carbon dioxide from the atmosphere. Since the beginning of Venice, they've been protecting the city and the lagoon ecology. However, these mudflats and salt marshes are eroding at an alarming rate. Venice is at risk of losing its natural protection and ability to absorb carbon dioxide. The huge wash from the cruise and shipping behemoths creates a massive, measurable erosion of the mudflats and marshes. The enormous volume of water dispersed by the ship pushes out, then sucks back in, diffusing the marshlands. Cruise ships create *depression wakes,* generating a type of wave that disseminates over the shores, re-suspending and breaking down sediment. Environmental scientists are constantly measuring this erosion in Venice.

Every time a cruise ship passes through, it also breaks down the bed of the lagoon. As the bed of the lagoon breaks down, the sea takes over, further eroding the lagoon floor. Without the lagoon, there will be no Venice.

When you see cruise ships in Venice, remember that they are emitting excess greenhouse gases and black carbon into the atmosphere *and* forcing the erosion of the lagoon and its natural protections *against* greenhouse gases.

Global warming is one major threat to this balance. The cruise industry is a super emitter of greenhouse gases and black carbon, even more so than the regular shipping industry. Most cruise ships burn the cheapest, most carbon-intensive fuel. They are more carbon-intensive than cargo ships because they burn fuel constantly, even while in port. Nobody forces them to adopt environmentally friendly practices, so they meander around the world with their enormous carbon footprint, exploiting beautiful places like the Great Barrier Reef, Bali, Santorini, Barcelona, and our beloved Venice. The crazy thing is they could choose to decarbonize and become more fuel efficient.

The natural water level in the lagoon reaches a maximum of about 1 meter deep (other than in the tidal channels). In the 1960s, deep shipping channels were dredged to accommodate big ships. Since digging the channels, the water depth in the lagoon has more than doubled. Doubling the water depth around a city that is already sinking, in a lagoon which relies on the careful balance of its ecosystem, is catastrophic.

THE BUILDINGS

Cruise ships cause extreme damage to the buildings of Venice and the pilings holding them up. As a ship passes, it disperses around 35,000 meters of water. This water causes damage when it hits the shores, but drastically more so in the return cycle. Like a giant suction cup, it sucks the muddy water away from the shores and the banks.

This sucks at the pilings holding Venice up and destroys the mortar holding the stones together. You can see this on the ground in San Giorgio, at the point where cruise ships enter the Giudecca Canal. Workers refill the gaps with mortar every week, effectively putting a Bandaid on the surface level of the damage, but not repairing the damage occurring below.

How Big are the Cruise Ships?

The MSC Opera is 275 meters long, exactly 100 meters longer than Piazza San Marco (roughly as long as three American football fields). This was one of the *smallest* of the 600 cruise ships to enter the lagoon in 2019. On 2 June 2019, this cruise ship suffered engine failure and crashed into the embankment of the Giudecca Canal. Google it and you'll see endless videos of this monstrous ship blasting its horn, people scattering in all directions as it crashes. Luckily no one died (this time). Pure luck, not ingenuity, stopped this from being a disaster.

Only one month later, on 6 July 2019, another cruise ship, the 292-meter-long Costa Delicioza, got knocked around so badly by severe winds it nearly hit the Riva Sette Martiri by Piazza San Marco. It missed colliding with a yacht and other boats by only a few meters.

Venice staved off invasions for 1000 years during the Republic, yet now it is under constant invasion by the cruise industry. The size of these monolithic cruise ships is hard to comprehend until you see them in the canal. They are taller than any building in Venice, their overwhelming mass dwarfing everything in sight.

An Act of Violence Against Venice

This is not just my personal opinion. Marine scientists, climate scientists and multiple international organizations working to preserve historic sites all say the same thing. UNESCO described the presence of these fuel guzzling cruise ships in the lagoon as being **physically incompatible** with Venice and the lagoon surrounding it. The cruise ships are described as an act of violence against Venice. So much so that in 2019, UNESCO wanted to add Venice to its list of endangered World Heritage sites, which prompted Rome to declare the Saint Mark's Basin a monument, affording it protection from the cruise ships.

At the time of writing this book, larger cruise ships are (supposedly) going to be rerouted and banned from traversing the Giudecca Canal. There are three proposals for what to do with the cruise ships in Venice:

1. One proposal involves using the industrial port at Marghera, which already has a port structure in place. Marghera is home to the chemical plants –the other super polluters in this area. Bringing more traffic through this already busy shipping channel would require widening the existing channel, creating substantially more damage to the lagoon.

   Marghera is home to oil refineries, gypsum phosporous deposits, petrochem factories. If a cruise ship gets out of control here (like what occurred in 2019), and crashes into the banks in Marghera, the environmental damage will be beyond catastrophic.

2. The second proposal is to route cruise ships through the commercial shipping route to Marghera, then into the unused Vittore Emanuele III Canal connecting Marghera and the current cruise port at Marittima. This option still involves dredging wider shipping lanes, and significantly increasing the shipping traffic through the commercial shipping route, again an extremely hazardous option.

3. The third proposal would require a new port in the Adriatic to be built, stopping cruise ships from entering the lagoon entirely.

Each of these options have pros and cons and I highly doubt anything substantive will happen in the immediate future. Ultimately, it comes down to supply and demand. If the demand decreases (if tourists make the choice not to come here by cruise), the cruise lines will take their supply elsewhere. Or they will be forced to become eco-friendly, which is absolutely within their power and purview.

There are many ways to travel to and enjoy Venice, and the decision to travel here by cruise is a choice –the choice to be an active participant in the destruction of Venice.

DON'T TAKE MY WORD FOR IT

There are masses of data to support this argument. Much of it is easily accessible for you to verify online. Do your own research *–don't just take my word for it.*

- See what internationally recognized organizations like UNESCO and the World Monuments Fund have to say.

- A quick Google search brings up information from marine biologists and environmental scientists, backed up with data to support their findings.
- Simply typing in Cruise-ships-damage-Venice brings up pages of information and news articles from all over the world.
- Google "We Are Here Venice", which is an organization run by environmental scientist Jane da Mosto and partnered with entities including the Peggy Guggenheim.
- Check out TED Talks about sustainable travel –you'll be delighted to see how many things you are already doing right and become aware of tiny adjustments you can make that will have a huge impact everywhere you travel in the world.

The crazy thing is, in every instance, just by making simple and small adjustments you'll also have a vastly more fulfilling and satisfying trip. Everybody wins.

Venice is aware they need to cut down the number of day trippers allowed there each day. A new command center monitors cellphone data, showing the provenance of each phone. Along with CCTV, they can now determine how many people are in Venice each day. There is talk of limiting the number of day trippers, and charging an entrance fee (which seems to me even more reason to stay a few nights in Venice).

34.
Save Venice & We Are Here Venice

Save Venice

I refer to Save Venice many times throughout this book. Although I must have seen their name around for years, they really didn't hit my radar until I read John Berendt's book, *The City of Falling Angels,* after which I became completely fascinated with them. Keep your eyes open as you explore the city and you will see them popping up everywhere.

Save Venice is a US-based non-profit dedicated to the restoration, conservation and preservation of artworks and cultural heritage sites in Venice. They celebrated their 50th anniversary in 2021, at which time they had funded the restoration of more than 1700 artworks. They raise extraordinary amounts of money and use it to repair specific projects in Venice, including many mentioned in this book. Their work is astounding, and their story is really interesting.

In a city bursting with incredible artwork and architecture, you can easily feel overwhelmed and not know how to choose what to visit. Sometimes I look through projects on the Save Venice website to find things to add to my daily itineraries. Check out their website: www.SaveVenice.org where you can read all about how they execute their projects, which makes visiting them even more intriguing.

We Are Here Venice

Another non-profit I want to draw your attention to is We Are Here Venice. Run by environmental scientist Jane da Mosto, We Are Here Venice is dedicated to the conservation of Venice as a living city.

When I talk about sustainable travel in Venice and the colossal damage wreaked on the city by cruise ships, I ask you not to take my word for it but to see what the scientists say. Jane is a scientist, and all of her information is backed by solid data. Jane is frequently on global panels addressing the conservation of the Venice lagoon, preserving essential wetlands and protecting Venice, amongst many other things. You can follow her on Instagram @WeAreHereVenice and check out the website www.WeAreHereVenice.org. You will be pleasantly surprised at the caliber of organizations and businesses who partner with this non-profit. The media section alone shows you how important this organization is.

Save Venice and We Are Here Venice both offer opportunities for you to contribute to the preservation and continued existence of this amazing city.

35.
Insider Tips for Travelers

Venice bewitches. Like many before me, I have been seduced by its art, architecture, poetry and beauty.

–Russell Norman

1. Stay several nights in Venice

You only get one life, and it deserves as may days and nights here as you can possibly get. The more things you do from this book, the more you will wish you could have just one more day in Venice.

2. Bring good walking shoes

You have to walk everywhere in Venice and comfortable walking shoes are essential.

3. Bring insect repellent

Venice is on the water, and it has plenty of mosquitos. If I'm in town too, they'll bypass you to come eat me alive, but in case I'm not there, douse yourself in repellent every day.

4. GPS is your best friend

The best way to get almost anywhere in Venice is by using the GPS on your phone. Printed maps are more a hindrance than a help. If you get the spinning wheel on your GPS, just step out into the nearest campo so the satellite can reconnect and re-route you.

5. Vaporetto tickets**

Plan on walking everywhere and only use the vaporetto when necessary. You'll waste a lot of time waiting for the next vaporetto, and Venice is best explored on foot anyway.

Public transport in Venice is expensive –a one way ticket costs €7,50 and a day pass is €20. However, do get a day pass when you want to visit the islands.

**Always validate your Vaporetto ticket. Always.

6. Art walking

Venice has an overwhelming amount of art, and sometimes it's hard to know where or how to approach it. One of my favorite things to do is have my guide Emanuele take me on a walking tour of *one artist.* I tell him to pick one –Tintoretto, Veronese, Tiepolo, Titian or whoever, then choose five or six works he feels passionate about and take me to see them, without worrying about chronological order or where they are around town. We walk the city together, he shows me where the artist lived and tells me about the artist's life, while showing me paintings he's especially excited about. It is a tremendous way to experience the city and its art. We'll stop for coffee or cicchetti along the way, and it's great fun. All the guides in my PDF list can do things like this with you.

6. Plan some day trips away from Venice

Be sure to allow enough time to take some day trips. Treviso and Padova are each only 30 minutes (or less) away from Venice by train. You can visit Prosecco country from here. Verona isn't far. Bologna is an hour away. Trieste is two hours away by train.

36.
What Next?

Thank you for reading *Glam Italia! 101 Fabulous Things to Do in Venice!* Now that you've made it all the way to the end of the book, I would like to ask you a favor. **Please leave a review on Amazon.** Reviews are crucial both to the life of this book, and more importantly to other travelers who are trying to find helpful, interesting books to help them plan their trip and add value to their time in Venice.

Glam Italia! Newsletter

Subscribe to my newsletter. Every month my newsletter tells you about secret little towns in Italy, festivals you won't want to miss and foods you'll want to try. It is full of information I don't share anywhere else.

My newsletter group are always the first to hear about new books, my tours, podcast appearances and other Italy-centric things I'm doing.

Get Social

My website CorinnaCooke.com has all the links to my socials, but you can find me here:

Instagram: @CorinnaTravels
Facebook: Corinna Cooke Author
Pinterest: @CorinnaMakeup
TikTok: @CorinnaTravels1

BE A *GLAM ITALIA!* TRAVELER

Check out the entire *Glam Italia!* series:

- *Glam Italia! How to Travel Italy: Secrets to Glamorous Travel (On a Not-So-Glamorous Budget)*
- *Glam Italia! 101 Fabulous Things to Do in Rome*
- *Glam Italia! 101 Fabulous Things to Do in Florence*

Glam Italia! How to Travel Italy is the first book in the series and teaches you how to put your own Italian trip together, covering all the things most first-time travelers find tricky. From how to work the trains, to which wines to choose, to what to do if something goes wrong –you'll find all the answers here.

Glam Italia! 101 Fabulous Things to Do in Rome and *Glam Italia! 101 Fabulous Things to Do in Florence* are designed to give you insider information for visiting these amazing cities. I'll tell you all about incredible, cool sites to visit –insider secrets hidden in plain sight, in the heart of each city's historic center. You'll learn where to find amazing places that the tour buses don't go and the tourists don't see. I'll tell you where you can get the most sensational aperitivo experience and where you'll find the best view of the city –without being surrounded by a crowd of tourists. I'll also tell you about the foods and wines found in each area, and I'll share my favorite restaurants.

All three books are bestsellers and are exclusively available at Amazon.com in paperback and as an e-book.

Ciao!

So, my friend, I hope you have enjoyed this book and that it has given you plenty of ideas for things to see, eat, drink, and do while you're in town.

Be sure to tag me in your social media posts so I can see what you are doing on your travels. Chances are, if you see a bright red ponytail bopping its way across the piazza, it's me, so please come over and say hi! I have met so many readers of my books while in Italy (even in airports and train stations), and it is such fun to be able to meet you! Sometimes I've been able to show them something cool nearby, and other times if we were heading in the same direction I walked with them across town, with me pointing out interesting bits and pieces along the way. After all, traveling in Italy is my favorite subject!

Finally, I wish you the very best for your travels. Have a totally fantastic time, do things you wouldn't normally do, and make it the trip of a lifetime!

See you in the piazza,

Corinna

XO

37.
Recommended Reading

I love reading books set in cities I travel to, and all through this book I have mentioned books which I have loved, and which are set in Venice. For your ease of reference, here is the checklist.

- John Berendt, *The City of Falling Angels* (2005)
- Laurence Bergreen, *Casanova: The World of a Seductive Genius* (2016)
- Giacomo Casanova, *The Story of My Flight* (1787)
- Marlena di Blasi, *A Thousand Days in Venice: An Unexpected Romance* (2002)
- Daphne du Maurier, *Don't Look Now* (1971)
- Alberto Toso Fei, *Venetian Legends and Ghost Stories: A Guide to Places of Mystery in Venice* (2002)
- Barry Frangipane, *The Venice Experiment: A Year of Trial and Error Living Abroad* (2011)
- Ernest Hemingway, *Across the River and into the Trees* (1950)
- Donna Leon, *A Sea of Troubles* (2001)
- Judith Mackrell, *The Unfinished Palazzo: Life, Love and Art in Venice. The Stories of Luisa Casati, Doris Castlerosse and Peggy Guggenheim* (2017)

38. Acknowledgements

To my ever-patient editor Anna Golden, thank you so much for yet another project completed together. I love all your ideas and am so grateful that you never squash my voice, but aways let my readers feel like I am chatting with them directly. Here's to many more books together!

To Marta Halama, thank you for the years of working together, for your brilliant ideas and your equally brilliant illustrations in all my books. You are a joy to work with.

Emanuele Ginocchi, thank you for all the years working together in Venice and for being such a good friend. I learn something new every single time we hit the streets together, it's still always great fun, and all my travelers adore you. Thank you for helping me plan amazing experiences in Venice, for helping me with this book and for answering my never-ending stream of questions.

Monica Cesarato, thank you for supporting this project and for being so incredibly helpful! I adore spending time with you, going on ciccheti walks and Prosecco tours together, and for the wonderful experiences you curate for my clients and my friends. You are an absolute treasure.

Jane da Mosto, thank you for taking the time to teach me about the lagoon and to answer my long list of questions! Your work in Venice is so important and I am grateful for all that you do.

Jennifer O'Bannon, thank you for being such a great friend for all these years, and for flying to Venice in the middle of a heatwave to walk the book with me. Despite the heat and humidity, that was one of the most fun trips ever!

Katy Clarke, thank you for your love of Italy, your amazing 'Untold Italy' podcast, and for being such a fun and fabulous friend! I am so looking forward to aperitivo hour together in Venice with a view and endless funny stories.

Jennifer Mary, thank you for your endless support and encouragement of all my crazy ideas, and for being the inspiration for a life of travel and laughter.

Tommy, thank you for being you. I am so proud of you every day of my life.

xo

Corinna Cooke

Corinna Cooke is a professional makeup artist and bestselling author.

A lifetime fascination with archaeology, art and history, paired with a love of languages, resulted in years of non-stop travel to Italy.

Her blog posts about exploring Italy and discovering off-the-beaten-path places led to her establishing an accidental private boutique tour business, Glam Italia Tours. Every year Corinna takes small groups of women on glamor-filled a la carte tours of Italy.

Originally from New Zealand, Corinna has lived all around the world, and now splits her time between Italy and the United States.

Made in the USA
Coppell, TX
18 March 2024